# Street Art, Public City

What is street art? Who is the street artist? Why is street art a crime?

Since the late 1990s, a distinctive cultural practice has emerged in many cities: street art, involving the placement of uncommissioned artworks in public places. Sometimes regarded as a variant of graffiti, sometimes called a new art movement, its practitioners engage in illicit activities while at the same time the resulting artworks can command high prices at auction and have become collectable aesthetic commodities. Such paradoxical responses show that street art challenges conventional understandings of culture, law, crime and art.

*Street Art, Public City* engages with those paradoxes in order to understand how street art reveals new modes of citizenship in the contemporary city. It examines the histories of street art and the motivations of street artists, and the experiences both of making street art and looking at street art in public space. It considers the ways in which street art has become an integral part of the identity of cities such as London, New York, Berlin, and Melbourne, at the same time as street art has become increasingly criminalised. It investigates the implications of street art for conceptions of property and authority, and suggests that street art and the urban imagination can point us towards a different kind of city: the public city.

*Street Art, Public City* will be of interest to readers concerned with art, culture, law, cities and urban space, and also to readers in the fields of legal studies, cultural criminology, urban geography, cultural studies and art more generally.

**Alison Young** is a Professor of Criminology in the School of Social and Political Sciences at the University of Melbourne.

# Street Art, Public City

## Law, Crime and the Urban Imagination

Alison Young

Routledge
Taylor & Francis Group
a GlassHouse Book

First published 2014
by Routledge
2 Park Square, Milton Park, Abingdon, Oxon, OX14 4RN

and by Routledge
711 Third Avenue, New York, NY 10017

A GlassHouse Book

*Routledge is an imprint of the Taylor & Francis Group, an informa business*



*British Library Cataloguing in Publication*
A catalogue record for this book is available from the British Library

*Library of Congress Cataloging-in-Publication Data*
Young, Alison.
Street art, public city: law, crime and the urban imagination/
Alison Young.
pages cm
1. Street art. 2. Graffiti. 3. Urban beautification. 4. Crime.
5. Public spaces. 6. Sociology, Urban. I. Title.
NA9052.Y68 2014
701′.03 – dc23
2013021441

ISBN: 978-0-415-53869-5 (hbk)
ISBN: 978-0-203-79691-7 (ebk)

Typeset in Garamond Three and Gill Sans by
Florence Production Ltd, Stoodleigh, Devon, UK

# Contents

# List of plates

# List of figures

# Acknowledgements

My encounters with individuals in the world of street art have been characterised by the great generosity of those I have met. Street art is often located within the economy of the gift, through which an artist creates an image and places it in public space, to be viewed at no cost by anyone who passes by; to that extent, generosity is a defining feature of street art. But it's never something that should be taken for granted, or forgotten, and so I'd like to note here at the outset of this book how indebted I am to the many, many people who gave up their time to speak with me, walk the city with me, send me links and images, and refer me on to other individuals. I could not have carried out this research without the fundamental generosity of these individuals with their time, ideas, words and images. So my primary thanks are to all of you who helped me in many ways: Alexone, Fletcher Anderson, Acoris Andipa, L'Atlas, Banksy, Blék le Rat, Kai Brethouwer, Garrison Buxton, C215, Cake, CDH, Civil, Satta Van Daal, Dave the Chimp, Dcide Now, Deadly Knitshade, Dora Dewsbery, D*Face, Ad Deville, Disturbanity, the Doctor, Brad Downey, Adrian Doyle, Dscreet, Eine, El Bocho, Luca Borriello, Elbow-Toe, Lorraine Ellis, Emess, Jean Faucheur, John Fekner, Thierry Froger, Ellis Gallagher, Ann Genovese, Samuel and Joseph Genovese-Ronfeldt, Ghostpatrol, Ha-Ha, Mark Halsey, Steven Harrington, Logan Hicks, Mark Holsworth, Russell Howze, Nasser Hussain, Nick Ilton, Ingo, Kurt Iveson, Jaybo Monk, Adeline Jeudy, JR, Just, Kaff-eine, Andrew King, Johann Lanzenauer, Steve Lazarides, Patrick Lerouge, Cedar Lewisohn, Anthony Lister, Ian Loader, Clare Long, Samantha Longhi, Andy Mac, Mary McCarthy, Lachlan MacDowall, Fiona MacKinnon, Shaun McVeigh, Tristan Manco, Mare139, Meggs, Angelo Milano, Esther Milne, Miso, Miss.Tic, MOMO, Alan Montgomery, Adrian Nabi, Nails, Sandy Nairne, Jeff Newman, Patrick Nguyen, Nikos Papastergiadis, Luna Park, Arnaud Oliveux, Ollie, Giuseppe Ottavianelli, José Parlá, Chris and Pam Pascuzzi, Alice Pasquini, Brice Pericard, Andreas Philippopoulos-Mihalopoulos, Pisa 73, Sandra Powell, Pure Evil, Puzle, James Reka, Marc Rigney, Roa, Jaime Rojo, Rone, Paul Ronfeldt, Remi Rough, Christian Ruggiero, Peter Rush, RJ Rushmore, Léanne Sacramone, Marc and Sara Schiller, Anton Schutz, Jordan Seiler,

Frankie Shea, Richard Sherwin, Shinobi, Slinkachu, Timba Smits, Mike Snelle, Sparcs, Jill Stauffer, Swoon, Dean Sunshine, Tony Taglianetti, Ralph Taylor, Tower, Various, Hrag Vartanian, Vexta, The Wa, Waleska, Nick Walker, Peat Wollaeger, xero, Sophie Young, Yz, Kid Zoom.

Research for this book has been supported by two Discovery Grants from the Australian Research Council. The first of these was a project entitled 'Urban Images and the Appearance of City Spaces', from 2008–10; the second is entitled 'Transforming City Spaces: Street Art, Urban Cultures, Transnational Networks', covering the period 2012–14. The latter is an ongoing project examining the reception of street art into the cultural field and its findings to date have particularly influenced the writing of Chapter 6 of this book. I'm very grateful to the Australian Research Council for their support of my research.

I also had the pleasure of working with some excellent research assistants, whose conversation always prompted new ideas and directions of inquiry. Many thanks to Tom Andrews, Sylvana Jahre, David Mence, Connal Parsley, and Cécile Taché. Thanks, Tom, for all the great conversations about the law, property and street art. And my gratitude, especially, to David Mence who has been working with me on the 'Transforming City Spaces' project and who not only revolutionised the various technologies used in carrying out the project but also proved a keen-eyed and thoughtful reader of the manuscript for this book. David, if it had not been for your encouragement, this book would not yet have been finished.

At various stages of my research, I presented conference papers and seminars to attentive and enthusiastic audiences, who provided thoughtful feedback and helped me to refine my ideas along the way. Many thanks to those audiences at the School of Social and Political Sciences, University of Melbourne (August 2008), the University of Oxford Centre for Criminology (May 2012), the University of Wollongong Legal Intersections Research Centre (August 2012), the University of Westminster Law School (January 2013), the Institute of Social Research at Birkbeck College (January 2013), the Centre for Law, Justice and Journalism at City University (March 2013), the Annual Meeting of the Association for the Study of Law, Culture and the Humanities held at Birkbeck College (March 2013), and the Research Unit in Public Cultures, University of Melbourne (May 2013). Thanks also to the audiences of various community or professional forums, such as the Melbourne Stencil Festival (in 2006 and 2008), 'Street Alliance' at Federation Square, Melbourne (December 2007), the Cultural Development Network (April 2008), the panel on 'Art, Advertising and Public Space' at ACMI, Melbourne (June 2010), 'The War Against Street Art', a Moniker Art Event at Shoreditch House, London (March 2013), Schmooze: Street Art, Kingston City Council (April 2013), and many others.

Some chapters or sections of chapters have been previously published. Chapter 2 is published in *Law and Literature* (2014). A small part of Chapter 3 appeared in a much extended form in *Street/ Studio: the Place of Street Art in*

*Melbourne* (2010, Thames and Hudson), the book I co-wrote with Ghostpatrol, Miso and Timba Smits. A version of Chapter 4 appeared as 'Criminal Images: the Affective Judgment of Street Art and Graffiti' in *Crime, Media, Culture* 8(3): 296–312. A far more detailed account of my experiences in the policymaking process can be found in 'Negotiated Consent or Zero Tolerance: Responding to Graffiti and Street Art in Melbourne' in *City* (2010) vol.14 nos.1–2, 99–115. As mentioned in Chapter 1, in 2008 I established a blog, *Images To Live By*, while conducting research in this area. Earlier, and rather different, versions of some of the material in this book can be found in various blog posts.

I am grateful to the Arts Faculty and the School of Social and Political Science at the University of Melbourne for their award of a Publications Grant towards the costs of image production for this book.

Special thanks are owed to Peter Rush and Sophie Young, who accompanied me on walks through cities, listened to my endless chatter about street art, came to gallery openings, and took note of interesting new street artworks for me to see. Peter and Sophie: no-one could have been better companions in the public city than you.

Chapter 1

# The situational artwork

## Histories of street art

When did I first notice an unauthorised intervention in the public spaces of the city? I was about sixteen years old, and sitting in a train carriage with a friend, who pointed out to me words that had been painted on a wall next to the train line that ran from Paisley, my home town, into Glasgow:

> MY DARLING FLOPS
> I LOVE YOU

My friend and I speculated as to who might be the author and the intended audience. Perhaps a commuter who would see the message from the train? We wondered how old the writing was and whether it would come as a surprise to 'Flops', if it was an affirmation of an existing love, or a declaration of a new one.

As an example of illicit writing in public space it is a charming one, likely to be inoffensive to most people (perhaps evidenced by the fact that it had not been removed by the train company, and indeed was to remain in place for many subsequent years). But what is important about this instance of unauthorised writing is that its communicative nature is apparent at the same time as its illegality. It was obvious to me that the writing was 'out of place' but also that there were ways of understanding why it had come to be there. Its very existence created the opportunity for speculation as to its author, its intent and its reception. Perhaps the unknown writer of these words sparked what was to become for me a long-lasting interest in illicit writing and images in public space.

Many years after seeing that declaration of love on the train lines, I carried out research on political slogan writing in Melbourne, on graffiti cultures in Melbourne, and on a collaborative project with Mark Halsey interviewing graffiti writers around South Australia. More recently, I started studying the emergence of what came to be known as 'street art', which soon showed itself to be both distinct from graffiti and intertwined with its history. My aim was to trace and to interpret the ways in which street art is both distinctive and interconnected with other cultural forms, in order to account for its complex history, as it has progressed from subcultural activity to mainstream indicator of 'urban cool'.

So much for the biographical history of my intellectual engagement with the activity. When did street art itself *begin*? Was there a day when someone created the first piece of street art? Unofficial mark-making in public space has a long history.[1] Some claim that Aboriginal rock art constitutes the first public art; others point to cave paintings in Lescaux and other locations. As Fleming (2001) details, mark-making in public spaces was common in Elizabethan England, and there is extensive evidence that for decades before modern graffiti came into existence, tourists wrote their names at places they were visiting and soldiers while on a tour of duty or overseas posting wrote messages such as 'Kilroy was here'. If we are seeking to pinpoint when the graffiti of tags and 'pieces' began, many point to the activities of Darryl McCray, aka Cornbread, a tagger in Philadelphia from 1967 onwards (Gastman and Neelon 2010), and others identify the 'sharpie' culture of Melbourne in the 1950s as having established tagging in the city. As is now well documented (see especially Castleman 1984; Chalfant and Prigoff 1987; Cooper and Chalfant 1988; Snyder 2009) graffiti originally took hold in American cities such as Chicago, Philadelphia and New York and was then exported to other cities and countries initially through books (*Subway Art*, 1988), films (*Style Wars*, 1983, *Wild Style*, 1983, *Beat Street*, 1984), magazines, 'zines and websites (the international website *Art Crimes* being one of the earliest and most wide-reaching).

At some point, maybe in the late 1990s, or maybe a little earlier, a new form of mark-making in public spaces came into existence, and this would later become known as 'street art'. It is not possible to specify the date of the advent of the first street artwork. Nor is it especially advisable. Thinking about street art in such terms depends upon imagining that street art had a definite starting-point – a moment when other kinds of image-making such as slogan-writing or graffiti had to make room for this new art form. Street art, while distinctive, is also related to other cultural practices (such as graffiti or writing political slogans) and this complicates any attempt to work out exactly when and where street art 'began' in the contemporary city.

The appearance of cities is shaped by the authorised activities of architects, urban planners, builders, advertising agencies and others. For many years, the cityscape has also been transformed by the efforts of unauthorised individuals: activists writing their beliefs on the walls; graffiti writers tagging and piecing along the train lines; skateboarders carving up the streets; and street artists

1 On the historical dimensions of street art, graffiti and other mark-making activities – 'wild signs' as the authors call them – see the essays in Oliver and Neal (2010).

placing stencils, stickers, paste-ups and other objects on the surfaces of the city. Some activities pre-date the street art that we are familiar with today, others have coexisted with it since its inception. Just as it is neither easy nor desirable to create a rigid categorical separation of street art from these other activities, so street artists should not be cordoned into a distinctive group: some of the artists now associated with street art began as taggers; others are motivated by their politics to write slogans on walls as often as they might create a paste-up; or a group of friends who skateboard together might also make art.

So what is street art? What is a street artwork? And why argue that our responses to the street artwork are crucially important in determining whether our urban centres can ever be(come) *public cities*? In thinking about street art and the city in this way, I draw on the work of many notable thinkers, including Amin and Thrift (2002); Butler (2012); Iveson (2007); Lefebvre (1996); Mitchell (2003); and Watson (2006). However, in the concept 'public city', I am intending something rather different to Lefebvre's 'right to the city' or Mitchell's 'social justice in the city': that is, a public city in which there exists a commons of the image (see Chapter 2), an aesthetically driven cityscape (see Chapter 3), networks of laws (see Chapters 4 and 5), and a landscape that is materially produced through hierarchies of taste and cultural capital (see Chapter 6). The notion of the 'public city' names a space and a moment in which citizens can inhabit all of these dimensions at once. To think about the street artwork in public space is obvious; to raise questions about whether street artworks can help create a public city is rather less so. The 'city' of a public city is more than its streetscapes, cartography, planning, economy and neighbourhoods; it is an image, a symbol, a mood, an atmosphere and a sensibility. The shift from a focus upon public space, important and necessary though it is, to a consideration of the public city itself allows us also to ask how we live in the city, and what we desire to experience there.

This is not to argue that physical place should be overlooked: far from it. The street artwork takes much of its meaning from its location in public space, on private property. From this complicated location, myriad questions arise, to do with conceptions of place, ownership, and boundaries. To write about the challenges posed to regimes of property, community and authority by street art necessitates the consideration of what the urban imagination involves, and what a street artwork can look like. While this sounds simple, the construction of such categorical frameworks is in fact fraught with difficulty. First, there is the issue of how street art and street artworks are defined (and therefore constituted). Is it the type of image created that determines whether we are looking at a street artwork – a stencil on a wall, perhaps, or an object hanging from a street sign? Or perhaps it is the particular creative activity that produced the artwork (stencilling, tagging, pasting up posters)? Alternatively, perhaps the artwork's production without permission results in an image being defined as street art? Perhaps street art is something that can be fixed within a particular historical period – the late 1990s and 2000s?

None of these characteristics is definitive, however. And, as the years have passed since street art emerged as a cultural practice, new forms such as yarn bombing and street sculpture have become commonplace on city streets. In the early 2000s, street art predominantly involved stencilled images; a decade later there is a far greater diversity of practices and images. This is not to say that the answer to defining street art is to adopt an inclusive stance, whereby any and all artistic activities and resulting images can be considered to be street art. For some commentators (for example, Grant, 2012) activities such as yarn bombing and cup rocking dilute the subversive challenges presented by illicit art, by virtue of their proximity to craft as opposed to art. Others point out that, despite many shared characteristics, graffiti and street art have very different historical antecedents and thus should not be homologised. The difficulties and undesirability of attempting to historicise street art by fixing its origins at a particular point in time are thus magnified when we take into account the lack of agreement among commentators as to what street art is (and whether it should even be called 'street art', rather than anything else, will be discussed shortly).

Invoking the illegality of an image as a central definitional feature is also problematic. Some street artworks are created without permission; others are created with the consent of the property owner. An implicit hierarchy within street art culture tends to give greater significance or credibility to works created without permission, and artists who call themselves street artists but who have never or rarely put up illicit work can sometimes be regarded as less authentic, or as attempting to benefit from street art's fashionability. Moreover, the spectator who stumbles across an artwork may not be able to determine whether an artwork was authorised or not; sometimes passersby assume a work is illegal simply because it is in public space or is painted in a particular style. (Artists recount instances in which local residents have called the police on the assumption that a mural is illicit despite the artist actually having permission; conversely some have tacitly relied on a passerby's assumption that a work is permitted when it was not.)

In terms of whether street art has a particular historicity, this is easy both to establish and to undermine. On the one hand, the term 'street art' began to be used in the early to mid-2000s, with reference to artworks placed in public space without permission and often, at that time, involving stencils and pasted-up paper images. However, such street-based images did not appear from nowhere, sharing connections with graffiti writing (which began in the United States in the late 1960s and 1970s), political protest (slogans had been written on walls in cities all over the world for many decades, and protest movements have for many years printed and pasted-up posters), punk culture (which emphasised the hand-made, local and subversive, and which utilised a similar aesthetic), Situationist art (which emphasised the alignment between art and politics and rejected any claim to separate the two) and drawing also upon a more general desire to make marks in public and private spaces, whether evidenced in 'latrinalia' (writing on toilet walls), carving initials on school desks and on the stone of ancient monuments, painting images on cave walls, and writing on walls within private homes.[2]

Street art, although a distinctive phenomenon with many discrete characteristics, intersects with a range of other activities and practices, and draws meaning from these other phenomena, while evolving attributes of its own that operate to constitute an image in public space as a street artwork (or not). For example, words stencilled on the pavement might well be the illicit work of a street artist, as in San Francisco when a group of artists called 'The Strangers' created a stencilled narrative that could be read cumulatively by the pedestrian walking in the vicinity of Dolores Park.[3] However, such stencilled words can also be created by government organisations and advertising agencies: in Melbourne, the Victorian Government placed stencils on the pavement exhorting individuals to use sunscreen, and companies such as Nike and Moonlight Cinema employed an advertising agency to stencil their logos on pavements around the city. In these instances, it is fairly clear that the resulting stencilled words are not a street artwork; in other situations, it is less apparent, such when I saw the words 'Taxi to the Dark Side' stencilled on the streets of Shoreditch in London; this turned out to be the advertising campaign for a documentary film.

For a long time, little was written in academic literature about street art. There was some engagement with graffiti, much of which focused on the question of whether graffiti could be categorised as art or crime (see for example Gomez 1992). Alternative approaches were provided by Ferrell (1994, 1995, 1996, 1997, 1998) and others who engaged with graffiti writing communities as examples of subcultural formations and awarded them a central position

2 On latrinalia, see for example Bartholome and Snyder (2004) and on graffiti by tourists at heritage sites see Dallen and Boyd (2006). On the practice by tradespeople of painting directly onto brickwork in order to advertise skills or wares, see Harvey (2006) who notes the oldest surviving example in London dates from the 1880s. Fleming claims that the habits of writing upon windows, walls and other surfaces in Elizabethan England 'invite us to imagine a practice within which writing and drawing are not fully distinguishable, and the page is no longer an important boundary' (2001: 9). Frederick (2009) provides an archaeologist's view of graffiti, drawing links between contemporary wall writing and the mark-making of Indigenous rock art. Finally, the affinities between street art and advertising practices is analysed by Droney (2010).

3 These could also be experienced out of order, resulting in a disjointed narrative: the first of the stencils that I came across was the last in the story, reading 'The owl drops the mouse in the street. She scoops it up and carries it home. She nurses it back to health and it lives out its life as her friend in her lonely apartment. THE END.'

in the development of what became known as cultural criminology. Initially focusing upon specific social and cultural practices (such as dumpster diving, graffiti writing, skateboarding and heroin use) in a way that constituted their practitioners as marginal(ised) or minoritarian, cultural criminology has since been expanded and refined such that these activities can now be regarded as components within culture generally, variously labelled and positioned within social hierarchies.

Other approaches seeking an alternative to the art/crime dichotomy include the Deleuzean stance that Mark Halsey and I took in arguing that graffiti writers see space differently, with vision operating haptically to construct a different mode of being in space (see also Haworth, Bruce and Iveson, 2013). Similarly, urban and cultural geographers saw graffiti writers as engaged in the construction and re-appropriation of urban spaces, sometimes able to contest dominant uses of the city and sometimes reabsorbed into the cultural mainstream (Dovey, Woodcock and Wollan 2012). Street art is often classified as being exemplified by a particular practice (stencil art, for example, or culture jamming), but as street art has continued to diversify, it is clear that there is no one determining art practice involved. Further, stencils have been used by advertising companies, corporations and local councils; billboard jamming is sometimes used by advertisers; graffiti can be incorporated into paste-ups just as paste-ups can be incorporated into graffiti. By the late 2000s, diversity and interconnectedness constituted key aspects of street art, complicating any straightforward definition of the activity.

How has street art been viewed in recent academic literature? From the mid-2000s, the idea of 'street art' as a distinct cultural practice has received newfound awareness in academic literature (Bou 2005; Lacayo and Miranda 2005; McGaw 2008; Ganz and Manco 2009; Lewisohn 2009; Austin 2010; Banet-Weiser 2011; Wacławek 2011; McAuliffe 2012). In sum, then, street art is sometimes regarded as a youth activity; at other times, as an evolution of graffiti, or a subculture, or a variant of artistic practice. Sometimes it is claimed to be a wholly new art form or new art movement. It is also regarded as transgressive behaviour. It has been analysed as a communicative practice capable of fostering new ways of being in public space; as a political practice; as akin to advertising; and as an aspect of urban space. Can something really be all of these things at once? Is the problem one of *definition*?

The difficulties of defining street art are noted by many. In her anthology of graffiti and street art, the gallerist and art dealer Magda Danysz is critical of the very enterprise of definition:

> Street Art is in motion and the simple act of giving it a name, of reducing it to a word or an expression is problematic. Style Writing, Graffiti, Subway, Art, Stencil Art, Street Art . . . How is anyone supposed to define the most important artistic movement of our brand new century?
>
> (Danysz and Dana 2010: 12)

Others have attempted to offer a definition, sometimes by virtue of what street art is *not*. Riggle (2010) notes that street art cannot simply be defined as art that is placed in the street. If this were the case then, as he notes, artworks being unloaded from a truck outside a gallery would have to be considered street artworks. Nor is the fact that such an artwork is in transit from truck to gallery relevant. It is not the length of time spent by an artwork in the street that constitutes it as a street artwork: some street art is extremely ephemeral, lasting only seconds, while other pieces may endure for years (2010: 244). Street artworks must also be distinguished from the communicative practices of advertising agencies (billboards, posters and so on). Riggle argues that street artworks are notable for making 'a *material* or *artistic use* of the street' (2010: 246 emphases in original) where that use 'is essential to their meaning' (255). Thus, in planning an artwork for the street, an artist might reflect upon the backdrop or context provided by particular urban surfaces, the work's visibility in particular public locales, its juxtaposition with certain buildings or architectural settings and, crucially, its existence within public space such that it is allowed to be subject to the vagaries of the public, other street artists, the weather, and the authorities.

For Riggle, then, the likely *ephemerality* of the street artwork is one of its defining features, along with the requirement that the artist or artwork makes substantive use of *the street as a setting or feature of the artwork*. Marc and Sara Schiller, curators, collectors and pioneers of street art blogging through their website *Wooster Collective*, categorise street art as 'free public art' (McCormick et al. 2010: 11), thus alluding to other aspects of the street artwork: its *accessibility* (the spectator does not have to visit a gallery in order to see such an artwork), its *democratic nature* (the spectator needs neither a background in art history nor to pay an entrance fee in order to view or appreciate the artwork), and its *egalitarianism* (in placing the work on the street, the artist may well be deliberately seeking to avoid the often exclusive institutions of the art world).

A wide-ranging definition, albeit of graffiti rather than street art specifically, is provided by Frederick:

> Graffiti in the broader contemporary context is a complex mark-making phenomenon, that may be seen as a kind of drawing or painting and, because it commonly employs language text, also as a kind of writing. Its sculptural forms and intervention in the surface textures and appearance of buildings make it an element in the liquid architecture of a mutating metropolis. However, the term 'graffiti' is most often applied to any form of unsolicited marking. Graffiti is generally understood as text and/or images that is made in shared spaces where it is generated and viewed publicly, be that a privately owned building, public transport or an alleyway. It is otherwise difficult to characterise graffiti because it is a

> mode of expression and communication which comprises a vast array of media, technique, subject matter, form, and meanings.
>
> (2009: 212)

Frederick's broadly generalist account is important in that all dimensions of street art certainly need to be acknowledged in order to understand its different affects and effects. If only a limited number of characteristics are considered (illegality, or aesthetics, or impact on urban space) then any analysis will be inadequate to the task of assessing how the street artwork is encountered in the contemporary city. In this book, I will thus be engaged in the enterprise of thinking through how a cultural practice can be art *and* crime *and* an aspect of urban space *and* a form of communication *and* a political gesture *and* constitutive of a new movement in art. But while such inclusiveness is desirable, my analysis will seek to avoid a conceptualisation of street art that is so broad as to lose the specificity of its practices and effects. There are many encounters in the contemporary city that might be comparable in various ways to the encounter with the street artwork – with a flash mob, a busker, newly installed public art, or a political demonstration. However, none of these incorporate the plurality of dimensions we find in the street artwork, and which contribute to the particular affective encounter generated when a spectator catches sight of a tag, a paste-up, or a stencil.

So as to frame the street artwork in a way that is both inclusive and particularised, I will be emphasising the following qualities: first, its placement in public space such that this placement becomes an integral aspect of the work and of viewing the work; second, the aims of the artist as primarily being the creation of an image such that commercial or informational concerns are secondary or absent; and, third, the illegality of the work existing either as a result of its placement without permission or through the assumptions about the work brought by the spectator. Such characteristics can be encapsulated in the term *situational*, which gestures towards the importance of the spectator's encounter with the work in a situation quite unlike other forms of viewing art, the artist's interest in placing the work in public space rather than in a gallery, and the law's desire to situate the street artwork as legal or illegal. In this book, I will refer to the street artwork as *a situational artwork*, when seeking to operationalise this nexus of connotations and characteristics.

At other times, I will use the commonly accepted and understood terms 'street art' and 'street artwork'. But this is not the only name that has been given to the cultural practice and to this type of artwork. Street art is sometimes called 'urban art'. Both terms advert to the artwork's location. The adjective 'street' in 'street art' functions as a metonymy: situational artworks might in fact be located in a wide range of places and on many surfaces, some located in or near a street, others with no proximity to a thoroughfare at all (such as inside an abandoned building, on the rear of a warehouse, on a fence abutting a train line). Certainly, the idea that all situational art can be called 'street' art condenses the vast diversity of places in which situational art could be located into a partial image that seems to evoke all of the possible places for such artworks – the image of a person writing or painting on a wall located in a street. This condensation then stands in for all the heterogeneous ways and places in which 'street' art can be made.

'Urban art' might then seem a more inclusive and accurate term. However, 'urban art' is disliked as a descriptor by most artists who make situational art in city spaces. 'Urban' specifies an artwork's location in the spaces of the city; yet it has also come to be used in relation to artists who have never produced work on the street and artworks that have never been outside of a studio or gallery. 'Urban art' has come to connote something about an artwork's appearance, or an artist's sensibility, or an aesthetic; a politics perhaps, or an affinity to a sense of 'cool'.[4] The term is also associated with auction houses, where it is used to specify a sub-category of contemporary art. The term is thus viewed distrustfully as saying something about the *sale* of art rather than the nature of the work itself.[5]

In this book, the term 'street art' is preferred to 'urban art'. It is the category most artists seem comfortable with and one of the guiding principles of my research has been to allow a relatively hidden population to voice their views, experiences and histories. However, it is worth noting that 'street art' is also a label, a construction, with implications for our understanding of space, place, the artist and the artwork. For this reason, in the following chapters I will use varying terminology (street art/ situational art/ uncommissioned art/ urban art), as appropriate to the context of the discussion.

This book will not offer an 'insider' account (such as an artist would offer), nor the sort of sociological or historical narrative that emphasises dates and landmark achievements. Instead, it is based on the experience of being a spectator to and researcher of street art as it has appeared and disappeared on the walls of cities around the world, as artists have been arrested (or not) and gone to court (or not), as street art has proliferated on computer screens through websites and blogs and in galleries and auction houses. It is an account that has developed while spending two decades looking at art on city walls. Many of the artworks that I saw twenty years ago are of course gone and now exist only in picture books or in the blurry snapshots I took when I first became interested in the activity. They have been painted over or replaced by new works. Some buildings have been demolished; new ones have been built.

4 One London interviewee commented to me: 'For example, Antony Micallef gets put into the street artist category, because he's young. But he's not a street artist, he's a fine artist and he doesn't pretend to be a street artist. There's certain people that call themselves street artists, but they don't really paint anything on the street, or if they do then it's not illegal, they've got permission. And then it's like, well, you're not really a street artist.'

5 Blogger RJ Rushmore commented about the term 'urban art' on *Vandalog*: 'Christ, five years after I first heard it and I still hate that term': at http://blog.vandalog.com/2012/10/weekend-link-o-rama-91/ (accessed 29 October 2012).

The constant turnover that keeps cities themselves in flux is a crucial aspect of street art: as new images are created, others disappear. An image appears overnight and might last a day or a year – its lifespan is never possible to predict, never possible to know. Street art does not happen according to anyone's plan; the passerby must therefore give in to the pleasures of uncertainty. Part of street art's charm (and challenge) to a city is that it is unplanned and unmanageable, despite what councils claim with their 'graffiti management plans'. As one artist wrote on a wall in Melbourne some years ago: 'our desires are ungovernable'.

## Genres of street art

Street artworks have taken an increasingly diverse range of forms. That said, there are certain conventions, histories and characteristics that have been prominent in the evolution of the situational artwork. The following section will sketch some of the most significant.

Street art has been associated with stencils since its inception and in the early 2000s the single-layer stencil became the stereotypical street artwork. So-called for the artist's use of a single layer of cardboard, which functioned as a template to be sprayed against a surface, the stencil created solid colour images and words, often humorous, sometimes political, with great popular appeal. While potentially indistinguishable from an aerosol tag (given that stencils involve paint being rapidly applied to a surface in a way that can be repeated hundreds of times a night) stencils tend not to be regarded in the same pejorative light as tags. Underlying this double standard is the likelihood that the communicative aspect of street art – which creates appealing images or thought-provoking statements – mitigates against the potential to view the stencil as damaging to property. Whereas a tag addresses itself to other taggers or to insiders within graffiti culture, stencils plainly take a more inclusive stance, involving the spectator in a communicative exchange.

It is hard to over-state the importance of stencils for street art. Stencils had long been part of political protest movement in Buenos Aires and elsewhere (Kane 2009) but what occurred in the late 1990s and early 2000s was a populist expansion of the activity far beyond those activities. In addition to the general appeal they present to the spectator, stencils have been taken up as a technique by artists worldwide. Tristan Manco's book *Stencil Graffiti* (2002) no doubt played a vital role in informing individuals about the aesthetic possibilities of the technique; the impact of the expanding Internet was also critical. For many artists, the advent of the website *Stencil Revolution* in 2002 introduced them to stencil art. Melbourne artist Ghostpatrol describes how he discovered the website when looking for information online about how to find images when making stencils:

> Stencil Revolution, obviously it was one of the bigger [websites], and it was the first online community that I joined. At first it was just uploading

> photos, but then I realised what the forum was and how it was this discussion site . . . And that's how I first got to see proper photos of the street and what was out there.[6]

*Wooster Collective*, the New York-based website, began in 2003 and initially focused on art seen by its founders, Marc and Sara Schiller, on the streets in that city; however, very quickly fans of street art all over the world began emailing photographs to the site, which then became a clearing house of information about new street art. And in the mid-2000s, the fact that stencils were frequently utilised by Banksy (well on his way to becoming the most popular street artist in the world) was a fact that did not go unnoticed by many aspiring street artists (see Plate 1).[7]

In more recent years, something of a backlash has set in against stencils within the international community of street artists and street art commentators. Although Banksy's command of the technique is beyond question, many have expressed boredom with stencils, especially the simple, single- or double-layered images so popular when the genre exploded into being. Stencil art now commands respect when it demonstrates high levels of difficulty, such as in the intricate, multi-layered images of the American artist Logan Hicks, or when it is incorporated into more complex imagery, one technique among others, as in the work of Australian artist Meggs (see Plate 2). Two brief issues should be noted, however. First, Banksy's work seems immune to the various expressions of *ennui* regarding stencil art, due to the skill involved in the design, execution and placement of his artworks, and to the fact that while stencils still constitute a mainstay of his artistic practice, Banksy has also diversified his techniques to include sculpture, animatronic objects and film.[8] Second, although the institutions of the street art world (and at the time of writing this book, street art has become mainstream enough for auction houses to have created urban art sales, for art journals to have spilled ink debating the aesthetics of street art, and for street artworks to enter gallery and museum spaces) have tended to promote artists whose work demonstrates complex technique, evidence of stencil art's enduring popularity can everywhere be seen on the walls and streets of London, Melbourne, Berlin and Paris. No doubt the ubiquity of stencil art derives in part from the fact that basic single- or double-layer stencilling involves an ease of execution and thus has a broad appeal, even for those with little artistic skill.

6 In interview with me. Unless otherwise stated, all quoted statements by artists, gallerists, bloggers, and collectors are taken from interviews conducted by me in the course of researching this book.

7 Banksy's work is discussed at several points throughout this book, including in the final encounter with street art, 'Banksy under glass'.

8 It should also be noted that, in 2012, the stencil-based artworks of the French street artist Blék le Rat enjoyed a great deal of critical and commercial success.

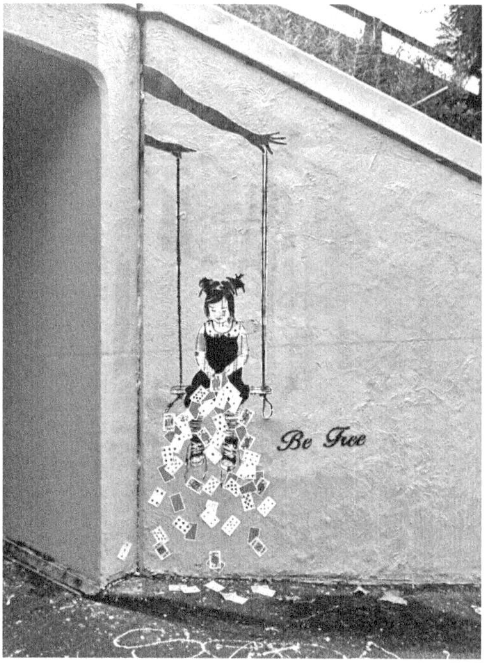


*Figure 1.1* Be Free, Melbourne 2011. Photograph © Alison Young.

Another archetypal form of street art is the 'paste-up' or 'wheat paste'. The name derives from a flour-based adhesive used to affix sheets of paper to city walls. As with many forms of street art, it is not the *medium* that is deemed problematic: stencilling is routinely used by local authorities and corporations; paper is conventionally glued to walls or other surfaces by advertisers. However, these urban significations are authorised, whereas a paste-up is glued to a wall without any such permission.

Paste-ups may be hand drawn, each one original, or they may be produced by way of copy shops capable of blowing up an image to a very large size.[9] Works on paper glued to a wall are extremely vulnerable: paper can easily be ripped down by a spectator or destroyed by council cleaning crews. Those that do not meet such an end can be destroyed by the weather. In 2008, at the height of the street art boom in London, many paste-ups were torn from walls by fans and collectors such that swirls of dried glue were all that remained of them in areas such as Shoreditch.[10]

9 For examples of hand-drawn paste-ups, see the work of Miso, Cake and Swoon; while printed and copied paste-up work is produced by, among others, Shepard Fairey and JR.

10 Paste-ups are produced through the same technologies of mediation that bring the imagery of billboards and band posters to city surfaces. Such images are, however, not regarded as

Finally there is the sticker. Stickers appeal to artists on many levels. An artist might 'bomb' the city with them and put up hundreds of stickers in a single day or night. For many street artists, the sticker acts like a tag: the artist will put up stickers in the same way that a tagger writes on a surface. Often small in size, they have the appeal of a miniature version of the artist's standard work (Stewart 1993), and stickers that are hand drawn, as opposed to industrially produced in bulk orders, have far greater artistic cachet. A sticker's adhesive attaches best to some surfaces rather than others (such as metal door grilles) and affixing a sticker becomes a means for the artist to indicate that all surfaces of the city may be transformed into the setting for art, not simply the more obvious walls (on the ways in which artists view the surfaces of the city, see further discussion in Chapters 2 and 5). Stickers can be traded with other artists for the purposes of collection or in order to put up the work of others. In terms of collectability, the sticker's ability to act as miniature artwork finds its apotheosis in Berlin's museum of stickers, Hatch, run by a sticker enthusiast and showcasing his collection of thousands of tiny adhesive images.[11]

Street art is not only about surfaces; it is also very much about objects within urban spaces. Some artists eschew the practice of adding a layer (of paper or paint) to a surface and instead focus their practice on altering the very contours of the streetscape itself.[12] Sometimes this involves creating a three-dimensional object and adding it to the conventional items seen within the streetscape; at other times it involves manipulating those items so that their conventional form is brought into question. Such 'street sculpture' can be found in cities all over the world. In New York, REVS creates his tag in metal and bolts or welds the word to suitable structures in the street, ensuring that the tag will therefore endure for months or years. In Sydney and Melbourne, the sculptures of Will Coles are easy to overlook: a Coke can turns out to be obdurate rather than crushable, placed on a ledge by the artist for others to find; the discarded bagel on a traffic bollard, on close inspection, can be seen to be made of concrete and to contain a perfect set of concrete teeth within it. London artist Slinkachu came to attention in the late 2000s for placing tiny objects such as painted miniatures and snails with tagged shells in a range of urban

street art, since they are intended to advertise products for consumption and profit. In 2010, debate took place in various street art blogs as to whether Banksy's use of commercial bill posting techniques and agents to advertise the upcoming release of his film, *Exit Through the Gift Shop*, betrayed his supposed politics as a street artist: see for example, posts on *Vandalog* and my own blog *Images to Live By* in April 2010.

11 Just as paste-ups are viewed as art while band posters are mere advertising, so the stickers of street art are regarded as having a different status to stickers advertising products such as CDs, shops and sneakers, any of which can be found near areas where stickers are placed by street artists.

12 A further discussion of the ways in which artists have used objects to alter the streetscape can be found in the encounter, 'Things on Walls'.

settings; unlike the long-lasting sculptures of REVS and Will Coles, Slinkachu's 'little people' were whisked off the street by fans almost as soon as they appeared.[13] In recent years, wool and other fabrics have appeared on the street: trees, telephone boxes, tram and bus stops, bicycle racks and other forms of street furniture have been wrapped in fabric or had knitted and crocheted decorations added to them. While some yarn bombing and guerrilla knitting risks being twee, artists have demonstrated the ways in which craft can provide moments of destabilisation within the public sphere. In London, members of the collective Knit the City have chosen high-profile locations in which to situate their knitted works, allowing the juxtaposition of knitted item and monument to create arresting moments for the spectator: see for example the knitted squid they draped over a statue of Charles Darwin or the herd of knitted animals trudging across London Bridge (see Plate 3). In Melbourne a group of 'craftivists' used wool to write anti-development slogans in cross-stitch on the chain-link fence surrounding a piece of vacant land; and in New York, the Polish artist Olek staged a picnic in Washington Square Park, in which she and other participants, along with all their picnic accoutrements, were 'fabricated', by being entirely covered in crochet.

Street sculpture for many is exemplified by Darius and Downey, who welded objects to street furniture, bent lamp posts out of shape and turned CCTV cameras into art objects. For many years they collaborated in New York and in Berlin; more recently, Darius returned to New York, working now under the name Leon Reid, while Brad Downey remains based in Berlin. Much of Downey's solo work has involved working with objects in urban space, sometimes made and placed there by him, sometimes destroyed by him (as when he dug up paving stones on Karl Marx Allee in Berlin) and sometimes using the possibilities afforded by movement through space to render the entire street a sculptural setting for his artwork (or perhaps even as an artwork itself).[14] It was skateboarding that first afforded Downey a sense of the ways in which bodies could transform space and helped him to see that urban space could be sculptural:

> I would consider my first 'street art' skateboarding. A bench is no longer a bench it becomes an obstacle for self-expression. My skateboard taught me how to be creative with my surroundings and question the fundamental function of things, I remember seeing Ricky Oyola roll up a hill, jump and grind vertically up one of the bars that held together a chain link fence. It's like ballet attacking architecture. These sorts of images paved the way.

13 London-based artist Pablo Delgado has adapted the appeal of Slinkachu's miniatures into a longer-lasting format, by creating tiny paste-ups of people, affixed low down on walls.

14 One of Downey's works is described in detail in this book's second encounter with street art, 'criminal damage?'.

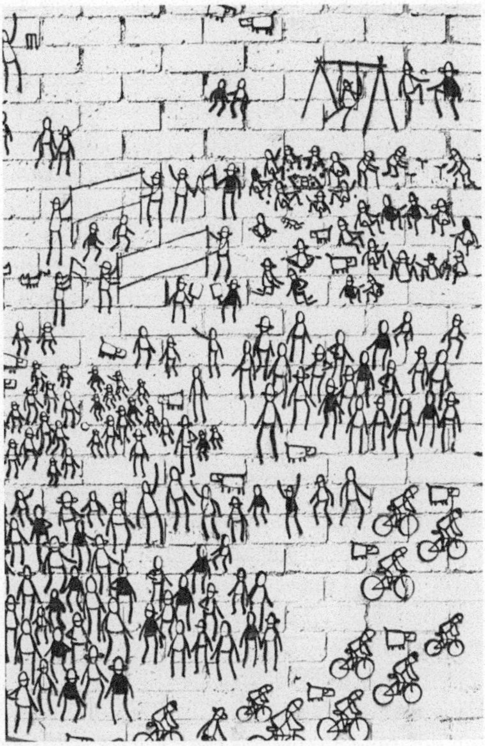

*Figure 1.2* Civil, Melbourne 2009. Photograph © Alison Young.

Sometimes the changes resulting from a street artist's intervention are tiny. Some images are placed almost out of sight. Some are situated low on a wall, or even on the pavement, visible only to a passerby who has dropped their gaze. I can remember walking through the streets of Melbourne one day, in 2003, when my eye was caught by a small stencil on a wall in the midst of a swirl of tags and throw-ups. It depicted a stick figure, with the word 'Civil' next to it, and an arrow pointing from the word to the figure surrounded by a square black frame. This small image had several meanings. On the one hand, it was the name used by the artist and so acted like a kind of signature for the image, which meant that the arrow pointing at the stick figure made it a self-portrait. But the image was also about people in general and the word 'civil' encouraged the view that people are members of civil society. These little stick figures later became a key motif in Civil's work, sometimes appearing in large numbers in much larger works.

But there was something perfect about the simplicity of this smaller version: the figure, the name, and the frame, placed on a wall in a public street.

The image is long gone, but I can still remember the delight of seeing it that first time.

Stumbling across an image in this way often feels like a gift from the artist to me as a passerby – I experience a palpable sense of lucky discovery. One day, I noticed a tiny splash of colour, high up on a brick wall. I had probably walked past it several times without noticing. But for some reason, on that day, it jumped into my field of vision – a small, brightly coloured image like a miniaturised Warhol portrait. It was a simple piece of work, nothing spectacular about it. But I liked the fact that it was placed so high on the wall, a good fifteen feet up, and thus was easy to miss (as I initially had).

Other works are impossible to overlook, created with massiveness in mind, demanding the spectator's attention. There has always been a fascination with size and scope in the production of street art and graffiti. Size is more obvious: to be able to paint a whole wall, to paint a 'burner' (which originally meant covering the whole of a subway car), or to create 'the largest' piece or paste-up.[15] But scale also drives many artists: to cover as much of an area as possible so that an individual work, which may itself be small, acquires status and impact through repetition. Some graffiti writers seek to 'bomb' the surfaces of their city, aiming for elusive 'all city' status, while street artists such as Tower, from Berlin, elicit admiration for the sheer number of stickers that they have put up around the world. Shepard Fairey is probably the artist most frequently cited with respect to scale: his paste-ups are often placed high above the city streets, on walls accessible only by climbing roofs, there for the noticing or not only if the spectator's gaze drifts upwards, and his painted walls often cover the entire side of a building (see Plate 4). Fairey's 'Andre the Giant Has a Posse' and 'Obey Giant' stickers number in the many thousands and have been placed in cities around the world since 1989. While the stickers are miniature, their accumulation over the years has created a different aspect to the very idea of the artwork, such that even when encountering a (now rare) Andre the Giant sticker on a lamp post or metal pole – as I did in New York City in 2010 – it is impossible not to view it as one of innumerable thousands.

In recent years, scale for many would be associated with the work of the French street artist and TED Prize-winner JR, who calls himself a *photograffeur*, a term derived from the French words for photograph *(la photographie)* and 'graffiti writer' *(le graffeur)* and constituting a near-homophone for the word 'photographer'. As an artist, he began his artistic career as a graffiti writer, writing his chosen tag around the city, but one day found a camera in the

15 In 2011, for example, Australian artist Drab covered most of an entire warehouse with an enormous paste-up. The act was described on *Land of Sunshine*, a Melbourne blog, as follows: 'The biggest paste up in Australia . . . 27 metres long by 8 metres high . . . 2 days, 1 scissor lift, 56 sheets of paper and 40 litres of glue', at http://deansunshine.com/drab-art-biggest-paste-up-in-australia-melbourne-2011/ (accessed on 26 January 2013).

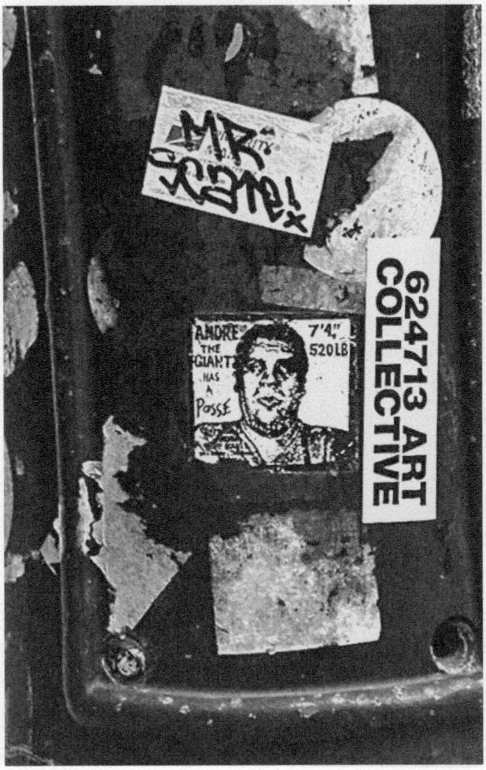


*Figure 1.3* Shepard Fairey, Andre the Giant sticker, New York 2010. Photograph © Alison Young.

Metro and began taking photographs, printing expanded versions of his images and pasting them up in the street. His work centres on a key device: his black-and-white photographs are almost always head-and-shoulders shots, waist-upwards shots, extreme close-ups of faces or of facial features such as eyes, the subjects often making caricatured expressions and grimaces. JR asks each participant to make a 'grimace' for the camera. Instead of smiling, as in conventional family snapshots, or staring expressionlessly at the lens as in portrait photography, JR's subjects screw up their faces and pull wild expressions in which eyes pop roundly, noses are scrunched up, or mouths are stretched open. These images are then blown up and either pasted in full on surfaces, or are divided into gigantic sections, such that a single eye might cover the entire wall of a building.[16]

16 See Young (2011) on certain tropes and themes in the work of JR, and see also the discussion of JR's filmed work in the first of the encounters described in this book.

Sometimes an artwork manages to balance the dichotomy between massive size and unassuming smallness. MOMO is a New York-based artist who in 2005 tagged Manhattan. This would ordinarily be taken to mean that the artist travelled around the city writing his or her tag hundreds of times on every available surface. Not in this case: MOMO certainly walked around and across the city, but he did so in order to create *one gigantic tag* using a brush to drip a continuous line of paint on the sidewalk. Only the colour of the paint changes; presumably as one can of paint ran out and the artist began another.

The tag can be viewed drawn over a map of Manhattan on MOMO's website. The map shows the word looping from the west side of Manhattan up and down and across to the east. As an artwork it is so large that it cannot be viewed in its entirety: even if one was able to hover at a height that cleared the tops of the city's skyscrapers, one would not be able to see the thin line of paint far below on the sidewalk. As Nick Riggle writes:

> One is confronted with the fact that one's senses simply cannot take in this work. What we *can* do is draw the piece out on a map; we can use *Google Maps* to visually imagine the piece. The resulting 'feeling of pleasure' would be a pleasure in the power of the imagination to recreate the piece in a digital medium – the sublime in the twenty-first century. (2010: 252–3)

It would be wrong, however, to give the impression that MOMO's 'Manhattan Tag' is a work that is all about size (although the audacity of the enterprise is certainly impressive). 'Manhattan Tag' also offers a much more intimate and modest dimension. Its massive scale is, in fact, something that exists cartographically, while the spectator in the street views the work as something much more simple: a thin line of paint on the pavement.

And that is all it is: one can stand on it, or look in either direction to see it turning a corner or moving out of sight. Something of its size can be experienced by treating it as a walking trail, but even so, all it offers is the sight of a line of paint upon the ground (see Plate 5). If a spectator chooses to view a small section of it, a thin strip of paint is all that will be seen; yet if the same spectator elects to walk its entire length, a thin strip of paint is still all that will be seen, except for a longer period of time and in a number of changing environments. Either way, it invites engagement with the smallest and simplest of aesthetic interventions in public space – a line – while standing or walking through the city. Thus, 'Manhattan Tag' demonstrates how the massive and the modest can exist in equipoise; and how even a single line of paint can transform the way we look at the city.

Images, objects, *words*. Much street art is text-based, as befits a cultural practice that derives in part from graffiti and in part from political activism.

Mobstr has become notorious for his sly, lettered interventions around London, which feature black capital letters stencilled onto walls, drawing the spectator's attention to the techniques of the art form while also following in the footsteps of the Conceptual art tradition in presenting a word as though it is an image: one of Mobstr's 2013 pieces simply states 'GRAFFITI'. Others satirise the recent enthusiasm for street art (one states 'OH WOW LOOK IT'S SOME STREET ART'; another says 'THIS WILL BE AVAILABLE ON CANVAS LATER'). Words also provide the lynchpin for the connection between street art and the lengthy history of street protest, whether via the 1968 *événements* in Paris or the culture-jamming activities of adbusters, such as Sydney's BUGA UP activists (Billboard Utilising Graffitists Against Unhealthy Promotions), who, throughout the 1980s and 1990s, targeted tobacco, alcohol and soft drinks, painting billboards with scornful slogans to subvert the allure of advertised products.[17] Such a strategy of *détournement* has persisted throughout much of street art: many artists express a distaste for mainstream advertising and for the limitations of the media, arguing that their activities create a broader range of information for the general public and demonstrating that the individual need not rely solely on mainstream news media (McGaw 2008). In Melbourne in the 1990s, it was possible to read the walls of certain neighbourhoods as providing an alternative conversation to that offered in the newspapers: certainly the volume of commentary written on pavements and walls was one of the factors that impelled me to take interest in situational art.[18]

Text has been important to street art for reasons that draw more on street art's intersecting history with graffiti writing, which centres upon the letter form, and its elaboration into a kind of pictoriality. In Melbourne, the artist Slicer, a member of the AWOL crew, creates enormous works that appear initially to be abstract fields of coloured lines; however, they are in fact attenuated letter forms, legible to the artist and encoding a range of comments and messages (see Plate 6). José Parlá's studio works, which create walls on canvas, incorporate similarly swooping calligraphy, as if the canvases had been tagged. The aesthetic nature of such textuality within artworks is clear; however, is it possible to make aesthetic claims for tagging itself, probably the most notorious word-based urban intervention?

Tagging is the writing of an artist's chosen name, often in a particular calligraphic style, often repeated many times on different surfaces. In one of the most thoughtful accounts of tagging within the cityscape, Sinclair

17 See also the practices and activities of artists such as Mobstr, Robert Montgomery, Jordan Seiler and the Public Ad Campaign and Mustafa Hulusi.

18 In 1997, the political graffiti in one suburb, Fitzroy, covered issues such as sexual assault, media images of women, party politics, gentrification and development, Aboriginal issues and homophobia.

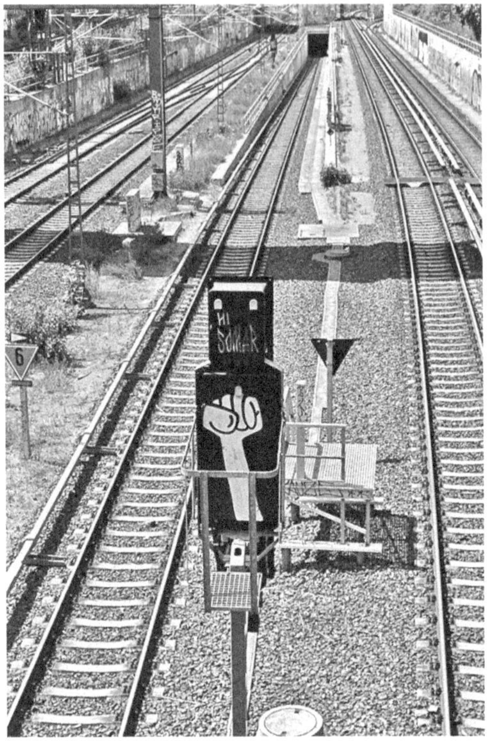


*Figure I.4* Kripoe, Berlin 2010. Photograph © Alison Young.

differentiates between the efforts of 'the purist' who writes a 'plain tag'; the 'clubbing tagger's E-vision', the 'hit-and-run calligrapher' who aims for quantity over quality of tags, resulting in a conglomeration of 'night scrawls, minimal adjustments to the psychic skin of the city' (1997: 12–13). Iconic images can also function as tags (examples can be found in Banksy's rats, which are as recognisable as any stencilled word stating 'Banksy', or the clenched fist of Kripoe in Berlin).

Tagging derived from graffiti is often hard to read, its calligraphy an elaboration of whorls, dots, arrows and lines. Other artists deploy a simpler style. This may be because they are bombers who are repeating the tag as many times as possible and thus need something that can be written fast, or the artist may have adopted an easy-to-read style for aesthetic or political reasons. In the 2000s, Melbourne's 70k crew evolved a particular calligraphy that was instantly recognisable as theirs, functioning as a brand of membership in their crew. In Berlin in 2010, writers were trying out variations on 'ugly' lettering, taking squarish shapes and attempting to push them to extremes. Brad Downey, in addition to the street sculptures described above, is also a prolific tagger. He decided not to tag under a pseudonym and simply writes his name, with the result that 'Brad Downey was here' and 'Brad Downey war hier' appear all over Berlin. Downey explained to me that sometimes property owners discover his website through Google and write to him, asking 'Why did you tag my building?' He then writes back, describing his attitudes to public space and mark-making and on most occasions an interesting correspondence ensues.

For many spectators, tagging elicits questions. Why do it? What is the point? Such responses indicate that the tag occupies a distinctive position within street art's ambiguous categorisation as 'possibly art' and 'possibly crime'. In considering the tag's aesthetic potential, let me begin obliquely: I was watching television one night, in 2009, when ABC Australia screened a filmed version of *The Eternity Man*, an opera which has been performed in London, Sydney and elsewhere, with music by Jonathan Mills and a libretto by the late Australian poet, Dorothy Porter.

*The Eternity Man* tells the story of Arthur Stace, who chalked the word 'Eternity' in meticulous copperplate script on Sydney's streets, walls and buildings for decades. His identity was unknown for many years and the reality of his existence – a formerly homeless alcoholic who was almost certainly schizophrenic – came as a shock to those who had speculated as to who might be behind such flowing 'penmanship'. Stace's handiwork, although initially decried as graffiti, was eventually recast as an idiosyncratic aspect of Sydney's identity. This process of redefinition reached its apotheosis long after Stace's death in 1967, when Sydney celebrated the arrival of the new millennium (and the Sydney Olympics) by lighting up the Harbour Bridge with thousands of fireworks spelling out the word 'Eternity' in what was clearly the style of Stace's handwriting. The opera continues this investment in the figure of Stace, representing him as a melancholic, enigmatic loner hallucinating his memories and anxieties around Sydney, and calming his fears through the repeated inscription of this single word.

While watching the film, it struck me that what Stace was doing was 'bombing' the city. The word 'Eternity' is like a tag, written over and over, and Stace's nocturnal wanderings and indiscriminate interest in any urban surface was a version of going 'all city', covering urban space with the author's tag. A few decades ago, when Stace was writing 'Eternity' in Sydney, his actions were regarded as graffiti, but now he is considered in a different light. What now prevents Stace being viewed as a 'vandal' and the word he wrote being thought of as his tag? While the retrospective revelation of Stace's probable mental illness assists in the romanticising of his obsession and the exoneration of his actions, the same admiration directed at Arthur Stace and his copperplate script could in fact be turned towards the effort it takes to develop and execute a good tag. In 2006, Melbourne street artist xero argued that, 'putting up a tag is not mindless. It represents imagination, dedication

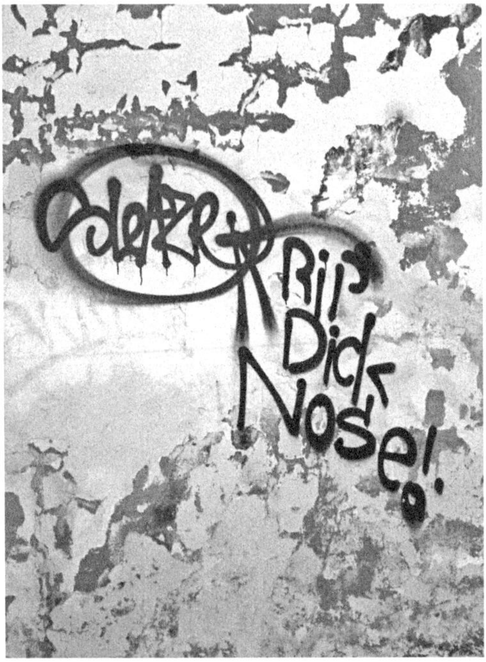


*Figure 1.5* Memorial tag for Dick Nose, Melbourne 2012. Photograph © Alison Young.

to an art form, and the willingness to take a risk in a public place to achieve an aesthetic outcome (even if it is one that we don't happen to like)'.[19]

*The Eternity Man* made me think about others who write words on a city's walls yet who are not remembered in the same Romantic light as enigmatic but admirable figures. The copperplate script used by Stace is in many ways as exacting and particular as the calligraphy used by taggers, who often spend hours refining and perfecting their letter forms. Despite their complexity, tags are often called 'scrawl' or 'scribble'; they are condemned for being illegible. Taggers are similarly criticised: news media has compared taggers to dogs urinating on lamp posts, and taggers often get called 'vandals' (Young 2005). 'Dick Nose', the moniker of an American living in Melbourne, a sometime poet, heroin user, and the city's most extensive tagger of urban surfaces, provides a point of comparison with Stace. Dick Nose would write his assumed name or its initials, DN, in blocky capital letters anywhere he fancied; as he walked the streets, any surface might be lettered by him. When, in 2012, it emerged that he had died of an overdose, his contemporaries covered the walls

19 In email correspondence with me.

of his favourite neighbourhoods with memorial tags: 'DN', 'DN', 'RIP DN' ('a Fitzroy requiem', as one local street artist described it). Both Dick Nose's efforts while alive and those that memorialised his death inspired conservative commentators to great ire, with one blogger expressing pleasure at his death.[20]

While Dick Nose's lettering had none of the unexpected grace of Arthur Stace's, it is hard to see why Dick Nose's actions should automatically be viewed as worthlessly criminal. As a form of urban intervention, the tag is certainly challenging, and Dick Nose's tags were among some of the least visually interesting tags it is possible to find. Nevertheless, rather than the tagger having to assert value in what she does, I believe that any move to create an exceptional category – in which the tag is separated out from other forms of street art – is untenable. Perhaps it is the ubiquity of the tag that makes it easy to single out for disapprobation; perhaps it is the assumption that it is easy to execute, or the product of mischievousness rather than intelligence. In this book, however, I include the tag in the repertory of street art techniques and genres, taking seriously the idea that the motivation for tagging might be to contribute something valid to the 'conversation with the street' (to use a phrase employed by the Berlin-based artist Dave the Chimp): to create something that is in its way an image, an icon, an urban text.

## The street artist

Who makes street art? The research for this book involved talking to artists about why they have placed artworks in the street. For a number of reasons, the stories and views of street artists are not often featured in public discourse. First, street artists, despite the increasing mainstream acceptability and appeal of street art, are often invisible to most members of the public, who come upon the after-effects of an artist's efforts – the artwork – without actually encountering the work's creator. Second, their views do not regularly appear in news media. Although many artists' websites put them within email contact, their opinions are less often featured in mainstream media articles about street art than the views of city council staff, local residents and police, who function as the 'primary definers' of the topic, to use the terminology of Hall et al (1978). Finally, despite the populist appeal of much street art, it is still illegal unless done with the property owner's consent, and street artists therefore risk self-incrimination when talking to journalists – and to researchers.

The interviews for this book were conducted with sixty-four artists, in several cities, over a period of years. Most were done in person and led to

20 The blog Fitzroyalty published a post, which stated 'Happy days! There is one less vandal in the world'. See http://indolentdandy.net/fitzroyalty/2012/03/13/one-less-vandal/ (accessed on 26 January 2013).

lengthy conversations; with some, repeat sessions were organised, owing to the range of their opinions or experiences. A small number were conducted by email. My attempts to meet graffiti writers when researching my earlier book, *Judging the Image* (2005), showed me how disastrous it can be to simply write to an Internet forum offering an email address and inviting people to contact me. Forum users found this suspicious: some sent me threatening messages, others simply stated on the forum that I was probably a 'pig' and a 'cop'.[21] Although I learnt how difficult it is to 'cold call' for an interview, I still attempted to approach some artists directly via email or websites. This was sometimes successful but more often led to silence (either because the artist was being cautious or as a result of the sheer volume of emails that a well-known artist might receive).

I had more success with personal encounters: at art openings, street art festivals and so on. These early interviews were important in establishing my *bona fides* (that I was not connected to the police and that confidentiality would be respected) given the suspiciousness towards outsiders in the street art world. Many artists referred me to others, especially when travelling overseas, drawing on contacts from the global community of street artists. Also important in establishing *bona fides* was my blog, *Images To Live By*, which I began in 2008. My aim was to create a space in which to think about issues I knew would be important in my research, to feature short essays on particular artworks I had encountered or artists whose work I was discovering. I also wanted to write pieces for a broader audience in a more everyday style than that found in academic publishing. I soon realised than an important aspect of the blog was its ability to act as a bridge between myself and various artists, since I was able to direct them to various pieces, and thus demonstrate how I was approaching the topic.

So who, then, are the artists that place work on the street? It is possible to answer that question using conventional demographic attributes about age, gender, class and so on, and some of those details will emerge in what follows. But my intention is rather to allow their identities to be read through their recounted histories, experiences and desires. In each interview, the conversation covered certain questions: their motivation for beginning to make images in public space (those early images may have been very different from the artworks they later become known for), memories of their first experience, and their intentions in putting up work in the street, whether initially or more recently. The resulting stories are diverse and the motivations heterogeneous, but they cluster around the idea that the placing of situational art in public space is, variously, cultural, communicative, oppositional, aesthetic and affective.

21 Their caution was not without foundation: in Australia police have monitored a range of websites and social media in order to identify writers for prosecution: see, for example, Croy (2013).

The *cultural* aspect of street art derives from the ways in which its practitioners see it as a means of belonging to a community of cultural practitioners. Many recounted their primary motivation as being a desire to join in with something others were already doing; others described their initial activities as inspired by the work of others and a desire to create something comparable. To that extent, street art is not just a cultural practice, but a culture in itself, with hierarchies, conventions, forms of inclusions and exclusion. Certain artists become aspirational figures, motivating others to emulation; alternatively it may simply be the activities that exert an attraction upon others, such that they desire membership of the street art community, something that can only be achieved through making street art.

It is not always street art itself that inspires the desire to join this cultural community. Although large numbers of interviewees stated that they responded to the work of other street artists or to street art itself, graffiti culture was even more significant. Older street artists traced their careers back to train writing or tagging, only later developing an interest in an expanded range of techniques or effects; even those with no background in graffiti commented that seeing it on walls prompted them to develop their own skills or to consider how they too could have an impact on public space. Although graffiti may be the initial motivating force, artists also expanded their interests from other cultural forms into the street. These include: punk, skateboarding, political protest, comics and 'zines, performance art and poetry. Younger artists who grew up with stencils as well as tags were inspired by seeing street art on the walls of their city. Some grew up with street art all around them and the desire to create and take part seemed like an incremental aspect of the world they moved in:

> It was a combination of meeting a young street artist who said 'Oh your work's really good. Why isn't it on the street?' and meeting friends of friends, who were friends with a street artist who had an exhibition, sort of being in there and seeing how much street art was around.
>
> (Kaff-eine)

For others, coming into contact with street art was more sudden. As Perth-born artist the Doctor described: 'coming to Melbourne when I was 17 it was definitely an eye-opener . . . It was like a light switch . . . everything around me was just screaming art.'

Where graffiti writing has an insular quality (many writers are famously indifferent or even hostile to whether their work can be understood by outsiders) most street artists regard communicating with others as an essential component of what they do. According to Ellis Gallagher in New York, street art 'is communication between [artists], it's also communication to the people, it's proclamations'. Street art is thought to be capable of communicating on many levels: as a political device, inviting reflection on attitudes

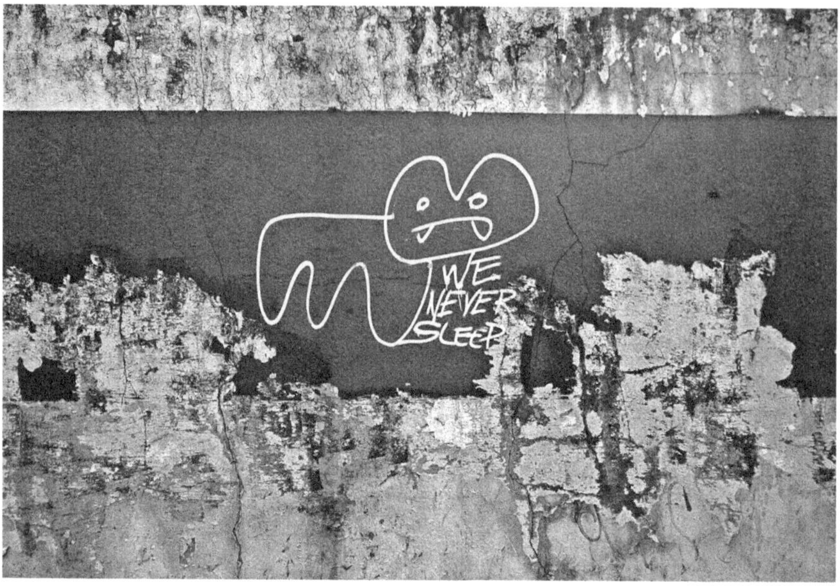


*Figure 1.6* Pure Evil, London 2009. Photograph © Mark Rigney – Hookedblog.

with a view to social change; to bring pleasure, by making the spectator smile; and seeking the spectator's emotional interaction with the work. Artists including Jean Faucheur in Paris, Tom Civil in Melbourne, Garrison Buxton and John Fekner in New York, and Pisa 73, Tower, Just and Emess in Berlin pointed to the links between street art and political activism: for them, street art is inextricably linked to their involvement in issues such as the militarisation of policing, globalisation, democratic social movements, gentrification and the privatisation of public space. Even when not protesting specific issues, the capacity of street art to function as a potent form of *political communication* was recognised by many artists. Pure Evil in London was typical in saying: 'it's important to be a political artist . . . If you've got a voice why not use it to try and make a change?' Many regard the act of putting up work in the street as inherently political: according to Tower, in Berlin, 'it was like a political statement to go out and make something', while Swoon, in New York, noted that 'even if you don't begin it as a political gesture . . . it's a form of active participation in public space.'

For many artists, such 'active participation' is focused on the idea that street art partakes in a conversation with the city by making marks within it. Sometimes this activity is evident only to the artist; for example, Ghostpatrol in Melbourne said he tried to make at least one mark a day, known only to him. At other times, it generates a much broader sense of communication:

Just (Berlin) stated that writing on walls allowed him 'to have a connection to the city' and for El Bocho (Berlin) 'it's a possibility to be a part of the whole construction of the city'. From this broader connection, many artists hope to encourage positive change by transforming the way the spectator relates to public space. Jordan Seiler, in New York, hopes his street art will demonstrate that '[this] place has a potential to be possibly better than it is right now' and Alice, in Rome, puts it thus: 'we want to transform [this place] so it's even better than it is'.

Two specific aspects of street art's political nature are worth emphasising. The first is that street art is often motivated by generosity: the artist seeks to make a gift of the artwork to the spectator, the neighbourhood and the city itself. This may not sound political. However, it is important to remember that two facets of contemporary image-making – the art market and the vast regimes of modern advertising – make the economy of the gift rare in contemporary culture. Pure Evil commented that in leaving a canvas in the street, 'it's a piece of free art for someone to take away'; and Kaff-eine said that much of her pleasure in the activity came from knowing that her artwork 'is going to make someone's day'. As John Fekner summed up: 'the spirit of giving is an inherent trait in all street artists'. A gift may not be appreciated or wanted (we all know the experience of opening a present and wondering why we have been given these socks or this book). But, if the street artist proffers the gift, it is then up to the recipient – the property owner, the city council, the graffiti writer, the passerby, the police officer – to decide what to do with it. CDH put it thus: 'the artwork is . . . gifted to the community. And that's it. I don't own it anymore . . . It belongs to each individual in the community and any individual can modify it.'

The second aspect of the political nature of street art relates to its perceived democratic nature (both in being made and being looked at). Street artists repeatedly assert that 'anyone can do it'; that is, make street art without special skills, education, materials, or access to the institutions of the art world. For Swoon, street art can be made 'with the simplest tool that everyone can get their hands on'; in Cake's view 'any kid on the street can still make a painting in his house and then put it up for free'; Just noted that 'everyone can join in'; while Roa joked that 'any asshole with a spraycan can make a difference'. Perhaps Mare139 put it best: 'Anyone can get involved . . . street art and graffiti democratised the act of making art in ways that no other art form has been able to do in history.' According to Ghostpatrol, the only obstacle between an individual and the act of making a situational artwork is 'you just have to have the balls to do it'. This could be formulated as a general rule with regards to urban space. Austin, for example, characterises the normal prohibitions of property and criminal law as 'a kind of invisible cultural repellent' that coats urban surfaces (2004: 221). This effectively deters individuals from looking at the city as a potential canvas. Among those who do not recognise the deterrent effect of criminal or property law (and I will return to this attribute shortly) 'anyone' and 'everyone' is able to make situational art.

Generality and inclusiveness (typified by the terms 'anyone' and 'everyone') characterise the discourse of democracy and reappear in the ways that street artists imagine their audience. The notion of 'making art for everyone' is a dominant feature in artists' stories. Remi/Rough says of graffiti and street art that 'it's for the people, it's for everyone', and Ad Deville is more prescriptive, stating that 'art should be for the people'. There is an almost philanthropic dimension to the way the audience is imagined, which fits neatly with the idea that street art is a gift. Peat Wollaeger, for example, described himself as 'bringing art to people who wouldn't normally experience it'. Such democratisation also exists in the sense that viewing street art in public space is a non-hierarchical activity. For Kaff-eine, all interpretations of a street artwork are valid: 'a kid, or a homeless dude, or an academic can walk down that same lane and read it any way they want'. Dscreet took this further and declared street art to be a way to resolve his 'dislike' for 'the elitism of the art system'.

That the artworks are freely accessible is also important, with 'free' connoting both available without payment ('it's public art', Remi/Rough) and also scattered throughout the everyday spaces of the city ('free for everyone to discover', Brad Downey). Street art means for Swoon that she is able to 'talk to people who don't feel welcome in [an upmarket gallery]' while, for Emess, street art is 'free for everybody to look at art and not only an élite cultural thing'. It should be noted that opponents of street art offer a different vision of democracy; namely, that street artists remove individual choice by imposing their works upon the passerby and by adopting an autocratic position with respect to other people's property. Such a vision is incommensurable with the views of street artists. However, my aim is not to reconcile competing views, but rather, to demonstrate how public space demands a discourse of democracy when debating the issue of entitlement to make images within it. Such questions of authorisation and entitlement will be taken up again in Chapter 5.

Although the preceding discussion makes clear that street artists see their activities as politically positive, it is also true that many artists consider their work as critical or oppositional. For some, opposition is concrete and readily identifiable: for example, a critical attitude to advertising or to the mainstream media (Tom Civil, Jordan Seiler and Garrison Buxton, Ad Deville, Jean Faucheur, CDH and The Wa). This view is also found in Banksy's writings. He repeatedly criticises the advertising industry for inflicting its commercial imagery upon the general public:

> The people who truly deface our neighbourhoods are the companies that scrawl giant slogans across buildings and buses trying to make us feel inadequate unless we buy their stuff. They expect to be able to shout their

> message in your face from every available surface but you're never allowed to answer back. Well, they started the fight and the wall is the weapon of choice to hit them back.
>
> (2005a: 9)

For others, what is more important is a sense that street art (and graffiti) is '*against something*' (Mare139) even if there is no clearly defined object of critique. Street art was called 'rebellion', 'rebellious' or 'subversive' by many (Vexta, Ad Deville, John Fekner, Remi/Rough, Garrison Buxton, Miso, Just, Nick Ilton, Sparcs). Early efforts at situational art were recognised to be fairly chaotic: 'drunken rampages of tagging' (Nails); and 'being an angry teenager with no intellectual content to it – just fuck you, fuck everything' (Kid Zoom). Once artists settled in to street art the notion of oppositional politics became more developed: 'once you start breaking the law, you start thinking, well, why can't I break the law, why is this the law, and these questions start breaking into your consciousness' (Swoon).

As Swoon's comments highlight, there is a legal dimension that is crucial to street art's oppositional politics. The illegality of the act was often described as 'thrilling' or otherwise pleasurable (Pure Evil, Elbow-Toe, Dscreet, Eine, Sparcs, Meggs, Laser 3.14, Disturbanity, Just). But, more importantly, it was characterised as crucial for street art to have meaning in order to distinguish it from the many other forms of mark-making in public space (advertising, official signage, public art, and so on). For Jaybo, illegality is 'the point', like C215, who commented that legalisation of street art would cause him to desist from making it: 'If it was legal I wouldn't do it. Because the poetry would be completely faded'. Issues of criminality and decriminalisation will return in Chapter 4. However, there is another dimension to street art's critique of the current legal arrangement of public space. Almost half of those interviewed spoke of a concern with property and public space: a desire to 'reclaim' the city, create new ways of thinking about ownership, and encourage people to feel a sense of engagement with and ability to transform public space (issues of property and authority will be considered in Chapter 5). *Oppositionality*, then, as a motivation for street artists, varies from an inchoate and unfocused sense of rejecting *something* to extensive and thoughtful arguments about street art's potential to contest social arrangements and indicate new attitudes to shared public spaces.

There are two further aspects of how street artists view their practice that I would like to elaborate. The first relates to the *aesthetic* attributes of the situational artwork: artists do not simply want to oppose, belong or communicate with the passerby in public space. The aesthetics of street art were important to over a third of interviewed artists, with another one quarter specifically invoking the idea that a situational artwork could *beautify* a location. Artists invoked diverse aesthetic influences, including Gordon

Matta-Clark's manipulations of space, Jenny Holzer's public interventions and text-based artworks, performance art, and Situationism.[22] In contrast to the critiques of street art and graffiti found in mainstream media (Young 2005) and the characterisation of graffiti in the criminological 'broken windows' thesis as precipitating factors in social decline, artists see their works as enhancing rather than destroying, creating rather than undermining urban amenity. Pisa73 said that 'those things we painted illegally ended up being nicer afterwards than they were before' and, for Kaff-eine, street art 'makes [a rundown space] a bit nicer and . . . makes it a more pleasant place for people to visit'. Banksy also subscribes to this view: 'some people become vandals because they want to make the world a better *looking* place' (2005a: 9).

More than this, however, beauty is specifically invoked either in the sense that the artwork itself is a thing of beauty or it brings beauty into the life of the passerby. CDH proposed that the street artwork acts 'like a magnifying glass for the simple beauty in things' and draws attention to textures, colours and shapes that would otherwise be overlooked. Cake, an artist who places hand-painted portraits on walls in New York, described a moment driving in her car when she encountered a street artwork by Swoon: 'Bam! We have a moment of beauty. That's fricking awesome. I didn't have to go to a museum. I didn't have to go to a gallery. I was just driving home from IKEA.' Given that the law fixates upon the notion that the situational artwork involves damage to property, it is important to remember that a great many artists engage in street art with the rather different goal of aesthetic enhancement.

The invitation to make art that the artist identifies as coming from the city, further discussed in Chapter 3, may in fact be experienced as a compulsion. A number of artists used tropes of addiction to describe the activity of making situational art. Almost a fifth of the artists characterised themselves as 'addicted' to street art, 'needing to do it', 'unable to control it' or 'compelled' to do it. It would be erroneous to interpret such statements negatively as proving the commonplace denunciation of situational art is problematic, antisocial or criminogenic (Berg 2004; Young 2005). Tropes of addiction are being used by the interviewees in the colloquial sense, as markers for desire and pleasure, rather than in any specific physiological definition. Many things may be described as 'addictive' (running marathons, playing Monopoly,

22 For an extended consideration of the aesthetic influences on street art as a genre, see Lewisohn (2008) and Daniel Feral's diagram, created in 2011, mapping the 70-year extant history of graffiti and street art as a valid mainstream art form, influenced by and influencing genres of art. Feral explains the diagram as 'utilizing the same graphic vocabulary as Alfred H. Barr, Jr (the first director of MoMA . . . in 1937) to create an impression of authority equivalent to [Barr's own] diagram. The Feral Diagram picks up chronologically where Barr left off, thereby subverting and redirecting the officially recognised historical trajectory', online at http://graffuturism.com/2012/09/24/daniel-feral-releases-feral-diagram-2-0-at-futurism-2-0-symmetry-across-centuries/ (accessed on 29 January 2013).

going to the movies, eating habanero peppers) and there is nothing in the artists' comments indicating that situational art is a problem requiring policy intervention, policing or disapprobation. If any lesson can be drawn from the fact that street artists refer to their work as addictive it is that any social policy will find it hard to deter people from situational art given that its *affective* qualities are so intense.

Affect, then, is the final feature that emerged in the interviews conducted for this research, and it is a profoundly important one. In Chapter 2, I will elaborate aspects of the affective dimension of the *spectator's* encounter with situational art; for now, I wish to emphasise the ways in which street art is affectively charged for the artist. Some describe it, as noted above, as addictive, denoting the experience of pleasure in an activity that they do not wish to stop. For others, it is thrilling, resulting in the literal intensities of the adrenaline surge. Banksy's account of his first experience of tagging captures this: 'That was the night that I discovered that beyond the "No Entry" sign everything happens in higher definition. Adrenaline sharpens your eyesight, each little sound becomes significant, your sense of smell becomes more acute, and tramps shit everywhere' (quoted in McCormick et al. 2010: 3). One surprising affective spur that emerged in my interviews was the therapeutic effect of making situational art: an eighth of interviewees mentioned a traumatic event, serious illness or personal loss as motivating them to begin or continue making street art.

Subsuming these various strands is the experience of pleasure, which was explicitly mentioned by half of the interviewees. Some called it 'fun' or 'enjoyable' and said that it simply makes them 'happy'; others referred to the stronger appellation 'joy'. The pleasure of street art in part draws upon the sense of executing objectives such as oppositional politics or the transformation of public space, but, much more than this, street art itself involves an affective corporeality that the artist may not experience at other times. Such pleasure is all about bodily sense, which is heightened in the demands of the work's illicit situationality. El Bocho identified the very *sound* of spray paint as pleasurable, and Tower, describing his activities as a prolific sticker artist, said that repetition becomes a source of bodily enjoyment: 'you do it hundreds of times and you become part of the flow'. The most extended account of the haptic pleasure of situational art was provided by Melbourne artist CDH:

> You have this sense of exposure . . . You know that if somebody, a policeman, comes around the corner, or a member of the public that doesn't like what you're doing, there's a risk to you now, or you're out in laneways in the middle of the night as well, so I guess you could be mugged or something, there's that sense as well, so there is a sense of a threat or a sense of exposure but you just kind of manage it and deal with it anyway. That brings a heightened sense of things. That's the only way I can describe it. So when you're painting in that kind of mindset or that

> environment, you're just feeling . . . for me, anyway, like I'm more alive, like I can feel, I just can feel the life going through me more intensely, sometimes you can kind of get into a routine and you go through life a little bit like a zombie. When I'm doing that kind of street art, especially when I first started out, it was like a sense of being awake. Truly awake, like things are more heightened, you're more attuned, obviously you're looking around more, and you're listening more carefully, and little sounds you hear and you're just aware of the sounds around you. But also touching the surface. Especially the smell of the paint. That was something always for me as well. And I know that smell so well now that I can – even if there's a little trace of it. If someone's painting, if someone's been painting with aerosol cans, even one or two days before, I can still kind of smell it. I'm kind of attuned to that smell. Yeah, the texture of the surface, the texture of the brick, the cold air on your skin, the feeling of the can in your hand, all those things, you just become aware of . . . it's just like everything is turned up. That's the best way I can describe it.

Cake names the intensity differently:

> It's pleasurable. It's spiritual. I'm not religious, but . . . when you're making work and you're in the process of making it, it's your connection to whatever 'God' is. Which means your most authentic self, your purest relationship to what life is and what you are.

Such affective intensity, experienced by the artist, may leave its traces in the situational artwork, haunting the spectator's subsequent encounter with it.

Affect has been receiving increasing attention in legal and criminological scholarship (see for example, Halsey and Young 2006; Hickey-Moody and Malins 2007; Buchanan and Johnson 2009; Young 2010b). As Massumi notes, affect invokes 'ways in which the body can connect with itself and with the world' (1992: 93). It is relational, responsive and productive. It is not a means of confirming the identity of the one who experiences affect (which would make it synonymous with identity); nor is it isomorphous with emotion; it refers instead to an intensity that registers in the body and is later named as emotion, or thought. As Massumi states, '[affect] is intensity owned and recognized. It is crucial to theorize the difference between affect and emotion' (2002: 28).

The encounter with situational art provokes affective intensities within the spectator herself, due to the spectator's recognition of two things: first, the artist's *desire* to make unauthorised images in the face of their prohibition; and, second, the fact of *trespass*, in the transgression of lines drawing distinctions between 'your' property and 'mine'. Thus the street artwork can never be encountered simply as 'an image', or even as 'an image in public space'. It is always encountered situationally: illicit, out of place, capable of re-purposing urban structures as settings for art, as a product of its situation. As such it is always already a *controversion* of values that are foundational to law, society and to images themselves (those of authorship and ownership, of boundaries and entitlement). In facing the controversion offered by the encounter with the situational artwork, the spectator is inevitably placed in a position of response and responsibility regarding the artwork, required to answer for herself the questions, 'what is it?', 'who made this', and 'why?'.

This book thinks through the ways in which these questions have been posed and the discursive frames shaping conventional answers to them. It would be easy to mistake the book's approach as stemming from an uncritical affection for situational art – to assume it is a 'fanboy' account that pays no heed to the opinions of those who do not share this point of view. While I am sure that my enjoyment of situational art imbues the tone of the book; its argument is not one that depends on personal taste. Indeed, its argument proposes that taste is something that comes *after* affect and is as mutable as the design and form of urban space itself. As will be set out in greater detail in Chapter 2, the street artwork is something that engenders an uncanny affective encounter for the spectator. Such affect can be interpreted as pleasure or as resentment: those are discriminations based on the shifting boundaries of personal taste. Instead, the book examines the ways in which affect intersects with notions of property, entitlement, ownership and propriety in urban space to such an extent that situational artists have been sent to prison and that anti-graffiti strategies have provided populist platforms for social regulation. The book therefore does not offer an argument based on 'liking' street art; rather it interrogates the effects of the ways in which we think about cities, law, boundaries and space. Such conceptualisations frame the passerby's encounter with the situational artwork and set the scene for the affective intensity that it generates.

To think, then, about the street artwork as an *encountered sign*, both the book and the research on which it is based have been structured around the idea of movement through the public spaces of the city. It follows a number of critics and writers in using walking as a methodology, drawing from the philosophies of de Certeau (1984b) and Benjamin (1999) and the writings of Sophie Cunningham (2012), China Miéville (2012), Iain Sinclair (1997), and Edmund White (2008).[23] In highlighting the constitutive aspects of walking, I do not mean to ignore other modes of movement: the individual travelling on trains, trams and buses is still able to notice and respond to a situational artwork. One day on a train in Melbourne, which runs at times on elevated tracks (with views of nearby warehouse walls), an elderly couple next to me tutted and said to each other, 'Look at all that graffiti, it's disgusting.'

23 On de Certeau and his philosophy as walking, see further Careri (2002), Meagher (2007), Morris (2004) and Pinder (2011); on Benjamin's *Arcades Project*, see Buck-Morss (1991).

Even when driving, a passerby can still encounter an artwork: when I realised that there was an Invader mosaic attached to a wall at a freeway entrance in Melbourne the sense of surprise was probably heightened by the fact that the artwork was seen so fleetingly. However, it is undeniable that the greatest potential for signification arises during an encounter with a situational artwork when we are on foot, on the street, in motion at our own pace, able to stop and look or walk on past. As befits a book based on the idea of movement through the city as constitutive of spectatorship and citizenship, subsequent chapters will thus pursue lines of inquiry as though following routes through the cityscape itself, tracing the directions and contours of the urban imagination at work in situational art. Interspersed between these chapters are short accounts of encounters with street art (or with its absence), in which I write as a spectator to the artwork, about the contours and consequences of particular interventions in public space.

Following on from Chapter 1's discussion of artworks and artists, the next chapter will consider the artwork as it exists within city spaces. It will continue to interrogate the signifying encounter with the situational artwork, drawing upon Jill Bennett's work on art and spectatorship (2005: 7), as she in turn draws upon Deleuze.[24] But where the opening chapter has focused upon the affective connection of the artist with the artwork, the second chapter pursues the nature of the spectator's encounter with the situational artwork, particularly as it arises out of the affect generated by the artwork's status as an uncommissioned, un-author(is)ed work, visible in public space and located on private property. The chapter also considers what situational artworks can tell us about the nature of cities and the possibilities for new kinds of citizenship through imaginative practices that produce a public city based on a commons of the image.

The perspective is widened in Chapter 3 by considering the effects of situational art upon the cityscape itself. Situational art can play multiple roles within a cityscape, at times beautifying run-down areas, at times contributing, deliberately or not, to processes of gentrification and urban renewal, and at other times associated with profit-making and the art market bubble. Above all, this chapter emphasises the lived nature of urban space as it manifests in the views and experiences of artists as they move in and through city spaces. It also constructs thematic portraits of several cities, based, for each one, on a key characteristic of the cityscape that street art has helped to produce.

The law's encounter with the situational artwork forms the focus of both Chapters 4 and 5. The street artwork is criminalised as criminal damage and under various anti-graffiti statutes; Chapter 4 considers the ways in which such criminalisation arises from the affective dimension of the law's encounter with situational art, examining the ways in which the criminal law

24 See also Grosz (2008) for further consideration of ways in which art can be viewed after Deleuze.

and criminal justice system utilise an 'exemplary jurisprudence' when judging the illicit word or image in public space, and elaborating the consequences of such a paradigm of criminalisation for graffiti writers and street artists who are arrested and charged. One of the animating aims of my research in this area has been the reduction of risks both of criminalisation and of harsh sentencing; the experiences of writers and artists detailed in this chapter demonstrate that there is an urgent need to find news ways for the criminal law to view the situational artwork.

It is all too easy to focus on the criminalisation of situational art without attending to other dimensions of the law's encounter with street art. However, part of the situational character of street art is its location without permission upon private property in public space. Chapter 5 examines the consequences of the law's conceptualisation of urban space as composed of pieces of *property*. The concept of property covers both 'things' (*res*) and the legal regime of their 'ownership' and the chapter considers the challenges that situational art presents to both. It also points out how the strategies of criminalisation elaborated in the previous chapter depend upon and are shored up by certain conceptions of ownership, land and space. On the one hand, the aim of this chapter is to set out the ways in which the law of property routinely excludes situational art, but on the other hand it will also emphasise that the very existence of situational art reveals other ways of thinking about land, boundaries and entitlement (and to that extent takes up the idea of the commons of the urban imagination considered in Chapter 2).

Having progressed thus far through urban space, the final chapter maps some of the transformations that street art has undergone in the years of its development from a relatively unknown subcultural activity to a cultural practice that is claimed by some to constitute a new genre of art and a well-established place-making activity in contemporary cities. As it transforms, two paradoxes demand attention. First, for all its increasing mainstream recognition (or perhaps even because of it), some claim that street art is dead. What could such an assertion mean? What prompts the making of it? What signs are thought to indicate its demise? If the claim is rebutted, by arguing that street art is not (yet) dead, what of its future?

The latter question brings us to the second unresolved paradox of situational art: mainstream recognition has not yet achieved any shift in the law's condemnation of graffiti and street art as a crime. Although (some) artists can command high prices for their artworks, although some homeowners seek out street artists to add adornment and cachet to their house designs, and although street art now constitutes a tourist attraction for many cities, an artwork installed on private property without permission is still a crime and the artist is still vulnerable to arrest, prosecution and punishment. Investigation of that paradox is the central purpose of this book, which seeks to find the place of street art both in the contemporary city and also in the public city that we can (as yet) only imagine.

encounter

# watching JR

Over the last five years JR has become one of the most internationally celebrated street artists. His considerable reputation can in part be explained by his aesthetic (described in the previous chapter) which centres on black and white portrait photographs, super-sized, printed onto poster paper, and then pasted onto walls and other surfaces. His reputation also derives from the politics animating his work: JR's goal is to remind the spectator of the discrimination and violence conducted in the name of race, gender, ethnicity and poverty, whether in the *banlieux* of Paris or in the villages of Liberia, Moravia, Kenya and Brazil.

In these places, JR met with women who have survived horrific violence at the hands of family members, government troops, rebel soldiers and police officers. He encouraged them to tell him something of their experiences and then photographed each participant, as per his usual style, making a 'grimace' for the camera. Putting up images of 'anonymous women' in public space is a political act for JR, in recognition of the ways in which men tended to occupy public space, while women are often officially or unofficially segregated in the home.

JR has also parlayed his images into a range of secondary representations, exporting them to places far removed from these original sites of violence. In London in 2008, I saw an exhibition from the '28 Milimetres' project at Lazarides Gallery. JR's portraits had been relocated from their countries of origin onto pieces of wood, old doors and conventional canvases, some small, some blown up. Some were pasted onto wooden panels or sheets of rough wood so that the face or figure in the image interacted with the texture of the wooden surface. The paper covering the wood was often scratched, as if scored with a knife or sharp nails, as if the images had registered an injury.

In the second gallery, on Charing Cross Road, an excerpt from the documentary 'Women Are Heroes' was playing in a room entirely covered with black and white portraits. And in the streets connecting these two spaces, JR's enormous portraits had been pasted over the walls and windows of intervening buildings.

In the film, JR is taking photographs of the inhabitants of Morro da Providencia, a *favela* in Rio de Janeiro. Morro da Providencia is Rio's oldest

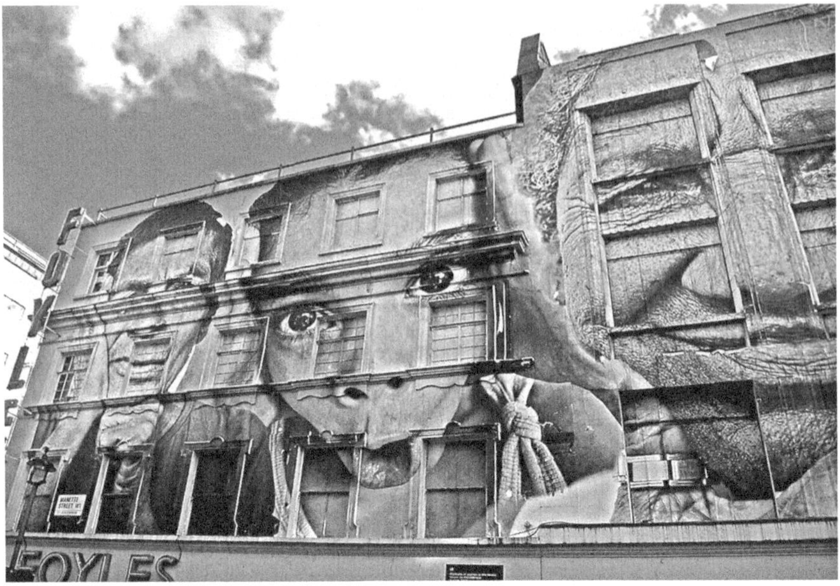


*Figure 1.7* JR, London 2008. Photograph © Alison Young.

*favela*, dating from the late nineteenth century, and is located on the side of a hill close to the city's port area. It has a population of around 5,000 and, like many other favelas, has for many years been a site of significant violence (from both drug dealers and the militarised law enforcement strategies of the Rio de Janeiro police). In Morro da Providencia, JR took photographs, blew them up and pasted them onto the sides of walls and buildings. The film features JR's artworks but it is also very much an artwork in its own right. For me, it was utterly arresting. I watched it three times in succession and found it an affective underpinning to viewing JR's artworks in the gallery and the surrounding streets.

The film opens with a news anchor relating a story about the police opening fire in a public square and shooting some of the *favela's* inhabitants. After this, JR's images are shown, in time-lapse, being installed throughout the *favela*. For this sequence, the camera was positioned at a distance and well below the cityscape so that the entire upward sprawl of the *favela* could be seen, with the eyes, mouths, foreheads and faces of JR's subjects gradually covering vertical surfaces. But while JR's objective may be individual portraiture, here he produced a multi-faceted portrait accommodating both individuals and the space of Morro da Providencia as a community coping in the aftermath of violence.

Such violence was being inflicted upon a community existing in the extreme poverty that arises from extensive governmental neglect. The camera shows litter not being cleared away, bare lightbulbs illuminating tiny rooms, houses made from concrete with corrugated tin roofs. Beds are often mattresses on the floor. Laundry is draped over an iron railing across a window without glass. There are few roads, only alleyways, paths and stairways, and a central public square (the site of the shootings mentioned in the news report, but in the film showing children playing soccer).

The remainder of the film mainly comprises sequences in which the camera races down alleyways and halts in front of an individual – sometimes a woman, often a child, occasionally a man – or follows someone through the interconnected rooms of their home. It often ends up with that individual (child, woman or man) standing on the flat roof of their home with the contours of the *favela* rising and falling all around them. Yet the camera never halts; cinematic stasis is never reached. The camera is in constant motion. It races through the streets and alleys. Even when apparently at rest, contemplating a face, the film plays at an accelerated speed, so that every single blink, glance or expression registers as a twitchy jitter. In this way, the film's cinematic form attempts to convey how trauma registers within the everyday life of the community and its inhabitants.

Meanwhile, various voices speak (in Portuguese, with English subtitles). These ghostly utterances are seldom directly related to the images on screen. In the disjunction between word and image, the film performs the inability of the individual to cohere memory and representation in connection with a traumatic event. While the camera races around buildings and alleys, voices narrate the affects of their experiences: a woman describes searching the garbage tip for pieces of her son's body after he was taken away by soldiers and killed. She says: 'It hurts your soul'. Another comments: 'I only give this interview because you are not from here and will take it far away, otherwise I wouldn't, for I am afraid of the violence'. A boy narrates how he witnessed the shooting of three children when police fired upon a demonstration in the public square. A woman relates how she did not grasp the nature of JR's installation until she saw it from afar, whereupon she cried 'Caramba! The eyes of the hill are open!'

The film occasionally shows a smiling face. A young woman breastfeeding her baby. A little girl laughing. Many of the voices say how much they love the *favela* and how grateful they are to live there. It seems to me that the film captured a tension between love for the *favela* as a space of community and the faces whose accelerated jitters are marked by the pain they have suffered. In revealing the tension between love and loss, JR created an artwork out of the *favela* itself, an artwork in which the faces of a community look outwards at the state that has inflicted such harm upon them. As night falls over Rio de Janeiro and these faces, bodies and eyes fade to black, the camera judders and neon streetlights blur. The film ends, in blackness, but there is no end to what we have seen.

## Chapter 2

# The cities in the city

Cities are made from stone and glass, concrete and brick. Streets convey traffic, vehicular and pedestrian, flowing around buildings. The movement of people and cars continually pauses and resumes, pauses and resumes. Every city block presents a succession of shapes, signs, populations. As an assemblage, a city's built qualities are initially the most readily apparent, and these manifest to the citizen both as tangible objects and things (concrete roads, bluestone foundations, glass windows, advertising billboards, sandstone buildings, and so on) and as a kaleidoscope of images, which jointly and singly communicate the identity of the space as 'urban'. Cities are also sites of cultural and aesthetic production, engaged in a continual process through which they develop and refine their self-image. They do so by means of a range of aesthetic practices, such as architectural innovation, statuary, control of signage and advertising, maintenance of the social environment through street cleaning, and through public art. Furthermore, a city's urban identity depends as much on its legal architecture as it does upon the arrangement of brick, stone and glass into thoroughfares, buildings and bridges. This chapter considers some of the intersections of law, space and culture in the city, in the context of the spatial, cultural and legal potentialities resulting from and embodied in the activities of street artists, who, by performing a 'commons of the image', point towards a means of conceptualising *other cities* within 'the city'.

Legal architecture produces a certain conceptualisation of urban space: the 'legislated city', a space in which a particular kind of experience is encapsulated and produced through the regulation of space, temporalities and behaviours.[1] Within the legislated city, citizens' experiences are framed by discourses of cartography, planning, criminal law, municipal regulation and civility. The legislated city has mappability, it has aspirational qualities expressed through social policies, statutes, local laws and strategic plans. Such a city depends

1 Another useful term is the 'lawscape', as coined by Philippopoulos-Mihalopoulos (2007); Philippopoulos-Mihalopoulos and FitzGerald (2008); see also Graham (2011). Alternatively, Delaney (2010) prefers the concept of the 'nomosphere'.

heavily upon law (whether criminal or civil). According to Philippopoulos-Mihalopoulos: 'a city without law is a holy city of justice, perpetually floating in a post-conflict space where everything is light and forgiveness. Likewise a law without a city is a law without materiality' (2012: 2).[2]

## Law's architecture: the legislated city

The legislated city is a city of order and regularity (or at least the attempt or desire to create a city of order and regularity). As de Certeau has noted, the 'scopic drive . . . makes the complexity of the city readable and immobilizes its opaque mobility in a transparent text' (1984a: 92). When we view a city from above (as de Certeau was doing from the top of the World Trade Centre) the streets below seem to conform most closely to urban space as set out by cartographers; order and regularity appear more tangible when the spectator is distant from the city's streets. As Brighenti notes, 'distance turns into the physical basis for the control of space and movement' (2010a: 223) and, in legislating its cities, law too seems to take a bird's-eye view, seeking order through municipal strategies, public order offences, local laws and environmental ordinances.

Such legislative efforts are anchored in place and time. Permitted noise levels vary according to the hours of the day and the location of the sound.[3] In Melbourne, various state governments have experimented with laws compelling clubs and pubs in the CBD to close at a specified time, in order to reduce alcohol-related violence late at night.[4] A statute in New South Wales criminalises swearing in a public place or near a school.[5] Other Australian states have enacted specific offences of marking graffiti in areas in or near public places.[6] Such strategies create legal territories in time and space: 'just like any other form of notation and writing, law, too, deals with lines, barring some and allowing others' (Brighenti 2010a: 225; see also Brighenti 2010b). In cities, the lines of law tend to coincide with the lines of cartography and of timetabling, resulting in an image of the city as smooth, compart-

2 The law-space nexus has been noted by many scholars (Blomley 2011; Brighenti 2010a; Cresswell and Merriman 2011; Delaney 2003; Philippopoulos-Mihalopoulos 2010a, 2010b; Valverde 2011).

3 See, for example, a series of regulatory strategies and statutory innovations in Victoria, Australia: the State Environment Protection Policy (Control of Music Noise from Public Premises) No. N-2 (1989) 'aims to protect residents from levels of music noise that may affect the beneficial uses of noise sensitive areas, while recognising the community demand for a wide range of musical entertainment'.

4 The '2am lockout' was trialled in Victoria for 3 months in 2008, and a '3am lockout' briefly operated in Queensland.

5 See the *Summary Offences Act* 1988 s 4.

6 See, for example, the Graffiti Prevention Act 2007 (VIC) s 6: a person must not mark graffiti that is visible from a public place.

mentalised, organised around boundaries and functional, although such a legal assemblage is based on a desire to control the city's perceived unruliness and fecklessness.[7]

The legislated city is conceptualised as existing within a cartographic space of readily identifiable thoroughfares and buildings, with conduct in this space governed, as noted above, by a grid of ordinances, regulations, and statutory and common law. In addition, the streetscape is constructed as a conglomeration of places and things whose ownership is framed within the dominant paradigm of property ownership (based on the sovereignty and probity of the title deed and according others, at most, the licence to act in a range of permitted ways within spaces owned by others). The legislated city is thus a city of legible spaces and objects with singular owners, licensing some behaviours and criminalising others. Historically, this ontology of ownership and authority has always designated certain spaces as exceptional. Singularly owned tracts of land might be situated next to a 'commons', a space that existed for shared uses (but note that deed-based 'ownership' and access-based 'use' are somewhat incommensurable frames) such as grazing animals, freely wandering or enjoying recreational activities. In contemporary cities, the remnants of such spaces can still be found: parks, piazzas and squares, to a greater or lesser degree, continue to provide individuals with a shared urban resource. In recent years, scholars looking for a concept that might undermine the dominant model of property law have turned to the notion of the commons and noted that it offers a model of physical space ordered by the activities that constitute a community as opposed to a collection of multiple singularities.

## Experience and encounters: urban enchantment

But how do we live in the legislated city? How do we experience ourselves as citizens and subjects within its spaces? The orderliness of the legislated city comes at a price: properties are often separated from each other not only by fences and walls but by ensuring that such boundaries are topped with barbed wire or broken glass, and dwellings are not only closed off from the street but sealed from the outside through the incorporation of alarm systems

7 I do not mean to imply that rural space is not subject to the law's desires to draw lines around properties. Such strategies of territorialisation are equally apparent there. Indeed, boundaries and properties in 'the countryside', are, in many jurisdictions, hotly contested: consider the history of land rights and native title cases in Australia, the histories of enclosures in Britain, the clearances in the Highlands of Scotland and the various disputes over the right to walk on or across rural land in Britain. Some of the street artists interviewed in this research have begun installing uncommissioned works in rural spaces; on 'country graffiti', see Oliver and Neal (2010) on 'arborglyphs' (letters carved into tree trunks) and Giles and Giles (2010) on graffiti by the horselads working the farmlands of the nineteenth and twentieth-century Yorkshire wolds.

or security personnel.[8] The normalisation of such devices in everyday life is driven by perceptions of threat to person and property; the basis of property ownership may, in fact, be the experience of ownership as something that can be encroached on or jeopardised by others. Paranoia, and the paramilitary architecture of security that it feeds, have no doubt contributed more than a little to the narrative of disenchantment that dominates many accounts of modernity after Weber. Sophie Watson notes the prevalence in accounts of the city of 'segregation, division, exclusion, threat and boundaries, where the story of city life as mixing and mingling is replaced by a story of antagonism, fear and exclusion' (2006: 1). Watson proposes a counter-narrative in which urban space can be thought of as:

> that space of delight which encapsulates serendipitous encounters and meanderings: sitting, watching, being, chatting in spaces that may be planned, designed and monumental, but more often may be barely visible to the inattentive eye, on the margins of planned space, or even imagined.
>
> (2006: 3)

For Watson, the key to revitalising a sense of belonging in urban space is to search out 'sites of magical urban encounters, hidden in the interstices of the planned and monumental, divided and segregated, or privatised and thematised, spaces that more usually capture public attention' (2006: 5). The experience of stumbling across a street-based artwork provides for many people this exact sense of serendipity:

> Walking down the street, on the way to work, a friend's house, dinner, a bar, a lecture, one haphazardly glances in the right direction and BOOM! – an unsolicited aesthetic injection. One is jolted out of whatever hazy cloud of practical thought one was in; one is forced to reconsider one's purely practical and rather indifferent relationship to the street, and a curiosity to explore the work develops.
>
> (Riggle 2010: 249)

For some, the dominant emotion when encountering street art is delight, as evidenced by bloggers who post photographs of their 'discoveries' online or fans who accumulate thousands of images on websites such as Flickr. Writing about the experience of viewing art in the streets, Emily Colucci (2011) says:

> When coming across an anonymous piece of street art, I always get a certain surge of excitement, finding something new that I don't have any proof anyone else has seen. Without the artist's identity, the work seems

8 On walls and other boundaries, see Brighenti (2009, 2010b) and Netz (2004) on barbed wire.

> mysterious as if it just appeared there by itself. As a frequent museum and art gallery goer where the work is so connected to identity, viewing anonymous street art is an almost freeing experience.

However, this sense of delight is not universal. Many encounter street art with irritation and outrage, experiencing a sense of trespass, offence and violation if they happen to own the painted-on property. Irrespective of variations in emotional temperature and character, each of us is *arrested* by the street artwork, halted in our passage through public space and everyday life, suspended in a momentary relation with an image or a word. As the Italian street artist Alice Pasquini puts it: 'the person passing by might be thinking about the bills to pay and other things and [the sight of a street artwork] gives him . . . a surprise'. To be 'surprised' is to be grasped or seized by something, captured, taken over, a sensation that can literally stop the spectator in their tracks as they pause to look at a word or image on a wall.

Even when the spectator continues on their way there may remain a residual sense of being struck by something unexpected, something out of place, something new. This is enchantment in Jane Bennett's conception of it: a state resulting in 'the temporary suspension of time and bodily movement'; 'to be enchanted, then, is to participate in a momentarily immobilizing encounter; it is to be transfixed, spellbound' (2001: 5).[9] It is, in other words, an experience that halts the spectator's movement through the city, that provokes questions in the midst of the unselfconscious flow from one activity to the other. Commuters are supposed to travel smoothly from one point to the next; consumers are expected to move from one point of sale to the next; halting, in this view, is only supposed to arise as a consequence of the citizen's own desires, as they idle, pause for a coffee, or browse but do not purchase goods. Whether strolling like a *flâneur*, or walking with utilitarian purposefulness, the legislated city expects that individuals will desire unimpeded flow, access, and destination: 'the city's public space is a site of circulation' (Brighenti 2010a: 222).[10]

The street-based artwork, then, can be conceived of as a tangle in the smooth spaces of the city. Out of such entanglement comes the potential for enchantment, by which I mean not an uncritical delight but rather, as Bennett (2001) states, a more complex and layered experience involving:

> in the first instance, a surprising encounter, a meeting with something that you did not expect and are not fully prepared to engage. Contained

9 See also, for a rather different version of enchantment, Del Nevo (2011).

10 See also Amin and Thrift, who, while stating that 'cities exist as means of movement', emphasise that such movement is a 'means to engineer *encounters* through collection, transport and collation. They produce, thereby, a complex pattern of traces, a threadwork of intensities' (2002: 81, emphasis in original).

> within this surprised state are (1) a pleasurable feeling of being charmed by the novel and as yet unprocessed encounter and (2) a more *unheimlich* (uncanny) feeling of being disrupted or torn out of one's default sensory-psychic-intellectual disposition.
>
> (5)

In the arrested moment engendered by such a surprising encounter, 'thoughts, but also limbs . . . are brought to rest, even as the senses continue to operate, indeed, in high gear. You notice new colors, discern details previously ignored, hear extraordinary sounds, as familiar landscapes of sense sharpen and intensify' (5).

A spectator might initially wonder who has authored an image or word, perhaps imagining an artist spraying a stencil at midnight or casually tagging a fence on the way home from the pub. The spectator's attention is focused upon a particular place in public space – the wall, the fence – and other aspects of the streetscape briefly recede into the background (see Plate 7). Such a telescoping of attention places the spectator in a position where they are 'simultaneously transfixed in wonder and transported by sense . . . both caught up and carried away' (Bennett 2001: 5). This accords with the experience of looking at a street artwork as recounted by Marc and Sara Schiller: 'when you first notice a stencil on the pavement, a sticker on the back of a mailbox, or a metal sculpture attached to a street sign, you are suddenly transported into another world – to a vibrant subculture that infiltrates and eradicates the monotony of daily life' (quoted in McCormick et al. 2010: 10).

Enchantment does not necessarily connote pleasure. On the contrary, the *unheimlich* disruption engendered by an enchanting image can be equally troubling. Bennett notes that 'fear . . . also plays a role in enchantment' (2001: 5) although, for her, it is crucial that fear is not the dominant response. The dislocations of enchantment – when a spectator happens upon an uncommissioned artwork and is unsettled by it – can frequently lead to emotional projections such as anger, frustration, disgust and outrage.

The American artist MOMO, whose 'Manhattan Tag' I described in the previous chapter, says his work has met with a 'whole range [of responses]. Confusion, anger, disinterest, obsession, amusement'. French street artist Yz states: 'I remember an old woman saying "Hell, what is this?" and "Why can't you put it somewhere else?"'. In Melbourne, Sparcs, while spraying a stencil, was accosted by a resident from a nearby building who was so angry he grabbed the artist by the shoulder and shouted, red in the face and 'getting a bit spitty' with him, repeatedly saying to him 'you're fucked'. While street artists and graffiti writers expect to be chased by security guards or police officers if they encounter them while installing or creating an image without permission, many also reported being pursued or assaulted by individuals who had no relation to the property in question, but who are simply responding to the appearance of an uncommissioned word or image in public space.

Tom Civil recounted his own and his brother's experiences of being assaulted by pedestrians:

> This guy, he caught me doing a stencil, older guy, he punched me full on in the head, full on, really freaked me out, gave me like a massive black eye. I had never been punched in the head before like that, and he was a really big dude. He pushed L., my partner, over, tried to rip my keys out of the car and punch me through the window of the car, full on dude. That really freaked me out actually, freaked me out for a little while, a year or six months after it, I was scared of drunk people on the streets and stuff . . . My brother got chased down by a jogger. They're a threat, joggers . . . They're fit and they're fast and they start early in the morning, and he dragged him by the hair to the police station, which is traumatising.

Enchantment, therefore, does not necessarily involve approbation, but it is a necessary precondition for ethical engagement: 'enchantment is something

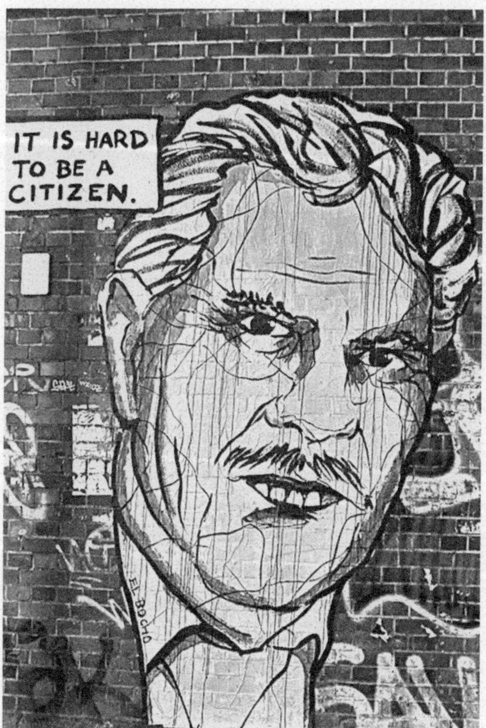


*Figure 2.1* El Bocho, Berlin 2010. Photograph © Alison Young.

that we encounter, that hits us, but it is also a comportment that can be fostered through deliberate strategies' (Bennett 2001: 4). Reading street art through the frame of enchantment can point us towards new ways of being citizens, and legal subjects, in urban space. Whether accompanied by delight or anger, enchantment marks the moment in which the citizen notices the existence of other ways of being in the legislated city; indeed *other cities and their inhabitants*.

## Other cities, other citizenships

What, then, is this altered sense of legal subjectivity in urban space? Where can these other cities and citizenships be found? Let us consider three tales of cities within the city. First, in 2010, the Australian artist Miso, in her exhibition *Tchusse*, transformed a gallery into a streetscape by way of a massive installation that filled the entire Gorker Gallery in Melbourne. Miso's installation involved layering drawings and objects on the gallery walls and hanging them criss-crossed above the space on string. Many of these drawings showed women in the midst of everyday activities. There were also objects made by the artist (for example, small models of buildings, lit from within); objects modified by the artist and installed in the gallery (wooden doors upon which pages from books or posters and notices were affixed, items of clothing suspended like laundry from washing-lines, tea bags drying in corners); and framed photographs of Miso's street-based artworks. The result, when one walked into the gallery, was a slightly discombobulating sense of entering *a city* rather than a gallery, suggesting also the possibility that the city's surfaces could be considered both as sites for the display of art and as artworks themselves.

It was not any city that was being evoked: it was Kharkhov in the Ukraine, the city that Miso comes from; the city which has inspired much of her art and which her art, in turn, remembers and recreates. Miso brought Kharkhov into Melbourne, through her drawings of its inhabitants, through her wooden doors covered with for-sale notices or pages torn from books, through her tiny scale models of buildings with bullet holes in them, through her hung clothing. It was not a *literal* Kharkhov that Miso created, but rather a representation of a city – a remembered city – a lost city that one sensed and experienced when standing in the gallery. And so the memory of Kharkhov, with its history of violence, its memories of loss, of family and community, became a part of Melbourne, at the same time as Kharkhov remained a literal city on the other side of the world. In this way, Miso's art made another city within the city and pointed out that any inhabitant of a legislated city may carry within them other cities whose memories affect their experience of the present.

Other cities can be *heard*. There was once a place in the centre of Melbourne, at the intersection of Flinders and Elizabeth Streets, known as 'Townend'. This area acquired a name for itself as a trouble spot. It was a run-down and unappealing group of streets, the sort of place through which commuters moved but never stopped; it was characterised by late-night violence, and packed with fast-food outlets, backpacker hotels, pubs and cut-price shops. In 2010, the City of Melbourne began canvassing opinions about the area, from residents, traders, commuters and so on. One might expect the council to simply carry out a letter-box survey and hold a few committee meetings with stakeholders to work out what should be done. However, to their credit, the council commissioned a group of artists, led by Jason Maling, Sarah Rodigari and Jess Olivieri, to find 'an alternative method for Council to engage with the city night-time experience to create a project that would engage with the precinct, by responding to the stories, interests and needs of commuters, residents, and traders'. Their aim was to discover whether or not a community existed within a precinct famous only for its 'bad vibe'. To do so, the artists formed a group called The League of Resonance, whose aim was to investigate the area's 'vibe' and uncover the literal and affective resonance of experiences in the area. The League described its activities as follows:

> [We] seek out the intangible and barely perceptible. We detect vibrations that form the backdrop to the mythical narrative of daily life. We situate ourselves in places of intrigue, we listen, we talk, we connect and we hum. In collecting and combining the resonance of individuals: their stories, perceptions and rituals, we unravel the backdrop to this myth. Together we create a new sound. This sound is The League of Resonance.

They invited anyone who used the area – commuters, residents, consumers – to go on a 'date' with League members, accompanying them on a walk around the area, sharing stories and experiences. Respondents took photographs of themselves in a photo booth and were invited to generate a 'hum' to summon up their affective connection to the area. These sonic manifestations were recorded and compiled on a CD, forming a collection that could counter the area's 'bad vibe'.

I was one of seventy people who went on such a date. Jason and Jess explained how their project aimed to investigate all the components of this area's 'bad vibe' and to discover where these vibrations came from. Their investigations were historical, aesthetic, architectural, sociological and ethnographic: they uncovered information about the precinct's origins including buildings that used to be there but have now been demolished. They walked around the area, in different weathers and at different times of the day, paying attention to everything. They documented businesses in the area and spoke with commuters, residents, the City of Melbourne, Victoria Police, employees, employers, punters and students. They photographed buildings in the area and created a dossier about various individuals who met with them and agreed to join the League (League members received membership cards).

They produced a newsletter in which they set out tiny snippets of information and ideas about the area and developed a programme of 'good works' based on suggestions by interviewees. On my date with Jason and Jess, I learned about a tram stop that is used as an informal shoe exchange (people leave unwanted shoes for the homeless) and a railway embankment that overflows with rats at night.

During our walk, one moment stood out. In a laneway populated with smokers from nearby office buildings, there was a lot of construction work going on. Smokers stood around, wreathed in grey cloud, in gloomy silence between hoardings tacked to the walls. But in this nondescript laneway I discovered an unexpected aesthetic activity: a line of chewing gum wads could be seen placed along a ledge on one of the wooden hoardings. They constituted litter, of course, but their placement indicated something other than (or more than) litter. This increasing line of different coloured balls of gum had become a visual punctuation against the bland beige of the hoardings. It might not have been sanitary, nor was it complicated – and perhaps the gum wads should have been in a bin – yet still I took pleasure in the fact that someone (or several people) had made the decision to line them up in a row rather than drop them on the ground. In a laneway that would seem to offer nothing significant, that would barely feature on a map of Melbourne, there was a small instance of aesthetic intervention in urban space, an intervention that bespoke a place-making quite different to that of monuments, public art and official signage.[11] My pleasure in this urban intervention no doubt resonated in the melodious hum that I found myself making in the Flinders Street Station photo booth used by the League as a de facto recording studio.

The project undertaken by the League of Resonance shows how multiple subjectivities can be unearthed within the legislated city.[12] Perhaps this

11 Dan Witz' first attempts at making street art resulted in something similar. He described his intervention as follows: 'Walking around I'd find all this tiny metal stuff laying on the ground – fittings, ball bearings, odd, tiny, inscrutable things – robot flotsam. When my pockets got full, I'd set up these ordered displays on window ledges or other flat surfaces. Carefully, like in a museum cabinet or store window, I'd line the objects up or make a regimented little circle or something and leave it behind. I don't think it ever occurred to me to photograph it. I liked thinking about people coming upon them and being mildly puzzled. This was also the first street art I made in New York when I transferred to Cooper Union. I still do this by the way. The stuff is mostly plastic now, which although more colorful, isn't as much fun' (quoted in Witz 2010).

12 The League of Resonance has been criticised for achieving little more than a new friendship circle for a limited number of people (Spiers 2011). Spiers also provides an account of a comparable attempt, entitled Agents of Proximity, to generate a peripatetic community within the Melbourne suburb of Brunswick. Agents of Proximity offered a 'localised, artist-run travel service' which 'aimed to explore urban space via the stories and experiences of the people who shared it. It was an exploration of the ways in which the rituals and mindsets associated with travel could be applied to the streets we walk down daily and the places that we think

premise can be taken even further. Is it possible that there exist cities within the city? Not just an installation within a gallery, nor a claim that the city accommodates many and conflicting viewpoints but *other entire cities* within the space of the legislated city? Is it possible that the legislated city actually *intersects* with other cities? Could every single street and building exist somewhere else?

Such is the premise of China Miéville's novel *The City and the City* (2009). Miéville's fictional city, Beszel, is located somewhere on the far edges of Eastern Europe and intersects with another city, Ul Qoma. People live in the same space but are citizens of one city and not the other. Some areas of Beszel are physically distinct from those of Ul Qoma; others exist within the same physical space, constituting a spatiality that Miéville calls 'cross-hatched'.[13] The inhabitants of Beszel speak a different language to that spoken in Ul Qoma; each citizen of Beszel must learn to 'unsee' the architecture of the other city and the presence of its citizens, and vice versa. The narrator recounts a moment in which he walks through a 'cross-hatched' area:

> I walked. I walked by the brick arches: at the top, where the lines were, they were elsewhere, but not all of them were foreign at their bases. The ones I could see contained little shops and squats decorated in art graffiti. In Beszel it was a quiet area, but the streets were crowded with those elsewhere. I unsaw them, but it took time to pick past them all
>
> (2009: 25)

*The City and the City* describes what it is like to live with 'others' (people who speak differently, who think differently about the same streets and spaces) whose cohabitation creates other spaces within the everyday spaces of the city. While Miso's work brought Kharkhov into the physical space of a Melbourne gallery, and the League of Resonance unearthed multiple subjectivities from beneath the weight of social policy, Miéville's book demonstrates that encounters with the *unseen* take place every day within the legislated cityscape.

we know'. Spiers argues that Agents of Proximity suffered from the same limitations as the League of Resonance: its participants were self-selected enthusiasts and no new or lasting connections were created.

13 Miéville has written about split, dual or parallel cities in other novels, notably *King Rat* (1998) and *Un Lun Dun* (2007), and similar themes appear in novels by other authors (see especially *Neverwhere* by Neil Gaiman, *Mind the Gap: A Novel of the Hidden Cities* by Tim Lebbon and Christopher Golden, 2008, and *Into the Nightside* by Simon R. Green, 2008). However, whereas those novels dealt with the idea of a second city *beneath* London (that is, out of sight to the denizens of the city on the surface, but able to be entered by the protagonist), *The City and the City* takes this concept further, to create a place in which two urban worlds are layered over each other within the same physical space.

## Uncommissioned cities

The legislated city, as we might extrapolate from *The City and the City*, is a discursive production that involves citizens learning *not to see* the bodies and places of others. If this is the case, then, such unseeing can almost certainly be undone. In other words, we can once more learn to see the citizens and cityscapes of the other cities enfolded within the legislated city. These other cities are founded peripatetically, nomadically and perambulatorily.[14] They are built from repurposed materials as when skateboarders turn stairs into the launching base for a kickflip.[15] They are founded when an artist uses discarded objects to create street sculptures or turns an alcove into a display site. Such interventions re-imagine the city as based on land that is 'neither owned nor occupied but rather crossed. Topologically speaking, it looks like a network or rhizome' (Brighenti 2010a: 219). Such interventions mark the existence of *uncommissioned cities* coexisting in the space of the legislated city. Even though citizens may have learned not to see these other cities, at times they catch glimpses of forbidden architecture and hidden inhabitants. In *The City and the City*, for example, when Ul Qoma is perceived by the residents of Beszel, an intense anxiety results:

> As I turned, I saw past the edges of the estate to the end of GunterStrász, between the dirty brick buildings. Trash moved in the wind. It might be anywhere. An elderly woman was walking slowly away from me in a shambling sway. She turned her head and looked at me. I was struck by her motion, and I met her eyes. I wondered if she wanted to tell me something. In my glance I took in her clothes, her way of walking, of holding herself, and looking.
>
> With a hard start, I realised that she was not on GunterStrász at all, and that I should not have seen her.
>
> Immediately and flustered, I looked away, and she did the same, with the same speed. I raised my head, towards an aircraft on its final descent. When after some seconds I looked back up, *unnoticing* the old woman stepping heavily away, I looked carefully instead of at her in her foreign street at the facades of the nearby and local GunterStrász.
>
> (2009: 12, my emphasis)

Such destabilisation is abjured in the legislated city: a raft of social, political and legal measures obscures the visibility of uncommissioned cities and their

14 See Brighenti (2010a) on 'motility' in the city; Cresswell (2006) on mobility; de Certeau (1984a), Lorimer (2011) and Blomley (2011) on walking and pedestrianism. Note also that much of the data collection for this book made use of the methodology of peripatetic exploration of the cityscape.

15 See Carr (2010: 992) on skateboarding and urban space generally. See also Borden (2000) and Chiu (2009).

inhabitants. 'Unnoticing' is habitual and commonplace. Once, I was telling a friend who lives in New York about how the tagging of subway trains using markers and aerosol cans had given way to tags scratched on window panes with keys and rocks. He firmly stated that no such marks existed. When next we went into the subway he was startled to discover these tags; over several years he had simply never seen them. In teaching students about street art and graffiti, I have heard many such stories of unseeing. One postgraduate student told me she was surprised to find that one of her favourite photographs contained a large wall covered in graffiti in its foreground; before my seminar on street art she had never noticed its presence in the picture.

Within the layered spaces of a city, encounters with uncommissioned street artworks constitute potentialities in which the alter-image can be erased or acknowledged. According to de Certeau, the 'ordinary practitioners of the city' walk paths that are 'unrecognized poems in which each body is an element signed by many others' thus 'elud[ing] legibility . . . as though the practices organizing a bustling city were characterized by their blindness' (1984a: 93). Graffiti writers and street artists speak of their desire to represent things otherwise, to change the way citizens experience cities and property, to point towards multiplicities within the singular city. Of the 64 artists I interviewed, 24 per cent saw street art as a practice that contests dominant conceptualisations of property, and 33 per cent spoke of it as a means of transforming urban space by complicating the textures of the city. Deadly Knitshade, a yarn bomber in London, said: 'I like the idea of encouraging other people to put their mark on the city.' El Bocho, in Berlin, argued that: 'if you work on the street it's a possibility to be a part of the whole construction of the city and to push it in the right direction.' Nails, in Melbourne, declared that 'street artists, architects or fine artists or urban planners or just guerrilla gardeners [are] engaging in an organic re-processing, re-configuring and evolution of the city experience'. Kaff-eine, also in Melbourne, saw street art as 'part of people claiming space for themselves, but also changing it for others' and that she now 'see[s] buildings, empty spaces, corners, curves, walls, pretty much every surface differently, through the lens of how they'd be as a canvas'.

Is the transformative potential identified by these artists just wishful thinking? What, after all, does a momentary encounter with an uncommissioned word or image really do to an inhabitant of the legislated city? According to Berlin-based artist Brad Downey: '[street art] shows people that the city is theirs. They need to see and question the objects that they engage with every day.' For Civil, the act of writing or painting an uncommissioned word or image can 'create a different kind of city'. These inhabitants of the uncommissioned city, then, though they occupy the same space as the legislated city, may embody the possibility of both another life and another mode of legality.

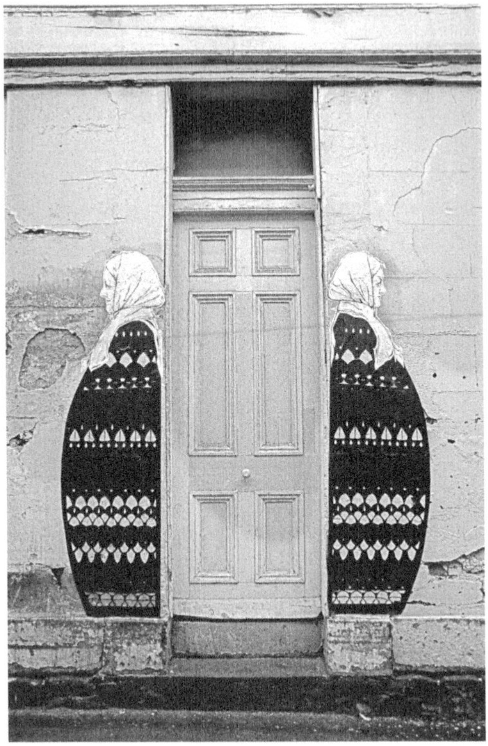

*Figure 2.2* Miso, Melbourne 2010. Photograph © Miso

In the legislated city – structured around ownership and the boundaries between properties owned by corporate or individual legal persons – the notion of the 'space-between' is repeatedly overlooked or taken for granted. Commuters travel along roads to get from home to work and back again. Consumers move from one shop to another. And certainly all of the thoroughfares required for such movement are owned and regulated. There is no conceptualisation of movement *through* urban space as a source of authority over property (instead, it is seen to generate a right to unimpeded passage and the responsibility to conduct oneself in various ways *en route*).

For the inhabitants of the uncommissioned city, however, through-passage gives rise to the potential to alter a streetscape in a range of ways. Knitted objects may be hung from street signs; words or images painted on a wall. Debates about ownership of surfaces do not have purchase for the citizens of the uncommissioned city because the very idea of entitlement arises through *proximity* to a surface and aesthetic reaction to what is already there.

Thus, a doorway may become a suitable frame for an image and a drab grey wall seem to be inviting the addition of colourful words or images.

Graffiti writer Zedz, in Amsterdam, acknowledged that this invitation is forever present: 'writers look at cities differently: every surface is for writing'. These citizens do not consider their actions deviant, criminal or troublesome. They do what they do so as to 'have a connection to the city' (Just, Berlin); to 'take part in a conversation' (Ghostpatrol, Melbourne), to make the city 'better than it is right now' (Jordan, New York), and to show that 'the walls are the commons' (Swoon, New York).

## Citizenship and the commons in uncommissioned cities

The commons has been much vaunted in recent years as a rallying-point for critical thinking in economics, law and political theory.[16] As a legal concept, 'the commons' referred to land customarily held in common, giving rise to a range of rights available to its users. According to Carol Rose, the extent of these rights developed to the point that 'customary claims did resemble the doctrines vesting property-like rights in the general public: custom too was said to bestow rights on people whose precise identity was unknown and indefinite' (1994: 122).

To be recognised, customary rights in the commons needed to be long lasting (preferably since time immemorial), reasonable, uncontentious and relatively uncontested. Many land usages were protected through the notions of custom and commons including grazing, access to materials and through-passage. Under common law, custom provided a different means through which to manage and negotiate property rights; 'a means different from ownership by either individuals or by organized governments' (Rose 1994: 124). It is not hard to see why Holder and Flessas have declared the commons 'a powerful polemical tool, as well as a legal or descriptive term' (2008: 305). Indeed, in recent years there has been something of an upsurge of research on the commons across a broad range of disciplines.

Within this broad terrain of commons research, a number of different paradigms can be identified. There is much scholarship re-thinking approaches to resources such as air, water, food and land as commons that are being encroached upon by private interests (see especially Ostrom 1990, 2000, 2008). Others have focused upon ways in which the commons – denoting a space in which all citizens share rights of enjoyment, use and ownership – might provide an alternative way of thinking about urban space (see Blomley 2008, 2011; Chatterton 2010; Foster 2011; Harvey 2011; Mitchell 2008). For some, the commons appears to offer a means through which to acquire the rights of ownership: Holder and Flessas have argued that 'the subject-position of the "owner", although privileged in law and society, is being

16 See for example: Blomley (2008); Hardt and Negri (2009); Harvey (2011); Holder and Flessas (2008); Linebaugh (2010); Linn (2007); Milun (2011); Mitchell (2008); and Ostrom (2008).

appropriated by flexible groupings of actors that would not formerly have been understood as being capable of supporting a claim to this position' (2008: 299). For others, drawing on Lefebvre, the commons reorganises the meaning of ownership by valorising use and action so as to constitute an obstacle to exclusion from the enjoyment of property or land (see, for example, Blomley 2008; Mitchell 2008).

Some accounts verge on a reiteration of the dichotomy between ownership and use; others position use as a means by which to wield the power of an owner. Such approaches either diminish the interests of a city's 'others' as minoritarian exceptions awaiting authorisation by the majority or else reauthorise the dominant paradigm of property that underpins urban space in the legislated city. Is it possible, I would ask, to think of the actions of graffiti writers and street artists as pointing to another kind of commons? In following this line of thought, I tread a similar path to those traced by Davina Cooper, who has argued for a 'social commons' or a 'space that constitutes, recognises, and permits multiple, overlapping uses' (Cooper 2007: 649; see also Cooper 2006), Kurt Iveson (2013), who draws upon Jacques Rancière and Henri Lefebvre to think through the 'do-it-yourself urbanisms' of graffiti, skateboarding and parkour in relation to the 'right to the city', and Kafui Attoh, who wants to see recognition of a general 'right to the city', following Lefebvre's 'notion of the city as an oeuvre, or as a work produced through the labor and the daily actions of those who live in the city' (2011: 674):

> If anti-panhandling laws prevent the homeless from asserting their right to the city . . . then the rights of the homeless are rights that stand *against a possible majority* who might believe that such laws are just and appropriate. When we argue that the homeless have a right to occupy a public park, it is a right that we would argue exists *despite the desire of a majority* (homeowners, renters, store keepers, developers) to deem otherwise. When we argue that protesters have a right to picket or occupy a street, it is a right that exists *despite a democratic majority* that may view such protests as nuisances, or disturbances.
>
> (2011: 677, emphases mine)[17]

But if there is a right to the city, it exists not only in the interstices, or in partitioned minoritarian spaces. The commons adverted to by street artists is not an exception, a custom that can be asserted if and when permitted by the dominant paradigm of property rights. The commons of the uncommissioned city must be an extensive one, *cross-hatched* (to re-purpose Miéville's term) into the landscape of the legislated city. The persistent acts of mark-making

17 For a detailed reading of Lefebvre's conceptualisations of law, space and the right to the city, see Butler (2012).

that constitute situational art enact a legality in which citizens are authorised by adaptation and by proximity rather than by use or ownership. In each act of installing a situational artwork, then, the artist demonstrates a way of thinking not only about the image of the city, but also the city *as image*, and an image crucial to the foundation of a public city.

A street is more than a thoroughfare for commuters on their way to work; it is also a space in which residents can set up communal gardens. A public park may facilitate recreation, but it can also be occupied by political protesters. A set of stairs, meant for climbing and access, may become a launch site for skateboarders. The possibilities for such activities should be included among the activities for which a space or object is intended: the fact that a metal surface provides a suitably adhesive backdrop for stickers means that doorways and street signs should be read as possible display surfaces when they are installed.

In future debates about the commons, the enforcement of the subject-position of owner might be set aside in favour of a debate as to how to expand the subject-position of 'space-adapter' or 'space-hacker', a subject-position bestowing rights disconnected from property ownership and embracing the 'enchanting possibilities inherent within contingent and provisional meanings' (Saler 2006: 714). In other words, I would like to propose a new kind of subject-position: citizen of the public city. In this, I am not claiming that the legislated city should be abandoned in favour of the uncommissioned city, but rather, that we should learn to be citizens of *both* and thus discover a space that is not reducible to either. In this chapter an appropriate last word can be given to Miéville who writes that the task is 'not to uphold the law, or another law, but to maintain the skin that keeps law in place . . . We are all philosophers here where I am, and we debate . . . the question of where it is that we live . . . I live in the interstice, yes, but I live in both the city and the city' (2009: 312). To conceive of citizenship as living in both cities might then involve the construction of a third space: what I call in this book the *public city*, whose existence is organised around *a commons of the image*.

# criminal damage?

In London in July 2008, as part of the Tate Modern's 'Street Art' exhibition, a series of public talks was organised featuring artists, curators, critics and collectors. Brad Downey was one of the featured presenters: he is an American living in Berlin, initially working as part of the duo, Darius and Downey, and then for many subsequent years as a solo artist. Downey's current work centres upon the interplay between movement, the body, objects and space to create a kind of 'street sculpture'. His aim is to 'come to public space with almost nothing, but to leave a monument.'

I was in the audience at the Tate when Downey showed a series of short films documenting recent pieces. One showed an artwork in which he dug up paving stones on Karl Marx Allee in Berlin, arranged them like dominos and tipped them over, leaving a tumble of stone slabs and a series of gaps in the pavement. The films made it clear that Downey's practice is about process as much as it is the final work and demonstrated to me that situational art is a *performance* of criminality, contestation and creativity.

One of Downey's films brought this home most clearly. The piece was called 'Ladder Stick-Up' and took place while Downey was in Aberdeen, exhibiting work at Peacock Visual Arts. He found a building under construction, its outer wall clad with scaffolding and covered with red plastic sheeting. The film showed Downey approaching the building carrying only a small bag. He disappeared behind the sheeting and for a time nothing seemed to happen. A hole appeared in the plastic sheeting and suddenly it was clear that Downey was standing on the scaffolding, cutting into the plastic sheeting from behind. Downey continued to cut the line as far as he could reach and then climbed to the next level where the cutting began anew. This went on, floor by floor, until we could see that a shape was being cut in the sheeting: a gigantic heart.

Finally, high above the street, he cut the last piece of sheeting holding the enormous red plastic heart in place. As the heart slowly fell out of the sheeting and billowed to the ground, I heard myself gasp, and I don't think I was the only person in the audience to do so. After the heart fell to the ground, the building's grey granite and metal scaffolding were starkly revealed (see Plate 8). It seemed both a shocking architectural anatomy lesson and a sublimely beautiful performance, a spontaneous sculpture indeed, created from material that we do not normally notice.

After the film, Downey said his aim had been to do 'a huge piece of damage', but to make it 'friendly and happy through the use of an image that everyone knows'. Was it damage? The building owner thought so. Downey was arrested when he climbed back to the ground (the owner called the police while he was working) and fined £2000. What was 'damaged'? Plastic sheeting (which cost someone money, no doubt, and which probably had to be replaced).

Downey's heart demonstrates how fluid is the nature of 'damage'. Downey's creation was both a performance in itself and one leaving behind an ephemeral piece of street art. It looked uncanny (the juxtaposition of heart shape and the now revealed innards of stone and scaffolding), it had a cute appeal (like a valentine card to the city), and yet it came into being through the violence of dissecting and discarding.

# Chapter 3

# Cityscapes

> When we walk down a street, what are the layers that are lying beneath what we see?
>
> (José Parlá, artist)

This chapter engages with the street artwork *in situ* by examining the place and impact of the image within the cityscape. In Chapter 1, I discussed how the street artwork is discursively framed ('street art', 'urban art', 'situational art', 'uncommissioned art'), and Chapter 2 investigated the contours of the spectator's encounter with the street artwork. In what follows, I will move outwards from this intimate focus to consider the street artwork within the space of the city and the city as space. In doing so, I will investigate the effect and influence of the presence of a large number of street artworks on the appearance and identity of the city. Artists often speak, as noted in the opening chapter, of engaging with urban space and of contributing to the aesthetics of a city or neighbourhood. The following discussion will trace the impact of street artists on the cities they live in or visit. Such an encounter necessitates a journey through *the cityscape* – a space both imagined and experienced.

The cities discussed all have a reputation for art in general.[1] London, Berlin, New York and Paris are known for their expansive and impressive art

1 Not all of the cities studied as part of my research on street art are included in this chapter's discussion of 'cityscapes'. For example, Amsterdam, where I interviewed a number of artists and conducted ethnographic and photo-documentary research, was not selected. For although Amsterdam is home to a number of significant street artists, such as The London Police and Laser 3.14, the culture of street art is not embedded within Amsterdam's city spaces in the way that it is in London or Melbourne. Furthermore, all the artists interviewed in Amsterdam spoke of the city's *lack of a street art culture*. Laser 3.14 commented: 'The whole scene [in Amsterdam] seems to be in decline over the last ten years. The government decided to move the artists out of the city – they cracked down on every type of dissent, everything that is a bit subversive or a bit different . . . It's really a shame because Amsterdam could be an amazing cultural centre. It seems to want to be known only as a certain kind of cultural

collections. For many, Berlin epitomises both the benefits of creativity and the way in which creative clustering can lead to gentrification, push up rents and ultimately displace artists, low-income residents and small businesses.[2] Rome is suffused with art and the display of art, focusing in particular on the ancient Roman world and the Renaissance. The city is expanding its holdings and display of more contemporary art in museums such as MAXXI and MACRO but the contemporary is still submerged beneath the past. Melbourne, known as the 'arts capital' of Australia, is a city whose self-image is entwined with creativity: while Sydney and Canberra have significant collections, Melbourne's artists, museums and numerous independent galleries have made art an intrinsic part of the cityscape. Indeed, in each of these cities, art is an essential part of self-image, marketed in tourism campaigns to attract potential visitors. Moreover, as described, vibrant street art cultures are found in each of these cities, although Rome and Paris are certainly not as suffused with street art as London, New York, Berlin or Melbourne.

The discussion in this chapter highlights issues common to situational art in any city (such as the tendency to prefer 'pretty' street art to the more opaque activity of tagging; and the dilemmas of preservation and conservation of an art form that subjects itself to the weather, the capricious responses of spectators, and the changing edicts given to council cleaning crews) but locates those issues within particular cityscapes. It also draws qualitatively on the ways street art can be interpreted through the phenomenological experiences of making and viewing art in various cities, to provide an urban ethnography investigating the citizenship that arises when we are *walking in the city*.[3]

## New York: elements

New York is globally associated with graffiti writing. Although graffiti's origins are variously attributed to Los Angeles, Chicago and Philadelphia as well as New York, it is the latter that has come to represent the very idea of graffiti, offering a distillation of styles, aesthetics, culture and history that cannot be found in any other urban setting. New York was famously home to writers such as Taki 183 and Iz the Wiz. Its graffiti stories have been immortalised by authors such as Jonathan Lethem (*The Fortress of Solitude*, 2003) and Don DeLillo (*Underworld*, 1997). Its images have been recorded by photographers (Cooper and Chalfant 1988), analysed by academics (Kramer

centre – for museums and galleries and so on. But that's a shame, because for those kinds of cultural experiences, you have to actually go to the gallery, you have to be ready to experience it. Art on the street, you never know when you are going to come across it.'

2 See Shaw (2005), Dovey (2011); Dovey, Woodcock and Wollan (2012) and Cook (2011) on gentrification.

3 It thus follows in the footsteps of Michel de Certeau (1984a) and to a lesser extent Walter Benjamin (see, on the *flâneur*, Benjamin, 1999; see also Buck-Morss, 1991).

2010; Snyder 2009) and honoured in museum shows such as 'Hip Hop Nation: Roots Rhymes and Rage' at the Brooklyn Academy of Art in 2000, 'Né Dans La Rue' ('Born in the Street') at the Fondation Cartier in Paris in 2009, and 'Art in the Streets' at the Museum of Contemporary Art in Los Angeles in 2011.

New York style has travelled. It has been written about as an experience or aesthetic appreciable only through transit. The philosopher Michel de Certeau, for example, described the images in the subway as follows:

> in the yellow-green and electric blue calligraphy that silently screams as it striates the city's underground – 'embroideries' of letters and numbers, the perfect gestures of spray-painted acts of violence, handwritten Shivas, dancing graphics whose fleeting apparitions are accompanied by the roar of subway trains: New York's graffiti.
>
> (1985: 137)

Graffiti writing has always been associated with trains and the subway. Graffiti writers developed a fondness for subway walls and subterranean spaces for a number of reasons: first, they were safe locations in which to write; and second, they made it possible for one's writing to travel, on the side of a train, thus increasing its visibility. Don DeLillo captured the essence of looking at a graffiti-covered subway train in his novel *Underworld*:

> The train came bopping into the drab old station like some blazoned jungle of wonders. The letters and numbers fairly exploded in your face and they had a relationship, they were plaited and knotted, pop-eyed cartoon humanoids, winding in and out of each other and sweaty hot and passion dancing – metallic silver and blue and cherry-bomb red and a number of neon greens.
>
> (1997: 395)

Claes Oldenburg famously remarked: 'You're standing there in the station, everything is gray and gloomy and all of a sudden one of those graffiti trains slides in and brightens the place like a bouquet from Latin America' (quoted in Mailer 2009: 23). New York graffiti has also been described as 'modern hieroglyphics' and a 'remarkable visual effusion' by Jon Naar (2007: 15, 19), the photographer who documented the early years of graffiti in the city. Norman Mailer, in his book *The Faith of Graffiti*, wrote:

> What a quintessential marriage of cool and style to write your name in giant separate living letters, large as animals, lithe as snakes, mysterious as Arabic and Chinese curls of alphabet, and to do it in the heat of a winter night, when the hands are frozen and only the heart is hot with fear.
>
> (2009: 12)

Notoriously, the subway also became the space in which the City of New York and the NYPD staged their war against graffiti (Austin 2001; Ziegler 2004) culminating in Giuliani's 'zero tolerance' strategy and 'Quality of Life' campaigns of the 1990s. This, it was claimed, brought an end to subway graffiti (a claim founded on a desire rather than a reality; there is still plenty of graffiti scratched onto train windows and onto other urban surfaces – mailboxes, newsstands, doorways, roller doors, walls and sidewalks). By 2011, the fashionable Ace Hotel in Manhattan even gave graffiti its own feature wall, made from tags and stickers.

In 2010, the Underbelly Project paid homage to the importance of the subway as a generative space for situational art. The project was located in an abandoned subway station, 'nearly the size of a small city block and able to hold six subway trains', unused for eighty years, unlit and filled with decades of grime. Two New York-based artists – going by the names 'Workhorse' and 'PAC' – curated works by a hundred artists, which they placed on the walls of this abandoned space over several months. Workhorse described the project as being conceived as 'a statement against the commodification of street art', and 'because it was fun' (Workhorse and PAC 2012: 14). Artists would be taken into the subway station at night, with lighting equipment, their works documented, and later viewed by specially invited journalists and bloggers.

There is so much street art and graffiti on display these days. The Underbelly Project, however, cannot be displayed. Until publication of *We Own the Night* (2012), Workhorse and PAC's compilation of photographs from the venture into a coffee-table book, these subterranean artworks existed only in the imagination. The Underbelly Project delved into a secret part of New York much as early graffiti crews did in the 1970s and '80s (as depicted in DeLillo's *Underworld*) to write purely for themselves. *Underbelly* resonated with many aspects of the history of graffiti and street art, but particularly the importance of trains and tunnels.[4] The sheer extensiveness of early subway writing is little known to most people, even today. Writers went into the tunnels and painted walls, train carriages, trapdoors, manhole covers, anything and everything. Far from reaching a wide audience, these images and tags were put up with the intention that only other writers – or no one at all – would see them.

Once, while I was riding the subway in New York, the lights came on in a section of tunnel as the train hurtled through it. Normally, outside the

4 Workhorse notes: 'We were never under the illusion that we were doing anything unique. We weren't tryng to be "first" or "best". We were (and still are) aware that wandering spirits such as Revs, Haze, Freedom, Control, Smith/Sane, and SP had wormed their way through tunnels decades before and left their mark before I had even dreamed of moving to New York' (2012: 14).

window is darkness, but for a moment this sudden burst allowed me to see the graffiti covering the subway walls from top to bottom. A huge canvas of text was wrapped around our train. It was only a momentary glimpse (the lights went off again after about a minute) but every time I travel on the subway I think about the layers of paint coating the tunnel walls – a testament to the commitment of graffiti writers – still there, even in the darkness.[5]

New York graffiti has also travelled by other means. In the 1980s, movies such as *Beat Street*, *Wild Style* and *Style Wars* were adopted as lifestyle texts all over the world. However, it was the book *Subway Art* that communicated the New York aesthetic to an international audience. By the mid-1990s, specialist magazines allowed aspiring novices all over the world in to study the styles of accomplished writers in Munich, Milan or Prague as well as New York City. The arrival of the Internet allowed graffiti culture to expand exponentially – initially through encyclopedia sites such as *Art Crimes*, then through the development of local sites showcasing the writers in specific cities, and more recently via websites established by individual writers to promote their own work.

Throughout this history of expanding frontiers, New York City has remained iconic as a place of origin, intensity and cultural value. It is partly the city itself – a global city (Sassen 1991), or the 'Maximum City' as Pye (1993) calls it in his 'biography of New York', the first city in the world where, as Robert Hughes once said, the 'land grab [was] in the sky' (1997: 405), where verticality, gigantism and massivity became incorporated into the everyday (and perhaps influenced graffiti writers' desires in the 1970s and 1980s to go 'all city' and become 'kings').

In such a context, it is no surprise that New York street artists often speak of their activities as a means through which people can connect with each other (an explicit counter-narrative to the Weberian story of modernity as alienation) or through which a spectator can gain a sense of personal attachment within a potentially dehumanising space (the kind of ethical engagement from a moment of enchantment in urban space discussed in the previous chapter). Where graffiti is so much about transit, about images that seem to be in motion or ask to be viewed on or from a moving train, the street artwork (by which I mean stencils, posters and wheat pastes, stickers and street sculptures) invites us to slow down, to pause and contemplate space.

New York has had an enormous importance in developing the precise grammar of this invitation to stop and look (or stop and think). In 1994, Dan Witz placed around seventy silhouetted figures in hoodies all over the Lower

5 As Jenkins comments, after the wholesale buffing of subway trains in New York in the late 1980s, 'just because passengers didn't see writing on trains didn't mean it wasn't still happening: writers would risk their freedom in order to paint trains no one would ever see except for themselves and their extended crews. It's a tradition that continues today – painting trains just for photographs' (2007: 13–14).

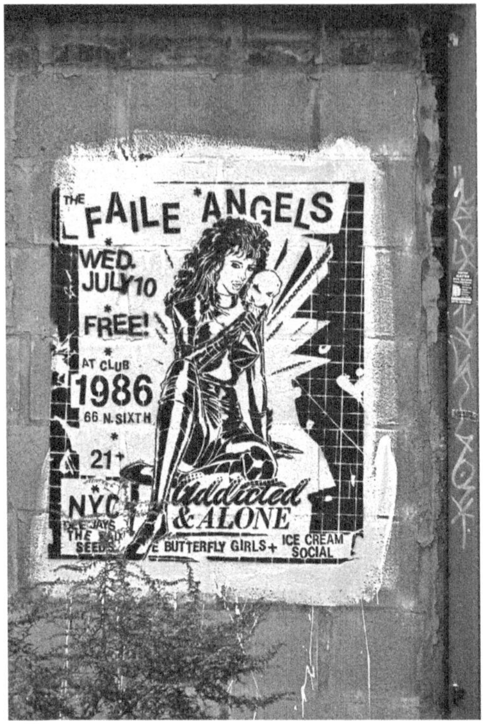


*Figure 3.1* Faile, New York 2011. Photograph © Alison Young.

East Side, referencing the illicit drug trade but also a wider sense of social decline (Witz's working title for the project was 'Plague Angels'). In 1979, Witz had painted hummingbirds as his tag, while in 2011, as I was walking around Bushwick, I noticed Witz had painted figures behind metal grilles, easy to miss, but turning a commonplace piece of urban architecture into something much more disquieting, since the individual appears imprisoned by the metal grid (see Plate 9).[6] In 1999, Bast and Faile began to create images on the streets drawn from advertising such that a spectator might be momentarily unsure as to whether they were viewing an old advertisement or a contemporary artwork.

Jordan Seiler has also explored the art/commerce boundary. Seiler replaces advertisements in the New York subway with his own paintings, and more recently has organised large-scale takeovers so that New Yorkers might awaken to a city in which hundreds of advertising spaces have had artworks

6 In January 2013, a series of works showing individuals imprisoned behind metal mesh was shown at Lazarides Gallery in London, entitled 'Prisoners'.

inserted into them. Other artists – such as Cake, Swoon, Elbow-Toe and QRST – paste-up figurative images, often delicately drawn or painted, that bring beauty into the everyday spaces of the city and invite pedestrians to share in a sense of commonality.

Such gestures hint at a different city from the vertical one (New York being a city with more skyscrapers than any other except Hong Kong), a city that '"talks" to the gentle stroller, revealing itself via . . . unexpected conversations with its inhabitants' (Bell and de-Shalit 2011: 5).

However, repressive municipal and criminal justice regimes have eroded some of New York's world famous street art culture. Mayor Giuliani's 'zero tolerance' approach has been mirrored by rapid gentrification in neighbourhoods that were previously significant for their graffiti and street art. SoHo and the Lower East Side have lost much of their situational art, although a few exceptions remain, for example, at the corner of Wooster and Grand Streets (Snyder 2006). Many artists moved from Manhattan to Brooklyn; even there, however, gentrification has forced artists out of Williamsburg and into Bushwick or Red Hook. This has resulted in a thinning out of street art. It is possible to walk for many blocks through different neighbourhoods without seeing much beyond tags and throw-ups. Garrison from Ad Hoc Art describes

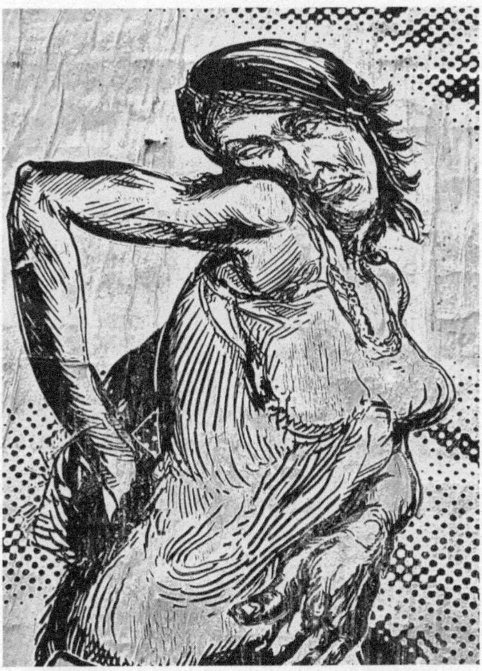

*Figure 3.2* Elbow-Toe, New York 2010. Photograph © Alison Young.

how the possibilities for viewing street art in New York are the product of an intersection of insider knowledge, the impact of the criminal law, and neighbourhood character:

> [New York] is a tough city because of the disincentives, the fines, the felony, it definitely makes people think twice. But at the same time for the people that actually get out there and do stuff it makes it that much more lively and interesting. And then again it's also a place where generally if you're just walking around you may walk for a long time and not see much, but if you have references from people, or know where to go, you can find places that have quite a bit of stuff going on. Most people given the option will choose to not go to jail, not get a fine, so there will be more stuff happening in places where say people have a lower risk of that. I mean, say to put up a piece in Times Square is way more problematic than a back street in Brooklyn. So yeah, it's really just about where you are. The police presence, it's like trying to break into a vault versus picking a bag of money up off the street . . . Our overall social and legal culture here makes it so people do stuff more in the nooks and crannies as opposed to out in the open. But again, not to say that – you know, people like Judith Supine, and lots of others, have done some really awesome big stunts that are very much in your face, and in highly trafficked places.

Despite new regulatory regimes and changing urban character, New York City remains an elemental city for situational art; synonymous with the origins of graffiti, where much of the world's best street art has flourished. But there is another sense in which the city provides an elemental setting: artists must accept the toll exerted by the weather on an outdoor, unprotected artwork. New York's winter is long and severe: rain, ice, snow, wind and low temperatures deter artists from putting up work and cause existing works to fade, erode or dissolve into pulp.

In April 2010, I was walking around Williamsburg with a local resident, who pointed out that work was looking ragged at the end of the winter and that the milder weather of spring would rejuvenate the images in the street by encouraging artists out of their homes and studios. Cake commented that she was going to stop using fluorescent paint in her artworks because the 'colour gets bleached out in like a week' by New York's weather: 'the two pieces [in Red Hook], they've been up for a few months now, and they're in really good quality right now. But that's going to be all over when winter comes'. 'Exposure' connotes a mode of display (from the French, *exposer*) in which situational artworks installed in public places are *exposed* to the public (some of whom, if they do not enjoy a work, may feel that they have been presented with an 'indecent exposure'). This exposure, then, must also include reactions from viewers: some may respond with a smile, but others will certainly try to remove a work, tear it into pieces, or paint over it. But in New York, as in other cities where the winter is long and harsh, the street artwork is surrendered to the effects of the weather – fading, eroding, bleaching, weathering – in a way that both confirms the street artwork's place as part of the cityscape (since the city's surfaces are constantly exposed to the elements) and as an all too temporary addition to the cityscape, whose presence may or may not be pleasurable, and may or may not endure.

## Paris: portraits

Parisian street artists appear to have a fondness for figurative artworks. This form is not the only one to be found on the walls of Paris, but it dominates the streetscape: animals (meerkats, tigers, giraffes) by Mossko et Associés; the urban characters of Jana und Js; C215's multi-layered stencil portraits of the homeless; the cartoon-like characters by Speedy Graffito; the subjects of PITR's portraits (including Michel Foucault); the knowing woman and the black cat in Miss.Tic's stencils; Nemo's black painted figure with umbrella; the accordion player or the giant Salvador Dali near the Pompidou Centre by Jef Aérosol; the abstracted black silhouettes of FKDL; and the *corps blanc* of Jêrome Mesnager (see Plate 10). Faces stare out at the passerby or turn to other characters as if there was another world to that experienced by the citizen, a narrative playing out on the walls, a world within the walls.

Those who experience street art and graffiti as destabilising and troubling often describe works as *defacing* the walls of the city streets. The term 'defacement' implies that a city's walls have an outward face, which has been altered, spoiled, or even destroyed by the artwork – literally de-faced.[7] This may seem odd, but then again, we are quite accustomed to speaking of the *façade* of a building. And both 'façade' and 'face' share the same Latin root (from *facia*).

In Paris, I encountered hundreds of portraits, a panoply of characters and animals adorning the walls and making me think about the pictorial appeal of such an aesthetic. It is certainly easy to find this kind of street art appealing: skillful images, in bright colours, in well-thought-out locations. Even the hundreds of mosaics by Invader, dotted around the walls of Paris, repeat the cheerful and amusing aesthetic. It seemed strange to me that anyone could find these images offensive, a disfigurement. The pictorial style so prevalent in Paris more than negates the criticism of street art as defacement; in fact, these works are not simply *not-disfigurements*, these actively *re-figure* the streets, transforming Paris for the passerby and opening up obvious moments of enchantment within the cityscape.

But it is important to remember that hierarchies of taste and preference still pertain. The artist Jean Faucheur, through M.U.R. (the Association

7 On defacement, see Taussig (1999).

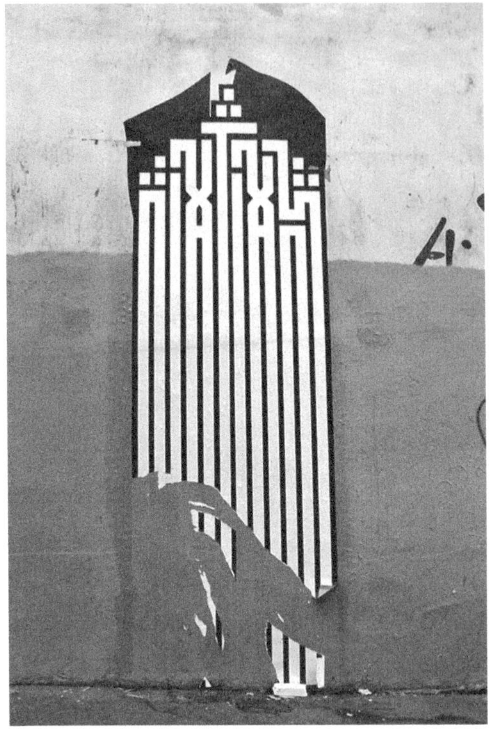

*Figure 3.3* L'Atlas, Paris 2010. Photograph © Alison Young.

Modulable Urbain Réactif), has created a space in which street art can be curated and displayed: a former billboard site, known as *Le Mur* (The Wall) on the corner of rue Oberkampf is painted by a different artist every month. They have an 'opening' – as would an indoor gallery for any new show – and *Le Mur* thus performatively suggests that street art can be regarded as consonant with gallery art. Although Le Mur's story is one of success, it took three and a half years to get permission for this one billboard space, indicating how difficult it is to enact such a philosophy within the municipal sphere.

Another successful site for street art (in that street art is 'tolerated' within it) is rue Denoyez in Belleville, which boasts an ever-changing range of artworks on the façades of the buildings. This area exists at the discretion of the Parisian authorities whose tolerance could be withdrawn if Belleville continues to gentrify. Around the corner from rue Denoyez the street artists, including Faucheur and L'Atlas, who used to occupy the studios known as La Forge, have relinquished the site to developers and moved further out.

As Faucheur put it, street art succeeds when it can find 'interim spaces', anything more than that and it becomes too threatening.

In Paris, then, graffiti and street art face several difficulties: gentrification (as in all cities); a perception of 'low' cultural status in a city filled with 'high' art; and, I would suggest, a need to develop work that *challenges*, so that Parisian walls may begin to speak of the city's diversity and struggles as well as offering pleasing and pretty portraits.

## Melbourne: communities

As in other cities, where the walls of Melbourne were once only tagged or pieced, now they display a variety of artworks. In the 1990s, as street art began to emerge as a distinctive cultural practice, particular styles, artists and places became synonymous with the idea of street art in Melbourne. Certain laneways in the CBD are now famous for their street art. Many artists choose to live and work in Melbourne displaying their work in galleries and on the street. In cities such as Paris or San Francisco, street art often still means stencil art, whereas street art in Melbourne can involve stencils, hand-drawn images rendered as wheat pastes, objects placed in public space, stickering, yarn-bombing and the application of paint to walls with fire extinguishers.

Where did this diversity come from? Geography provides one answer. Melbourne is remote from many other centres of street art and isolation has made its street art scene intense and insular. The tyranny of distance may explain Melbourne's distinctive street art scene in much the same way as it does Sao Paulo's highly characteristic graffiti style.[8] The scene may be geographically isolated, but it is has been a welcoming and inclusive one, attracting artists from every other city in Australia as well as overseas (there is a significant population of European and Japanese artists in Melbourne). Melbourne has also attracted famous visiting artists: Futura, Barry McGee and Chaz Bojorquez have visited Melbourne as guests of art and design festivals, and images by Herakut, Faith47, D*Face, Blék le Rat, Lister, Banksy, Tower, Eine, Peat Wolleager, Eghz, Sixten, Fafi, Invader and Nelio have been seen over the years on Melbourne's streets. And geography has played another role in influencing Melbourne's street art scene. Looking to cities such as New York and Washington DC, Melbourne was laid out in the 1830s according to a formal grid system. In the centre of the city, grand streets intersect with narrow laneways or alleys that were originally not noted on maps (since they existed only to service the buildings on the main thoroughfares).

For many years, Melbourne had a reputation for the extent and quality of its stencil art. Yet Melbourne's street art scene owes just as much to its histories of graffiti writing, political protest and skateboarding. Graffiti first arrived in

8 Note, however, that many Melbourne artists travel in order to make art in other cities and to connect with overseas artists. Miso, Ghostpatrol, Vexta, and several of the artists in the Everfresh crew (Meggs, Reka, Rone) have spent time in cities such as Tokyo, Vienna, London, New York and Berlin; while Civil has worked with artists in Indonesia.

Melbourne in the 1980s as copies of *Beat Street* and *Style Wars* circulated through the suburbs. Writers began to imitate the New York style of writing and later converted it to the character-driven style associated with crews such as Wild Child Artists. Crews such as DMA evolved a style that spoke distinctively of Melbourne by drawing on New York influences and pushing the representation of letter forms in new directions. In the 1990s, graffiti was harnessed as a means of political expression, marking the beginning of disaffection with mainstream media and a search for an alternative means of expression on issues such as urban development, Aboriginal politics, the environment, refugees and migration, consumerism and globalisation.

When stencils started to appear in the late 1990s they were often linked to political protest. But stencil-making offered benefits beyond political expression: images were sometimes placed on walls with no intention other than to give pleasure to the passerby. Artists would go out and spend hours walking or driving around the city putting up stencils much like a graffiti writer bombing a tag. But unlike tags (which tend to be unpopular) the stencil became *positively* associated with Melbourne's identity as a city. Films such as *Rash* (Nicholas Hansen 2005), books such as *Stencil Graffiti Capital: Melbourne* (Smallman and Nyman 2005) and the advent of the website *Stencil Revolution* all attest to this. Stencil art has never been policed in the same way as graffiti (to the resentment of graffiti writers). And while the official position is that stencils done without the property owner's consent are illegal, by the mid-2000s it was clear that an unofficial hierarchy had developed in which stencils were tolerated, while tagging and piecing was not (a differential attitude also shown to street artists and graffiti writers by police, as will be discussed in Chapter 4).

This is not to say that all street art was seen as permissible, far from it. A major component of the early Melbourne street art scene was the Empty Show, which involved artists taking over abandoned buildings in order to stencil, piece and draw over a period of days. Police would periodically raid these events. Key figures involved in the development of the Empty Show were Civil, Ha Ha, DLux, Psalm, Sync, Meek, Prism, Vexta, Tusk and Optic. Between his stencilled robots and countless portraits of Ned Kelly, Ha Ha's work at one time seemed to cover the entire city. Vexta was one of Melbourne's first female street artists, making political stencils about war and immigration alongside more dream-like images of kissing skeletons or a woman flying like a bird. In 2002, Prism was responsible for setting up 'Stencil Revolution', the first website devoted to stencil art (unlike sites such as 'Wooster Collective', which looks at all forms of street art). It included tutorials in stencil-making, interviews with artists and information about shows and events, and although its audience was international, most of its images were of Melbourne. This led to a great many travelling to Melbourne to participate in the scene themselves.

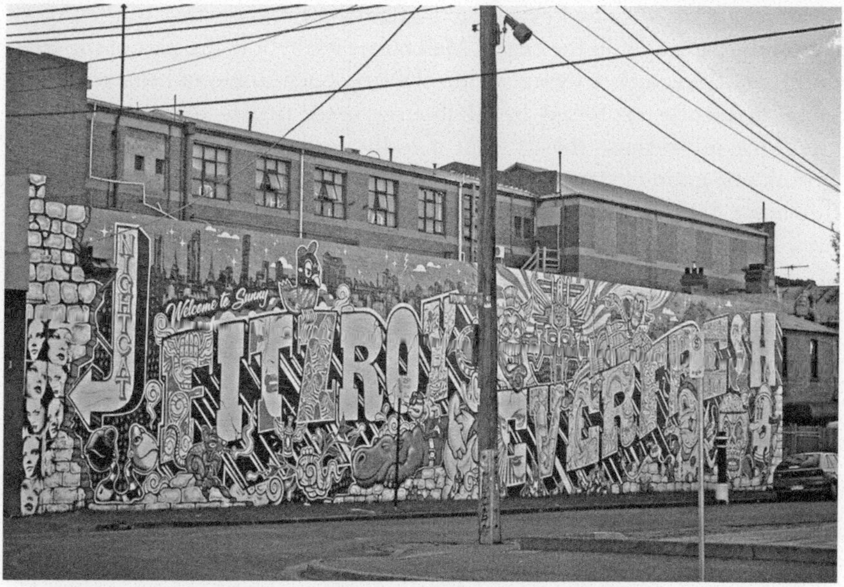


*Figure 3.4* Everfresh, Melbourne 2009. Photograph © Alison Young.

Around 2005 Melbourne's street art scene rapidly expanded, as artists began to experiment with new styles and techniques. The tags of Stan, Bones, Meow and Renks, members of 70K, one of Melbourne's most prominent graffiti crews (see MacDowall 2006) became ubiquitous. Many street artists become similarly prolific and began to look for more ingenious ways in which to fill the city's high-profile spaces. Some were attracted to stickers for their small size, portability and easy application; or to paste-ups, large paper images made at home or in a studio and then glued to a surface.

Public response has also contributed to the distinctiveness of Melbourne's street art scene. Many people in Melbourne enthusiastically welcomed street art as a part of their culture. While it is true that there is a counter-current of repression (see Chapter 4 as well as Young 2005, 2010a, 2010b, 2010c), Tourism Victoria has also made use of Melbourne's graffitied and stencilled laneways in its promotional materials. School groups, bridal parties and tourists also routinely head to places like Hosier Lane to be photographed in front of Melbourne's walls. One large wall became something of a local landmark after it was covered with an enormous monochrome mural by the Everfresh crew.

Laneways provide the backdrop for fashion shoots and music videos and an episode of *Rush* (a network television crime drama) featured a stencil artist putting up work in Rutledge Lane. According to Miso, graffiti and street art are 'a big part of the ethos of the city'.

Many artists described experiences of belonging – whether to the overall community existing in the city of Melbourne itself, or being part of the community of street artists living within the city. Such stories of belonging were more frequently expressed by Melbourne-based artists than in any other city. Miso put it thus: 'the art scene is really, really supportive and there isn't I think one grain of competitiveness between people which is a little bit of a difference I think to some of the bigger cities [elsewhere]'. Within this network, individuals are committed to a collaborative ethos and a sharing of ideas. As Nails commented: 'There's not the external support like in a big city like New York, where there's galleries and media and a big audience . . . people have to be here for each other, and to create a community, so that there is the prospect of propagation of ideas'. And one artist mentioned that, when she travelled abroad and described the mutual supportiveness found among Melburnians, her hosts were variously puzzled, surprised or concerned that it would jeopardise her individual success.

Ghostpatrol emphasised that this network also exists to protect artists from exploitation by others, an issue that has become increasingly relevant as auction houses, galleries and corporations have begun to view street art as a marketable commodity:

> All the [information about] the commercial stuff . . . it's all shared amongst our network. If I have a bad time, I'm going to tell [other artists] because I don't want them to get in to the same kind of trap . . . Even though they try and convince you and lie, lie, lie, you have to hold your own and say, 'No money. Fuck off. We don't want your money. We want dignity'. Because of the strong network and friendship, we share that information . . . [You get] guys saying, 'You're ruining your careers. You've got to be part of this market' and things like that. So, we have had to unite as a community – and you have to send [information] to other people . . . Everybody needs to share that. What's good for one of us – so, when Kid Zoom [an Australian artist now based in New York] is going well in New York, that's good for all of us. When Meggs has another show in London, that's good for everybody. When the *Young and Free* show [a group exhibition of Australian street artists at White Walls gallery] takes place in San Francisco, that's good for all of us . . . It's no good one person excelling and the rest suffering.

And although commercial imperatives have in recent years encroached upon some of the mutual supportiveness shown by artists to each other and within the city's responses to street art, it is still these intersecting attitude of communal ownership of street art and protectiveness towards street artists that characterises Melbourne's production of situational art in its cityscape.

## Berlin: ghosts

The walls of Berlin are crowded. Not just tags, pieces, posters, paste-ups and stickers, but thick layers of them. Street art climbs the walls, reaching up around drainpipes, testifying to the agility of Berlin's street artists. Buildings sometimes look as though they have sprouted an engulfing vine or creeper. And it is not only the walls: artists in Berlin seem to view *any* area surface as a potential writing surface and to a much greater extent than in other cities. I saw signal boxes at train stations, windows and windowsills, pavements and the undersides of tunnels all painted or written on. As the artist Emess says: 'It's painted everywhere'.

Berlin artists write on surfaces that in other cities might well be deemed too difficult to reach. It is not simply that a signal box at a train station will have been tagged; but rather that the tagging will have required feats such as hanging from a bridge or overpass (as Kripoe from the CBS crew seems to have done at many of Berlin's stations) (see Figure 1.4). Although it is not unusual for graffiti writers to use a rooftop in order to reach a high (and perhaps highly visible) wall, in Berlin, it is common to find that the roofs themselves have been tagged with enormous letters that can be seen from a great distance. When Just said that he wants his tag to be read by a lot of people ('I look for spots that are the most readable') what he means is that he is willing to scale a building five storeys high, with a fire extinguisher or paint roller, so that

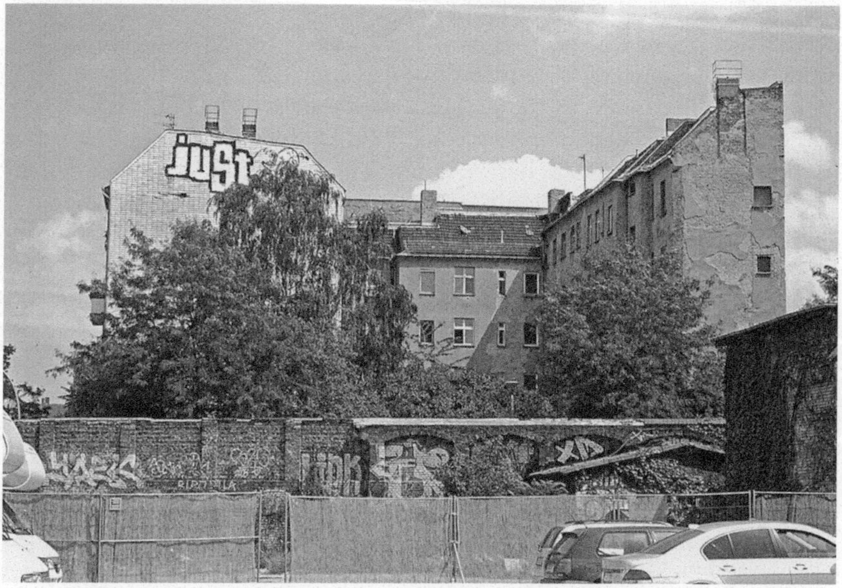


*Figure 3.5* Just, Berlin 2010. Photograph © Alison Young.

his tag 'JUST' can be read all the way from the Cassiopeia skate park in Revaler Strasse, several streets away.[9]

In addition to massive tags, Berlin boasts large-scale murals by os gemeos, The London Police, Dave the Chimp and Blu, all curated by Adrian Nabi, whose 'Backjumps' exhibitions gave street art great prominence in the city and inspired a number of local artists to begin making street art. Local and international street artists exhibit in Berlin galleries such as Circleculture. In fact, Berlin has a vast number of galleries, and during my visit several people mentioned proudly that it has 'more galleries per capita than any other city in the world'. One artist said: 'If you cannot get an opening in Berlin you must be a really terrible artist'. Berlin was also home for several years to what was known as the 'Papergirl' event, through which works by street artists (sent to the organiser by artists from all over the world) are freely distributed in Berlin's streets by volunteers on bicycles.[10] Berlin also has Hatch, a Sticker Museum, in which visitors can admire the stickers of local and international artists. The museum's proprietor describes himself as a curator and archivist: 'Maybe in 10 years I will be able to show a bit the history, the development of all this. Maybe some artists in a few years will be happy that I have the first pieces and I can show also the development of these signs'.

The extensiveness of street art in Berlin has resulted in part from the city's inability to fund graffiti removal, and from the fact that (as many artists noted) the Berlin police rarely arrest street artists (although they do arrest graffiti writers on trains). Various summed up the thoughts of many artists when she wondered whether '[the police] acknowledge that it puts attraction to Berlin as a cultural city or whether they have other things to do'. Berlin's atmosphere of intense creativity attracts artists from all over the world. El Bocho said: 'Berlin is really a good city for [art] because it's always changing and it's very easy to find good spots, to find a studio.' Brad Downey, an American who has lived for several years in Berlin, said: 'The city is so alive and full of possibilities. Berlin is constantly under construction, socially and physically, and nothing feels permanent. This impermanence is a big inspiration for my work.' Berlin, home to artists from London, Australia, the United States, France, Holland and from elsewhere in Germany, is so attractive to overseas artists that it can be hard to find local ones. Tower, a prolific sticker artist, was the only native Berliner out of the fifteen artists I interviewed. As the French artist and Berlin resident Jaybo Monk wryly noted: 'It's quite hard to find a Berliner right now in Berlin.'

9 Writing with fire extinguishers has been taken up by graffiti writers all over the world but it seems particularly prevalent in Berlin.

10 When Papergirl began, in the mid-2000s, around ten or twelve volunteers distributed approximately thirty artworks. In 2010, when I observed the event, dozens of riders handed out 584 artworks to people on the streets of Berlin.

Emess hoped that Berlin's international appeal would help to preserve its street art: 'Maybe in the end there are . . . more people who say, "Well, we need this for our culture. It's part of Berlin. Please don't clean every wall outside". Because . . . that's why a lot of people come to Berlin, to experience the rough, urban art scene.' However, appreciation of graffiti writing and street art does not permeate all sectors of Berlin society. Ingo, from the collective Klub 7, noted:

> I think it depends on the borough or the part of the city. In Friedrichshain, where we live, a lot of students live there and they like it . . . But there are parts of Berlin where old people live or people who have their own house and don't rent and then I think that they hate it. Perhaps they've got a restaurant on Kurfurstendamm and want the street artists to make the artwork but they hate it on their own house. But I think a lot of graffiti artists think that too. On their own car, please not.[11]

The one thing that Berlin does not have is a thriving art market. Its intense creativity tends to generate works that are bought and sold elsewhere: in Munich, London, Australia or New York. Jaybo commented on this: 'Berlin is a very poor town. There are galleries on every corner, but nobody sells in Berlin. I make my money overseas.' Meanwhile, the creativity that has characterised many of Berlin's neighbourhoods has also given rise to gentrification.[12] Emess was already worried about a potential downturn in the city's creative economy:

> We don't have any industry here, so artists are important. I hope that we will have this feeling for the coming years because it's changing a lot. There's a lot of new money in the city. It's changing also the streets. It's getting cleaner and cleaner. And then some day it won't be interesting . . . It's a little bit like Barcelona. It was very hip ten years ago and then they cleaned [it up].

Over the last decade, areas with large working spaces and low rents have been crowded out by the middle class (Prenzlauer Berg being the most obvious example). Although this process has been found in many cities, and thus is

11 Ollie, the owner and curator of Hatch, noted that despite being located in Friedrichshain, an area associated with street art, 'neighbours, they don't like it that there are all these stickers [on drainpipes and windowsills outside the museum] and they try to put them away . . . A lot of people still don't like tags, but it's not so easy to get rid of them because you have to cover a tag with something, paint something over it, but to remove a sticker is easier so I always see people, older people sometimes, that pass on by and when they see the stickers, start to peel them off and then they throw them away . . . Some neighbours nowadays they prefer to have a perfect clean-looking house.'

12 On gentrification in Berlin, see Drissel (2011); Jacob (2008); Papen (2012); and Shaw (2005).

not unique to Berlin, it is testament to the city's self-identity as a location that values creativity over profit that gentrification is now an abiding concern in Berlin with many artists and activists actively resisting its effects. Some spray-paint slogans critical of property development along the river banks in Kreuzberg ('Fuck off Media Spree') while others join organisations such as Platoon, which provides a physical and online platform for investigating the effects of urban change through gentrification, social media, art and political activism. Artists such as Various and Gould address gentrification issues in their works, and Various noted that, 'after a while we will move away, we will have to [as rents increase]'. Ollie from Hatch said:

> It will become more and more difficult for projects like [the sticker museum] or galleries to be in areas like [Friedrichshain] because of gentrification. The real estate companies prefer to have good perfect looking buildings to take higher rent . . . I have to look now for a bigger place [to expand the museum] and it's impossible to find something here at a price that I'm able to pay and you notice that the buildings are getting cleaner, the people who move here have more money, the shops now here are more and more exclusive.

But while Berlin may gentrify, it also carries with it an array of ghosts from its wars and their horrors. As I walked through the streets of Berlin, I felt the presence of these ghosts in various ways. At Potsdamer Platz station, I was startled to see the station's name written in a Gothic script I associate with Nazi Germany: this prompted in me a recognition of the violence these spaces must have seen. Of course, Berlin's ghosts are explicitly acknowledged in memorials and museums. Any pedestrian who walks into Grosse Hamburger Strasse in Mitte cannot help but notice the statues marking the assembly place for those transported to concentration camps during World War II.[13] The tourist who wanders down Unter den Linden may notice a strange Perspex-covered gap in a square (Bebelplatz) outside Humboldt University's Faculty of Law: it is a memorial artwork indicating the site where the Nazis notoriously burned hundreds of books on 10 May 1933, and its interior, subterranean space appears to open downwards into a book-filled library. The massive Monument to the Murdered Jews of Europe occupies an entire city block near the Brandenburg Gate. And nearby, another form of state violence is memorialised: white crosses on a fence represent those who were shot trying to climb the Berlin Wall and escape the East. Meanwhile, at Birnauer Strasse, small fragments of the bulldozed Wall have been concreted into the pavement – a literal insertion of the past into the present – so that what has disappeared might remain within the everyday spaces of the city.

13 On encounters with the ghosts of Berlin's past through monuments and public art, see Whybrow (2005), especially Chapter 5.

The Berlin Wall can even be purchased, in small containers, at the Museum of Checkpoint Charlie. A long unbroken stretch of the Wall remains, close to the River Spree, and constituting what is now known as the East Side Gallery featuring civic-minded murals about human rights, peace, friendship and global politics. Very few draw on the aesthetic that covered the historical Wall, that is, graffiti and punk art. What the Wall looked like in the 1980s, however, can be seen on a section preserved at the museum in Birnauer Strasse. Tags, slogans and images cover its concrete surfaces, much as they do the walls of every surface in contemporary Berlin, and much less decorously than the contemporary murals on the Wall at the East Side Gallery. Indeed, it is important to remember that it was the Wall's effect on the topography and organisation of Berlin's society that helped to produce the prolific, extensive graffiti that covers Berlin's surfaces today. As Jaybo recounted in his interview:

> I came [to Berlin], and we had the Wall, which is like very special because just one metre over the side of it was already the DDR, but then there was this in between space that was not anything, and nobody could tell you anything. So we were painting there and we would have the police just come and look at us, and they could do nothing . . . so everybody tried to do things there. Big artists, little guys like we were, everybody. Then came this hip hop thing, and everybody start to tag, and it became easy. Berlin is *the* place for this. And suddenly the Wall falls down, and it was just virgin walls everywhere in the former East Germany . . . So everybody could try it, and everything happened then.

The Wall's originary status has certainly been diminished. Jaybo noted that the Wall is 'gone a long time' and that, when people come to Berlin, visit the museum and Checkpoint Charlie, they feel that it is 'so "back in the day"'. But is all the history gone? The Wall may be a civic gallery, a tourist attraction and a collection of painted fragments sold in small plastic boxes, but walls all over Berlin continue to speak of creativity, memorialisation and protest. And though Berlin is rapidly changing – and re-shaping its present – it cannot forget or escape the ghosts that inhabit its streets.

## London: the node

When newspapers, magazines and websites publish lists of the 'top ten cities in the world for street art', London is always included.[14] And when talking

14 Examples include *Reuters* (www.reuters.com/article/2009/07/10/us-travel-picks-art-idUSTRE56913420090710); *Huffington Post* (www.huffingtonpost.com/bootsnall/the-worlds-best-cities-fo_b_1327741.html#s766462&title=Melbourne_Australia); *Travel and Leisure* (www.travelandleisure.com/articles/the-best-cities-for-street-art); and the *International Business Times* (www.ibtimes.com/articles/69974/20101008/best-cities-street-art.htm) (all accessed 2 July 2012).

with artists or people interested in street art, London's centrality is often reiterated. According to Eine: 'it's the hub . . . the mecca for street art'. In conversations with people interested in street art, London's central status is taken for granted: 'oh, you must visit Milan/ Berlin/ Barcelona/ wherever . . . and London, of course'. What gives London this status?

There are a number of factors making London the central hub of the street art world. First, it is proximate to Bristol. In many ways Bristol is a more accurate point of origin for street art in Britain given that it is the home of Banksy and many other street artists and graffiti writers. Nowadays, Bristol has 'come to London': the cultural shift that began in the regional city is now more associated with the capital. At one point or another there have been so many Banksy artworks in London that you can buy guidebooks showing their locations (such as Martin Bull's guide, *Banksy Locations and Tours*, now in two volumes).[15] And key individuals in the street art world – such as Steve Lazarides, gallerist and art dealer, or Mary McCarthy, who worked for a number of years at Dreweatts auction house – have moved from Bristol to live and work in London. Second, London's topography has lent itself to a number of prominent street art areas, in particular, the East End: Brick Lane, Shoreditch, Hackney and Dalston. Third, artists, collectors, dealers and aficionados flow in and out of London with ease, as do information (blogs such as 'Hooked', 'Vandalog', 'Street Art London', and 'Art of the State' discuss London's street art scene) and wealth (London is the global centre of the art market and even many American clients buy direct from London). It was no coincidence that London auction houses such as Bonhams achieved the astonishing prices that characterised the 'art bubble' of 2007–2008 (Thompson 2008; Leung 2009).

London has also been the location for many events in which street art is the centrepiece or is incorporated in order to lend a sense of cultural currency. Consider 'Banger Art', organised by London gallery Nelly Duff, in which ten street artists (including Pablo Delgado, Eine, Sweet Toof and the Toasters) painted cars to be displayed at a music festival. Other events have become key to street art's sense of its own history. These include Finders Keepers, the annual Santa's Ghetto organised by Banksy, and more recently (and more fine art-oriented), Hell's Half Acre, organised by Steve Lazarides and located in the Old Vic tunnels, displaying work by David Choe, Todd James (REAS), Conor Harrington and Paul Insect. Most significantly, London was the location for the Cans Festival, which cemented the idea of London as a node to and from which people would travel in order to make and view street art. Held

15 The association of both Banksy in particular and street art in general with London is demonstrated in John Lanchester's novel, *Capital* (2012), which features a thinly disguised version of Banksy in the form of a character called Graham who goes by the alias 'Smitty', lives in Shoreditch, and stages conceptual art in the streets of London, aided by a team of assistants sworn to secrecy as to his identity.

in late May 2008, artists from a range of countries (Australia, the United States, Holland, France, Portugal and many more) were flown in to take part in this massive exhibition and celebration of stencil art.[16]

Part of the impact of the Cans Festival derived from its sheer scale. Housed in a disused tunnel in Leake Street, near Waterloo Station, hundreds of people queued for up to three hours at a time to enter the tunnel and see the artworks. The space filled with people, some adding their own stencils or tags to the walls, other photographing what they saw. But its impact was also a product of the volume of work on display. Official works, commissioned for the event, by artists such as Vexta, Civil and DLux (Australia), Vhils (Portugal), C215, Blék Le Rat and Jef Aérosol (France), Sten e Lex (Italy), Kaagman (Holland), Logan Hicks and Faile (USA), Pure Evil, Eine and Banksy (Britain) were joined by unofficial additions. The tunnel was crammed with images to the point that railings and posts had been sprayed as had the ground, painted by the Canadian artist Roadsworth with a stencil version of a Scalectrix track, complete with cars, racing through the tunnel.

Art in general is important to London's sense of itself as a city. As Eine commented: 'London has a good art scene, so people are more open to [street art] . . . We've got good art galleries. We've got the Tate, we've got the Turner Prize, Channel 4 [is] always reporting on art and artists'. The way in which art is ingrained in the city's self-image has no doubt made it easier for street art to find a degree of institutional acceptance in London. This may seem paradoxical given street art's anti-institutional sensibility, but it is in London that the greatest institutional absorption of the street artwork has occurred. In 2008, the Tate Modern gave its façade over to six street artists (JR, Faile, Sixeart, Nunca, Blu and os gemeos) who covered its entire outer wall with massive images. Private galleries have also been swift to capitalise on the public interest in street art. In 2007, Andipa Gallery in Knightsbridge organised the first Banksy exhibition in an art gallery (and was criticised for fuelling the secondary market in Banksy images), and lists Banksy and Slinkachu alongside artists such as Miro, Matisse, Bacon and Warhol. Artists associated with street art or graffiti have been shown in many well-established commercial galleries in addition to Andipa (such as Opera Gallery and Haunch of Venison), while other galleries primarily focused on street art have opened (and sometimes closed) over the years.

Can London's status as the node for street art be maintained (or even justified)? In 2008, London was bursting with street art and street-art-related activity: the Tate Modern was exhibiting street artists on its exterior (although not inside); the Cans Festival had been an overwhelming success; and the walls

16 The May Cans Festival was repeated later in 2008, this time showcasing the work of graffiti writers. The tunnel in which the festivals were located now functions as a semi-official painting site for all artists and writers.

of Brick Lane and Shoreditch were full to capacity. Laser 3.14 compared the scene in his home city of Amsterdam to that of London at the time:

> The whole scene [in Amsterdam] seems to be in decline over the last ten years. The government decided to move the artists out of the city – they cracked down on every type of dissent, everything that is a bit subversive or a bit different. The artists went to Rotterdam – where the city said, yes, we want artists, and provided space for them, and everything in the city is improved as a result. Like in Shoreditch – in that area there was not much happening, but now it's full of artists' spaces, and galleries and art everywhere on the streets.

Although Shoreditch was indeed vibrant at that moment, it also had a slight air of a street art theme park. Work was being put up in and around Hoxton Square partly to meet the expectation that people could find street art in that area (as opposed to the idea that artwork might work well in a space or add something to a wall). It also felt somewhat quarantined. As Slinkachu commented: 'I imagine other councils probably quite like it that everything's confined to Shoreditch and around . . . I don't think other councils like people scrawling things on walls'.

But even mandated and segregated vibrancy could not last long. By 2009, much of Shoreditch and Brick Lane had been buffed – painted over or blasted with water hoses. Surveillance cameras spread and buffing became much more vigorous in London, so much so that, in early 2010, Dscreet described the process of putting up work as 'a combination of art and extreme sport'. The deterrent effects of the combination of CCTV and buffing has been so effective that much of London's best situational art now exists in memory rather than in the city streets. Activities have sedimented in side streets and other hidden areas; the abundance and randomness that was so noticeable in 2008 has been lost.

London is a horizontal city (the opposite of New York) whose demographics shift as you cross the road, travel one stop on the Underground, or pass out of one postcode and into another (as Zadie Smith describes in her novel *NW*). It is gentrifying like all the other cities in which street art has become significant (since street art plays a large part in that process). As artist and gallerist Pure Evil said of the East End in general and Shoreditch in particular:

> About fifteen or twenty years ago this place was a no-go area for black people. The National Front and British National Party were here, and in fact this was a no-go area for a lot of people, but now it's changed, it's like yuppie paradise. You've got all these estate agents, you know, they have little special Minis to take people around to look at apartments. So it's definitely become a lot more gentrified.

Many of the artists I interviewed in London spoke of moving eastwards, away from Shoreditch and further into Dalston and Hackney Wick and beyond. They cited skyrocketing rents and new residents in expensive apartment blocks who lobbied councils to keep the area free of graffiti and street art.[17] Street art can still be found in Shoreditch and around Brick Lane, but, while impressive, some of it feels more 'stage-managed', in the form of commissioned mural projects, than when the scene was exploding in 2008 (see Plate 4). Unlike Berlin, where gentrification was regarded by artists, academics and activists as something to be fiercely resisted, in London there seemed to be greater resignation to its inevitability, tinged with a sense that it was also possible to create new spaces in the interstitial areas of the city. Eine summed up the cycle of creativity and commerce as follows:

> Artists as a rule don't particularly make that much money and are prepared to suffer for their art. So they'll move into a studio in an area that no one else would move into, they'll slowly get the area up. So artists used to live around [Shoreditch], because it was one of the very last run down areas, Whitechapel is still a bit like it. Hackney is one of the poorest boroughs in London. So lots of artists live around here, and to a degree Hackney Wick when you go quite a bit further out. So they move into places that other people don't want to live . . . [Other people], they're quite enterprising . . . They're into film and into music, they'll put on nights, they'll start up nightclubs, coffee shops. And artists are interesting people, so that begins to bring people into the area and then somebody gets a sniff of that and then starts buying up property, renting them out. It's not that the property developers are following the artists, it's just that they're all chasing the next place to do up.

London is a city of art galleries both public (Tate Britain, Tate Modern, National Portrait Gallery, The Hayward Gallery, the Victoria and Albert Museum, the Courtauld Institute and more) and private (the White Cube, the Saatchi Gallery, Andipa). There are also galleries that specialise in street art or urban art (Stolen Space, Lazarides's two establishments, Signal). Within that list of sets and subsets lies an embedded chronology. In 2008, a number of galleries proclaimed themselves to be 'street art galleries', and yet by 2012 some had gone out of business while others had varied their holdings to make the most of artists demonstrating longevity of activity and depth of market interest. Thus, a range of artists initially associated with graffiti or street art are now enfolded within a range of London galleries as 'contemporary artists'.

17 On questions of 'place identity' and gentrification in Dalston, see Davison (2012).

As is shown by the example of the shifts in gallery presence, holdings and reputation, London, perhaps more than many other cities, is a city of flows. Artists fly in from the United States, or South America, or Australia; they come by train or on budget airlines from Europe. While in London, they put up work on the walls: 'anyone who comes into town will make a mark and say here I am, hello everyone' (Pure Evil). The streets of London display work by Colombians, New Yorkers, Parisians, Poles. 'London street art' is a misnomer; it could be better said that situational art from all over the world coalesces on the walls of London in ways and to an extent that cannot be seen in any other city. 'London street art' is constituted by its very *un*-Londonness.

Thus art flows through London, following transport routes, the word on the Internet, the memory of the days when Cans happened, or when the streets were filled with Banksy stencils, or when the buff was not so rigorous. London sutures itself around these flows, holds them in place, lets them ebb or intensify, and then moves on. As Lacan would put it, the city is a *point de capiton*, a 'quilting point' that draws together threads and fragments, rendering them a heterogeneous conglomeration that is neither the sum of all its parts, nor identifiably something distinct from them. It is an intensity, it is an accretion. It is a node in a transnational network of bits, bytes, desires, bodies, cash, credit and walls. It is insuperably itself, reminiscent of all the other cities in the world and distinct from all of them.

## Rome: layers

I was staying in a hotel near the Campo dei Fiori, a popular location for tourists in the *centro storico* of Rome. One evening I had an appointment at a gallery, Wunderkammern, to interview its director. I went to the taxi rank near Campo dei Fiori, got into a cab, and gave the address: via Gabrio Serbelloni. The driver indicated that he did not know where it was. I did the same; although I had looked at the address on Google Maps I would not know how to drive there through Rome's tortuous streets. The driver looked it up in the street directory and turned to me, saying 'No, it's impossible'. He thought I must be mistaken. But I insisted and showed it to him written in my notebook. He drove off, muttering. Once closer to the area in question (Torpignattara), he became lost, driving around a series of one way streets, cursing as he went: 'Que zona brutta! Questa zona di cazzo! [What an ugly area! This fucking area!']' Eventually, he deposited me in a street and pointed: 'It's down there, you need to walk!' I found the gallery. But I kept thinking about my driver and his destabilising experience: the gallery's location had jarred with his idea of what it means to be a visitor to Rome (and where such a visitor should want to go). Identity, I realised, is spatial.

A similar realisation fascinates and motivates the gallery, Wunderkammern, which seeks to 'explore themes related to the marvellous, the paradox, the relation between the inside and the outside, the conventional and the unaccepted, privacy and voyeurism'[18] and is deliberately located in Torpignattara so as to problematise ideas of place, image, territory, history, memory and experience. This can be seen most clearly in the collaboration between Wunderkammern and MACRO (Rome's gallery of contemporary art). In 2012, Wunderkammern and MACRO worked together on a project called *Living Layers*, which involved a series of exhibitions featuring artists brought to live and work in Rome. The project aimed to 'explore the depth of territory and to read its cultural heritage . . . Living Layers [is] composed of those practices, representations, expressions, learning and knowledge that the community recognises as part of its own living cultural heritage'.[19]

However, there is another sense in which the notion of 'living layers' applies to Rome more than to most cities. One can stand on a street corner and see a Renaissance palazzo built right on top of the Emperor Augustus's Teatro di Marcello, which dates from 13 BC, and note, a few feet away, how the ruins of the first century Portico D'Ottavia is incorporated into the eighth-century church, Chiesa di Sant'Angelo in Pescheria. The very experience of the Roman cityscape is one of *living a city's layers*: the visible strata of the city embed history into the structures and edifices of the city. In order to exist in Rome, you must actively live (in) its layers. Visitors to sites such as the Palatine Hill often declare awe at the vertiginous (if slightly inaccurate) sensation of treading exactly where Cicero must have walked 2000 years before. And unlike other cities, in which historical ruins are often segregated from functional domestic, governmental and corporate zones, in Rome the layers of the city are enfolded within the contemporary and visible to all. A walk through the Roman forum is accompanied by the thunder of trucks and buses from the major arterial road adjacent to it. Apartment buildings and offices cannot help but lay their concrete foundations deep in Roman ruins. During the construction of an apartment building in the central area a column, many hundreds of years old, was discovered; the solution was to construct an alcove around the column, so it would be visible from the street, and to carry on building the apartments.

Rome reveals a geological temporality not normally on display in a city: millennia are visible. On street corners, buildings of different historical periods jostle with each other, while beneath one's feet cobblestones transform to concrete, to brick, and back again. Before I visited Rome for the first time, someone said to me: 'Being in Rome is like a hallucination', and I found that description did indeed encapsulate something of the destabilising experience of place and time in the city. The Roman cityscape offers proof of the fact

18 See the gallery's website at www.wunderkammern.net/whoiswunderkammern/intro.htm (accessed on 14 October 2012).

19 See the gallery's website at www.wunderkammern.net/markjenkins/markjenkins.htm (accessed on 14 October 2012).

that the 'Eternal City' remains constant throughout the passing of time, and yet simultaneously the city changes while appearing to stay the same. This paradox – that stone persists while it weathers, that buildings crumble even as they remain – can also explain some aspects of the discomfiting nature of the street artwork. Installation in urban space subjects the situational artwork to the inevitability and impact of change in ways that gallery-based artworks never experience, and in Rome, where the inconstancy of urban surfaces is constitutive of the city itself, it is all too obvious that street art is a temporary thing.

Viewing street art in Rome is a curious experience. First, Rome is obviously dedicated to the conservation of its monuments and artworks. Frescoes must be preserved so that colours do not fade, tourists must not climb on the ruins of the Forum and further erode already weathered stone. Against artefacts with such incontestable heritage, the situational artwork's claim to cultural value seems more marginal than in other cities. The street artwork, unlike the ancient fresco, is regarded as transient: if it fades, it fades; if it is torn down, it is not mourned; if it is chipped from the wall (as has happened to many of the mosaics installed around Rome by the French artist Invader), it is not a scandal. Although Rome is synonymous with the idea that conservation of

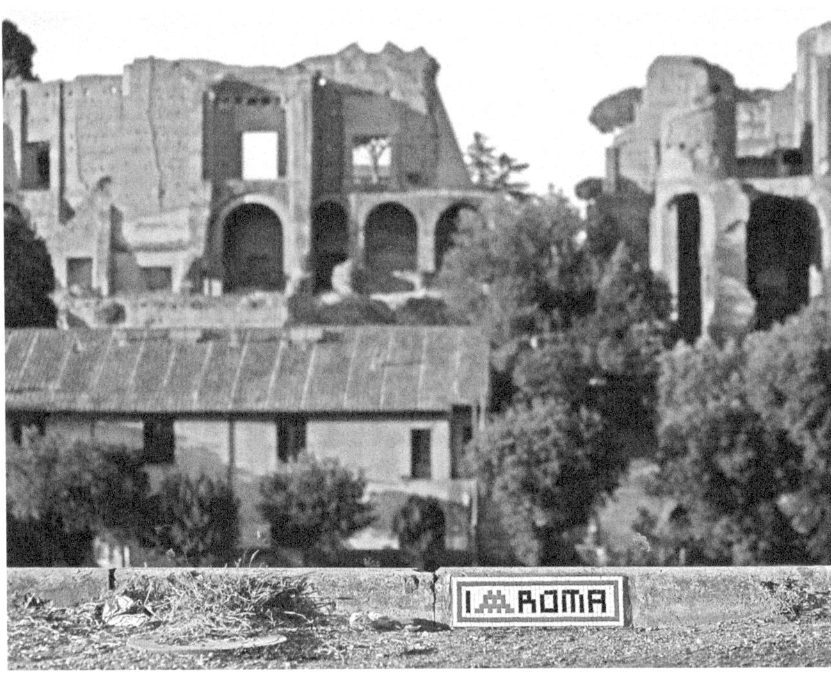


*Figure 3.6* Invader, Rome 2010. © Invader and Wunderkammern Gallery.

art is essential (even if it can only retard, never freeze, time), street artworks in Rome come into being and disappear without any comment. The artworks installed around Rome by Invader are mosaics, small renditions of the well-known 'space invader' icons from the 1980s computer game. Although their reference point is a computer game from the recent past, the techniques of their execution and installation create points of consonance and resemblance with some of the ancient artworks being assiduously conserved around Rome.

Invader's mosaics are highly desirable collector's items: when sold through galleries in Paris, they are priced at around 12–15,000 euros. Their fashionability in art circles may have led to them being chipped from walls by unscrupulous collectors or profiteers, or it may be that municipal authorities have decided to remove these illicit works. However, their disappearance from the walls of buildings around Rome has attracted little criticism. To point this out is neither to argue that all street art should be preserved (since ephemerality is regarded by many as a constituent feature of street art), nor to imply that Rome should allow its ancient artworks to crumble into disrepair. Rather, it should be easy to point out that all citizens are potentially the poorer when any artwork is chipped from a wall in public space in order to be privately possessed or sold for profit. Such claims for street artwork, however, are hard to make in most cities. In Rome, it is even more difficult, despite the extensiveness of the city's commitment to conservation, as evidenced by the silence around Invader's disappearing mosaics. Street art is rarely discussed in the context of preservation, partly because its ephemerality is interpreted by street artists themselves as positive, but also because it is categorised as undeserving – lacking in cultural heritage. The vast extent of cultural heritage in Rome, of all cities, means that in Rome a conversation about the preservation of street art could never take place.

The interpretation of street artworks as lacking in cultural heritage is underpinned by shifts in municipal politics in Rome, which has recently seen a change at the mayoral level. The new mayor, a conservative one, has increased the numbers of police on the streets and is overseeing efforts to remove graffiti. The impact of this change is visible: where, in 2010, street art was plentiful in areas such as Parione or Trastevere, in 2012, those districts have been buffed (and were being maintained in such a way as to deter street artists, with frequent removal of any stray artworks that dared to reappear). Graffiti writers and street artists have been pushed out of these central areas into outlying neighbourhoods such as San Lorenzo, Ostiense and Pigneto. Even there, tags and throw-ups are being painted over. It is not clear, at present, whether Rome's graffiti will disappear into the past and become another one of the city's living layers or whether it will be allowed to remain, so that one day it might be possible to have a conversation as to whether contemporary wall-painting and wall-writing has any of the value that is taken for granted in respect of those from the city's past.

## City/art

Each city, as the preceding sections have shown, *produces* its own situational art. Graffiti writers and street artists are always already responding to a city's surfaces, spaces, architecture and aesthetic. Laser 3.14, who writes poetic aphorisms in Amsterdam on temporary hoardings and scaffolding covers, sees his work in relation to the city's own efforts to change itself through construction:

> I like temporary surfaces like hoardings because it seems cool that my work appears and disappears all around the city. It's also important that the temporary coverings are over a building or next to a building where construction work is being done. So something is going on underneath the sheeting at the same time as the line of my writing has appeared on the outside.

Many artists describe themselves as having a different understanding of the city from other citizens (as argued in Chapter 2, the street artist inhabits an 'uncommissioned city' as opposed to the 'legislated city', resulting in a distinctive sensibility as to city surfaces). Interviewees often saw themselves as responding to an invitation from the city – from its surfaces – to create work. (Such an invitation is not perceived by citizens of the legislated city, who do not view the city's surfaces as awaiting the addition of paint, sculpture

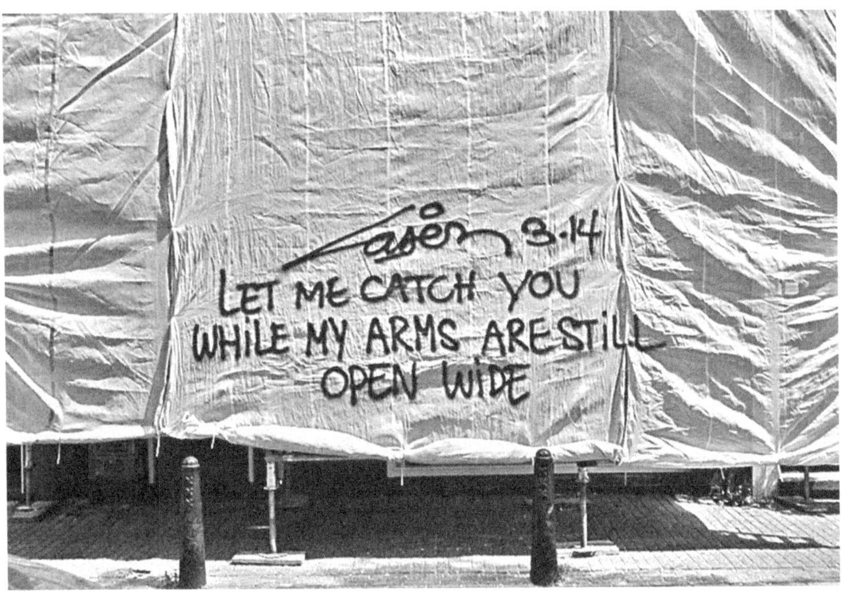


*Figure 3.7* Laser 3.14, Amsterdam 2008. Photograph © Alison Young.

or paper.) Kaff-eine said: 'I now see buildings, empty spaces, corners, curves, walls, pretty much every surface . . . through the lens of how they'd be as a canvas, and how my work could interact with them.' Erris described himself as 'constantly being influenced by the city', and Morcky commented:

> I've got a totally different relationship with the city . . . I know the way to interpret objects, places, walls, surfaces, if a surface is going to keep the paint for long because the surface is good enough or from which distance [the artwork] is visible. You know, like it's all a part of . . . the relation you have with the surroundings.

Street artists also actively seek out spots in which to place their work (on the 'spot' see Ferrell and Weide 2010). There is great pleasure to be derived from the serendipity of discovering a good spot, and a planned location can be superseded by a site that offers a better fit for an artwork. Laser 3.14 recounted: 'Usually I'm cycling around the city and I see spaces that have appeared, and I'll think, ah-ha, I should put something there'. The 'ah-ha!' moment may be enjoyable, but artists more often than not appear to search for spots methodically, that is, by actively scouting out locations. Brad Downey described 'going around and finding the perfect spot'; and Kaff-eine keeps a notebook in which she lists spots to come back to when she has created the right image for them.

Once a spot is found, many artists plan out the placement of their work, monitoring the site for pedestrian traffic, security guards, CCTV, accessibility and so on. Shinobi agonises over choosing a site: 'I'm the sort of person that will look at a spot for months and go, "No, do I really want to do that?" And then I suss out how to get up there, and suss out everything about the place before I go and do something.' Morcky is also extremely cautious: 'I do a lot of trips also during the day to check the places.' Anthony Lister described how he maintains successful sites by continually repainting them whenever he visits a city: 'I try to choose good spots. Like I've got areas in LA that I go and paint every time that I'm there. And in London, I'm just trying to maintain spots that I've painted for the last ten years . . . You choose a good spot and then hopefully it stays there.'

Beyond the pragmatics of site selection, artists seek locations that will assist in having an impact on the city. Just, in Berlin, looks for 'readable' sites so that his work will be seen by people. Morcky tries to find locations that balance solitude (necessary for painting) with a ready-made audience once the work is completed. C215, based in Vitry-sur-Seine near Paris but a prolific stencil artist in cities all over the world, described his work as 'turning bad architecture and context into nice pictures'. Civil sees his stick figures as a way to 'humanise the city' while Swoon declared that it is 'a really beautiful thing to write on the walls and let it get seen'.

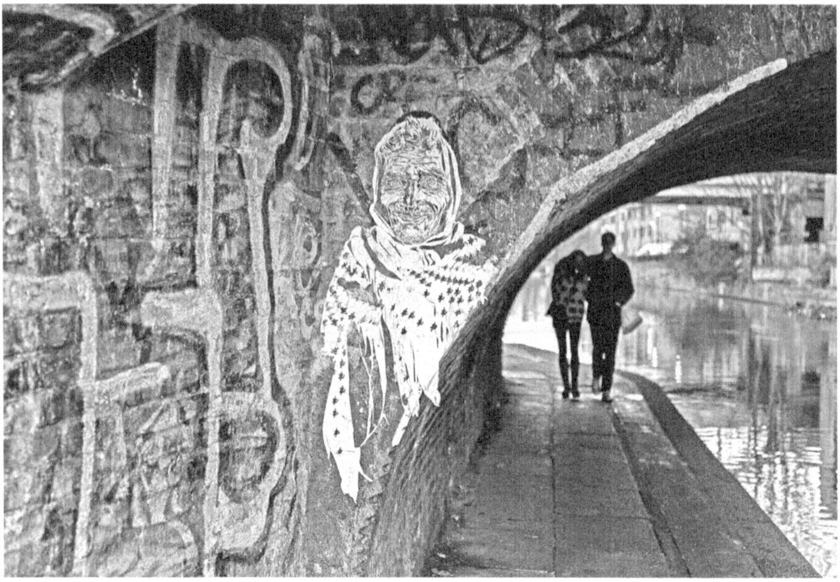

*Figure 3.8* Swoon, London 2011. Photograph © Mark Rigney – Hookedblog.

Artists thus project a relationship between the space they find themselves in, the artwork they create, and the range of effects flowing from the artwork, through the particular space, and encompassing both the spectator and the city itself.

This chapter has traversed a range of different cityscapes that I lived in or visited as part of my research on street art. In each city, street art has a distinctive character, and this has been recounted from the experience of *being in them*, which enables us to talk about them 'with a degree of confidence about the prevalent way of social and political life of those cities' (Bell and de-Shalit 2011: 8). What conclusions, however, can be drawn from these discussions? How can a consideration of 'the cityscape' help us understand art in the city and the city as art?

Walking in the city is a constitutive act; citizenship arises, and varies, as we traverse the streets and train lines, sometimes in haste, sometimes as part of a herd of commuters, sometimes strolling at leisure, sometimes lost, and in hot sun, in humidity or cold, and in darkness or daylight. To take such a citizenship of experience seriously, the urban ethnography developed in my research also noted repetition and change, making multiple visits to places, at different times of the year, during day or night, in different weather conditions. I recorded variations at sites and in neighbourhoods over time, as artworks faded or were buffed, buildings were torn down and rebuilt, areas gentrified and artists moved on to new neighbourhoods. Through this ethnography of the cityscape, my aim has been to elucidate the place and time of street art – what Swoon calls 'that beautiful temporary gesture'.

Temporariness has become one of the defining attributes of situational artworks: in the cityscape, they appear, and disappear. Often this is due to 'buffing'.[20] Cityscapes are as marked by the effects of the removal of graffiti and street art as by the addition of images and words to city surfaces. Residents who wish to paint over graffiti or street art can acquire paint kits from local councils. It is also possible to buy special solvents that will remove unwanted writing or imagery. Councils sometimes mistakenly remove commissioned art as happened to Anthony Lister, as discussed in Chapter 5. In some jurisdictions, removal is even mandated by legislation. The Graffiti Prevention Act 2007 in Victoria, Australia, gives local councils the power to enter property and remove graffiti, even without the property owner's consent, if they have received no notification that the owner wants to retain the graffiti. In San Francisco, the election in 2003 of a mayor with a strong anti-graffiti stance led to the passing of an ordinance compelling property owners to remove graffiti from their property within thirty days or be fined.

Graffiti writers and street artists seem to be engaged in a perpetual dance with municipal authorities. The artists put up, the authorities take down, and so it goes. Buffing aspires to a graffiti-free cityscape. For street artists, this produces an aesthetically depressing cityscape. Swoon explained: 'When I go to a city that doesn't have any graffiti I just always feel like there's something missing, you know, that there's a lack of vitality, there's a lack of inclusiveness, there's a lack of, I don't know, a kind of grooviness, a lack of a certain energy'. Garrison, in New York, said: 'If a city had no graffiti or was entirely buffed, with brown, grey, drab, boring façades with nothing going on in them, I mean, that's very boring and antiseptic'. After walls had been buffed in St Louis, Peat Wollaeger said 'everything was whitewashed, everything was white. White, white, white, white, white. Ugly. Horrible.' Kaff-eine took the same view: 'It would be so boring if we lived in cities with no imagery except imagery that was paid for'. Shinobi, on the other hand, saw potential for new works in the buff: 'I like buffing. I reckon the buff is good; some people get really upset about their stuff getting taken down, but I think changing walls is awesome.'

Artworks appear; artworks disappear. Cities are continually in flux. Where some artists spoke of beautifying the city through their actions, others

20 Buffing occurs when a local council or property owner removes or paints over a situational artwork. It can be done with a high-pressure water hose (often used on wheat pastes but also in relation to painted work) or with paint or with solvent chemicals. Council cleaning crews have vans equipped with the hoses and paint rollers. (Such equipment necessitates fairly large vehicles to transport it around: at a municipal briefing on graffiti management in the City of Yarra in Melbourne, a representative from the Community Crime Prevention department of the State Government showed a slide depicting a newly designed graffiti removal van, and pointed admiringly to its streamlined shape.)

emphasised the already beautiful nature of urban space. Beauty was often identified with neighbourhoods in decline: street artists tend to find value in areas that many citizens would pass by fearfully, or would discount as ugly. José Parlá, in New York, stated: 'there's beauty in the ghettoes, there's beauty in the streets'. Elbow-Toe preferred street art 'in decrepit spaces', and Swoon said she was into 'decay'. Erris, in Amsterdam, said: 'I really like the parts of a city in which people, especially older people say, "Oh they should really straighten this out, this looks horrible".' He described how he and his artistic partner respond to such areas:

> Most people when they see [places] like that, people will be like, 'It's interesting, but also like a little bit almost scary'. And of course also dirty and you don't want to be there, but if we go there, we are like small children, we are really happy and just taking pictures.

And whereas many citizens would see such places as holding little or nothing of usefulness or aesthetic appeal, graffiti writers and street artists are strongly attracted to the kinds of surfaces and textures found in such areas. In Berlin, Tower collects objects to use in his artworks, 'old things, old signs, old buckets', that most people would discard as useless. In New York, Cake prefers 'dirty grimy surfaces, because it makes for the most beautiful kind of spot [in which to put up an artwork]' (see Plate 11). Dscreet, in London, is drawn to 'run down surfaces and things that have got character and energy [because they are old or used]' while the Belgian street artist Roa said that he looks for 'walls that have a bit of a story . . . I like abandoned buildings, interesting surfaces'.

Like Roa, many street artists are drawn to areas of dilapidation and make works in the midst of dereliction. Cake said: 'I like spots that are like really isolated. I love abandoned buildings and I love scaffolding, but my favourites are abandoned spaces'. In Melbourne, there has been a tradition of using derelict buildings for the temporary exhibition of situational artworks, notably the Empty Shows in the early 2000s, but many artists still place works within these overlooked and run-down buildings today. Kaff-eine says that she works in spaces that are 'crumbling and decayed and forgotten' and that it has brought her 'incredible joy, to be able to combine my love for these decaying, grand, forgotten urban spaces with my artwork' (see Plate 12). The Doctor says, 'Abandoned spaces are great, like I find myself really comfortable in them . . . some of the buildings are stunning' and for several years Meggs painted 'dead, forgotten, in between spaces'. Indeed, contrary to public perception and claims that graffiti inevitably leads to social decline if not removed (discussed in greater detail in Chapter 4), oftentimes graffiti writers and street artists contribute to the revival of dilapidated neighbourhoods through the creative clustering that can ensue when galleries, clothing stores, bars, coffee shops and so on are attracted to areas associated with situational art.

Having begun the chapter with the notion that the situational artwork offers a means of interaction with the surfaces on display within a city, it seems appropriate, in ending, to acknowledge a paradox: not all situational art is about *display*. Some artists intend their work to be visible; others place works in seclusion, in buildings that look empty, unused, abandoned. As is characteristic of citizens in an uncommissioned city (see Chapter 2), street artists and graffiti writers have rejected the relegation of a derelict building as worthless, instead re-purposing its walls as canvases and seeing gallery space within its architecture. It is this insistence on finding an aesthetic through adaptation that will always be incompatible with imperatives of pure profit and commercialisation. From the desire to write and paint in the street comes a city whose hidden spaces are filled with tags, pieces, stickers, stencils and wheat pastes that no one, other than artists and writers, will ever see.

Such spaces are still contested. Even without the risk of an artwork being removed or destroyed by avid collectors or through buffing, artworks are still temporary. The Doctor noted that inside some of Melbourne's abandoned buildings, situational artworks have been tagged over, part of a continuing antagonism between graffiti writers and those they consider 'street artists': 'it's horrible to go into [buildings] and see that [artworks have] been ruined by the odd destructive teenage boy or someone who can't control his anger'.[21] However conflict-ridden the abandoned space may be, it demonstrates that 'street' art always exists in the in-between: in a space that is categorised as derelict but that can be re-purposed as a gallery; in a space that constitutes the boundary to someone's house but that also forms the wall adjoining a street; on a train that travels around the city and thus provides a mode of display for a tag as well as transport for commuters. Situational artworks are located in the cityscape for reasons that might include the desire to create beauty in a neighbourhood that seems unloved, or through the aim of showing citizens how to create DIY images around them. But it also arises from an aesthetic appreciation of the look of the paint or paper or sculpture against a particular surface. And if we build our cities with a particular set of materials, to what extent does the landscape of the city itself then invite a particular aesthetic to engage with it, even as it is crumbling into ruin?

Cities, in the end, are made of stone and brick and wood. The ephemerality and precariousness of graffiti writing and street art may seem to underline the

21 In interviews, a number of artists who had backgrounds in graffiti expressed resentment against street artists as parvenus seeking hipness without having served their apprenticeships writing on trains, and benefitting from the public preference for 'pretty' images over graffiti, despite both activities being executed through the illicit application of materials to surfaces. At the time of writing, Melbourne has seen a period of turbulent turnover on walls, with the efforts of street artists being frequently crossed out or gone over, apparently by graffiti writers. In April 2013, the following comments had been added to a large piece in Fitzroy done by an emerging street artist, Shida: 'writers united against street art'; 'no legals'; 'commodification of culture'; and 'leave it in your studio'.

permanence of the built structures of the cityscape, but as a stencil on a wall in Melbourne stated: 'Our art dissolves the stone'. The act of making art dissolves the obduracy of cities. It renders their permanence open to the effects of change; it questions, revises, transforms and opens them up to new forms of attachment. We city dwellers live our lives in the textures of urban spaces; situational artworks invite us to look more closely at the non-monumental corners of the cityscape – disused buildings, vacant land, run-down areas, alleyways, subways, railways, byways. At its most powerful, situational art can help us to understand the exigencies of time and memory in urban space. It can reconfigure the city as a place where citizens play an active role in the construction, revision and imagination of public space. It can show us new ways to inhabit the cityscape.

# losing the image

Losing an image can result in an uncanny intensity for the spectator. Most often, images are deliberately removed ('buffed') by councils, property owners, or offenders sentenced to clean graffiti from walls. Different cities, just as they have distinctive cultures of graffiti and street art, have different removal policies. Some cleaning crews use water sprays. Others paint over images. Graffiti removal is big business; private removal companies abound. Sometimes 'concerned citizens' get involved: Neighbourhood Watch groups; organisations such as Graffiti Hurts Australia or R.A.G.E (Ratepayers Against Graffiti Everywhere); even dedicated individuals such as 'Guerrilla Joe' in Doug Pray's documentary film *Infamy*.

San Francisco has put the onus of removal upon the property owner. Property owners are obliged to remove graffiti within thirty days. If they don't, the city's attorneys can obtain a court order to remove the graffiti, at a cost to the owner of at least $500. But the law doesn't specify that the paint must match. The result is often a patchwork as people use just enough paint to cover a tag or stencil so as to avoid being fined. Does it look better or worse than when the wall had a tag or stencil on it? The answer may be in the eye of the beholder, but one thing is for sure, these aren't 'clean' or 'blank' walls. And when local councils decide it is time for a removal 'blitz', hundreds of images can be buffed in a day.

For many works, the buff is their fate, sometimes far sooner than the artist would like. One day the image is there, the next it's gone, painted over or scraped off. But sometimes an image evades the buff and remains in place for a long time. Its longevity might derive from being tucked away in a hard-to-notice spot. Or it might have been placed somewhere that's hard to reach, hard for the artist who put it there, but also hard for any cleaning crews. Sometimes, even when a work is visible, easy to access and illicit, it *still* escapes the buff and slowly disappears, fading back into brick, stone or wood.

In street art culture there is great admiration for 'fresh' work: images that look glossy and shiny and haven't been weathered or degraded in any way (by the addition of tags or the application of posters on top, for example).

And I've heard people say that work which is fading 'looks old' or, 'tired' and so on, and to a certain extent that's true.

But some artists welcome the effects of these external forces and circumstances on their artworks. Miso, for example, is interested in the peeling and fraying that occurs when a pasted-up image experiences the effects of hot sun, rain and wind. And JR's pasted-up photographs swiftly register the impact of the environment – his work on the façade of the Tate Modern had to be repaired after only a few weeks in place, thanks to a damp British summer. For these artists, though, the possibility of deterioration isn't a problem, but rather an integral part of their artistic practice – it's something they actively invite.

Faded artworks raise interesting questions, even when deterioration and disappearance isn't part of an artist's intentions. How should we make sense of a fading artwork? Do we dismiss it as occupying some transitional zone between freshness and oblivion? Do we paint over it so that new work can take its place? Does its faded nature mean that it is no longer worth noticing or thinking about? In some ways, I think it is the very 'in between-ness' of the fading image that makes it interesting. Not quite here and not quite gone. It has an almost historical value as a record of what was done in the past but is gradually relinquishing any claim on our attention amidst the visual hubbub of the contemporary city. It's important to acknowledge these fading images, these survivors who have, through chance or circumstance, escaped being erased by the buff or covered over by new work.

What attachments are interrupted when an artwork *suddenly* disappears? In London in October 2008, I met with a gallerist in Shoreditch. Afterwards, I went for a walk, to see what was on the walls. I had come across some impressive images when I was walking the streets a few months earlier. I thought I would revisit one in particular, a work by the French artist C215, a diptych of portraits of two children on the tiled panels on the outside wall of a pub (see Plate 13). I first encountered it by accident. The work really felt like a gift. Walking down a side street, I had suddenly seen the image, quietly and perfectly placed close to the ground.

On my subsequent visit, however, I walked purposefully to find it, almost as if I wanted to say hello to an old friend . . . but it was gone. The panels had been buffed – whether by the council or by the pub's owners, I don't know. Several years later, I'm still struck by the depth of the loss I experienced. It was more than a momentary flicker of disappointment, more than a sense of annoyance at my objective being thwarted. I actually felt quite disoriented – I found myself looking around, as though the image might have migrated somewhere else. I felt saddened by its disappearance, and the same feeling resurfaces now, when I think about those blank panels.

I'm not sure why. Images on the street come and go. It's meant to be ephemeral. I know all that. But clearly I had become attached. Maybe because I enjoy C215's work generally. Maybe because that particular image seemed *so* perfectly placed. Maybe because when I came across it initially it delivered to me that fantastic sense of being a gift from the artist to the passerby, to the spectator – *to the city*.

At any rate, it was gone, and I registered its absence, both through the photograph I took of the buffed panels, and in the corporeal ache of loss that I could not fully rationalise. Images appear and images disappear. Their disappearance says something about time and its passing. The way we respond to the loss of an image on a wall says something about how we see street art itself – do we celebrate the empty space, as the opponents of graffiti and street art do? Do we plan the next image for that empty space, as an artist might do? Is a lost image something that we can mourn?

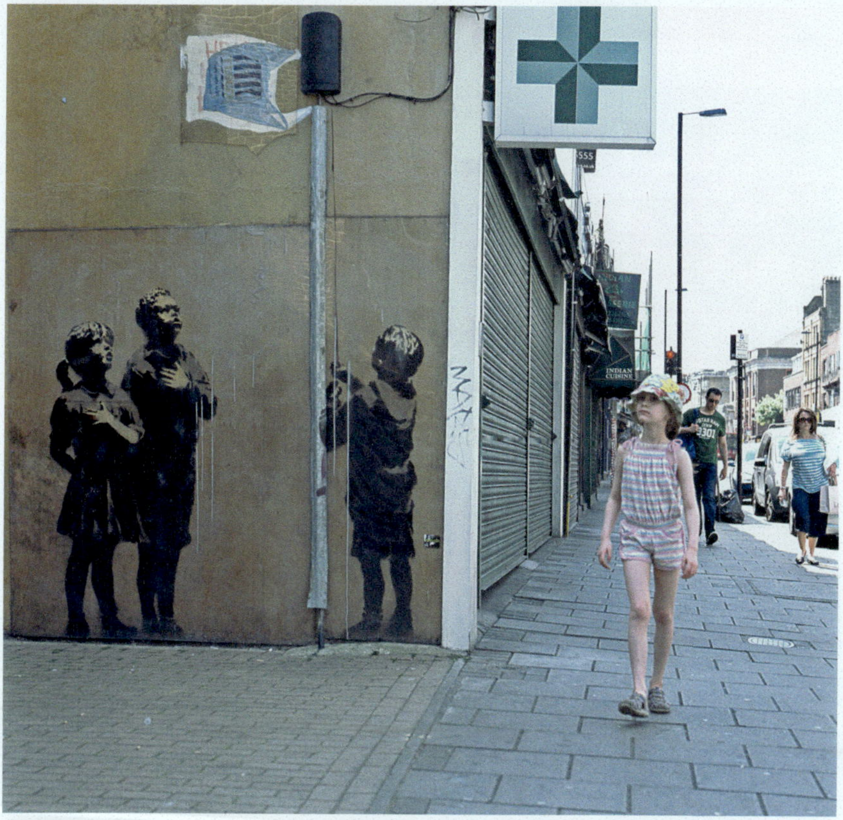

*Plate 1* Banksy 'Very Little Helps', London 2010. Photograph © Miriam Douglas.

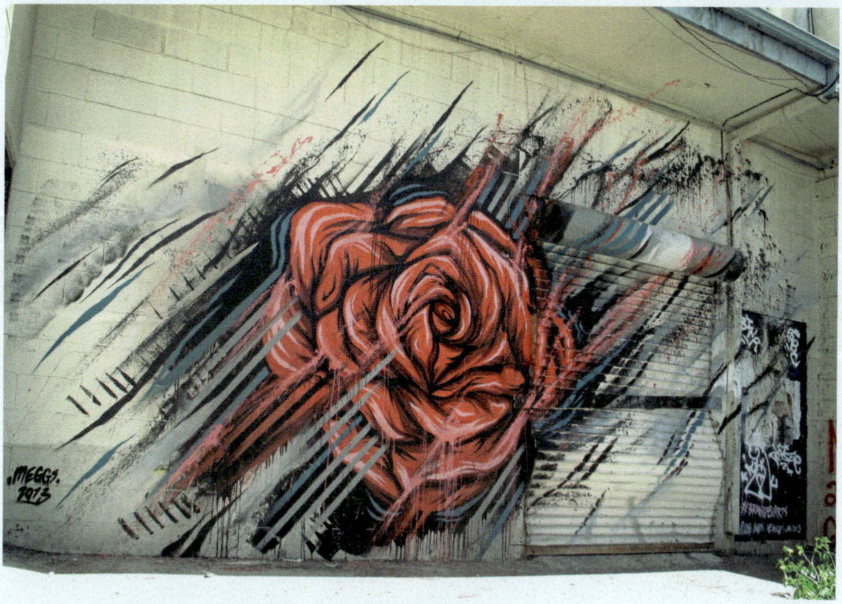


*Plate 2* Meggs, Los Angeles 2013. Photograph © Meggs.

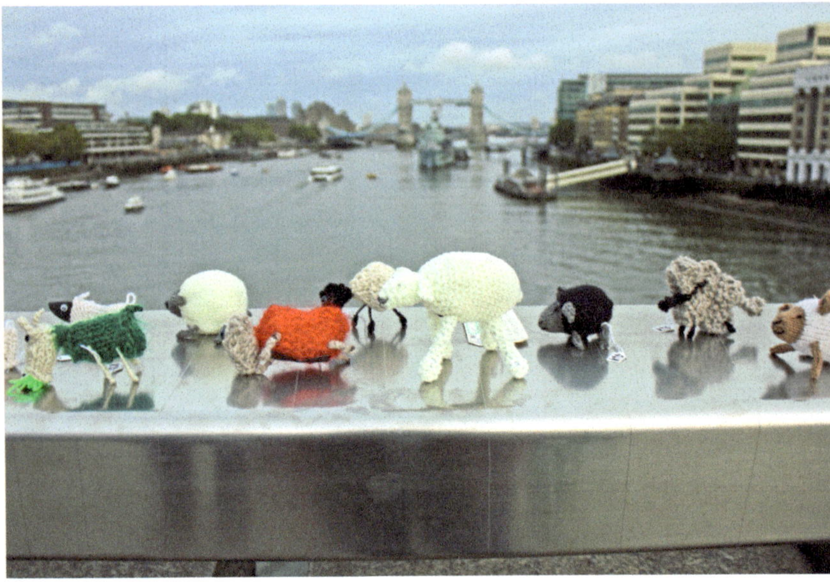

*Plate 3* Knit the City, 'Handmade Herd', London 2011. Photograph © Lauren O'Farrell.

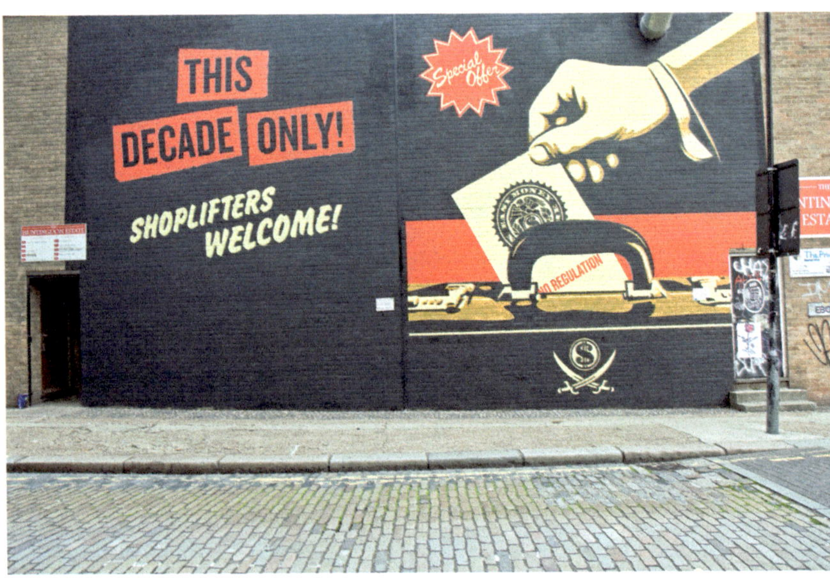


*Plate 4* Shepard Fairey, London 2012. Photograph © Mark Rigney – Hookedblog.

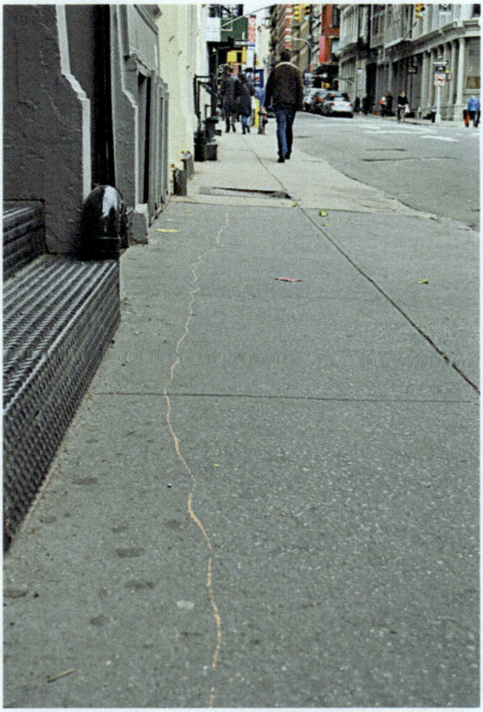

*Plate 5*
MOMO, 'Manhattan Tag', New York 2010. Photograph © Alison Young.

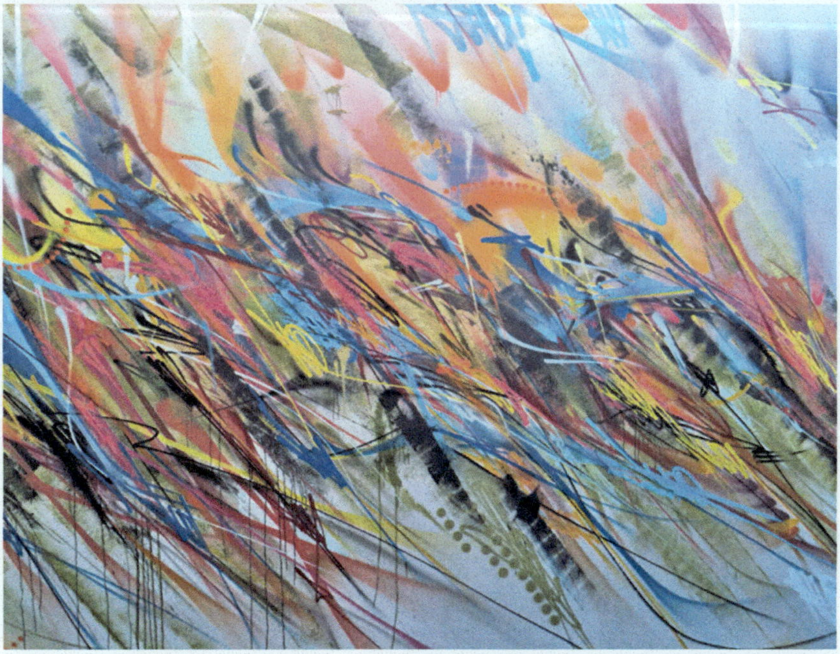

*Plate 6* Slicer, Melbourne 2012. Photograph © Alison Young.

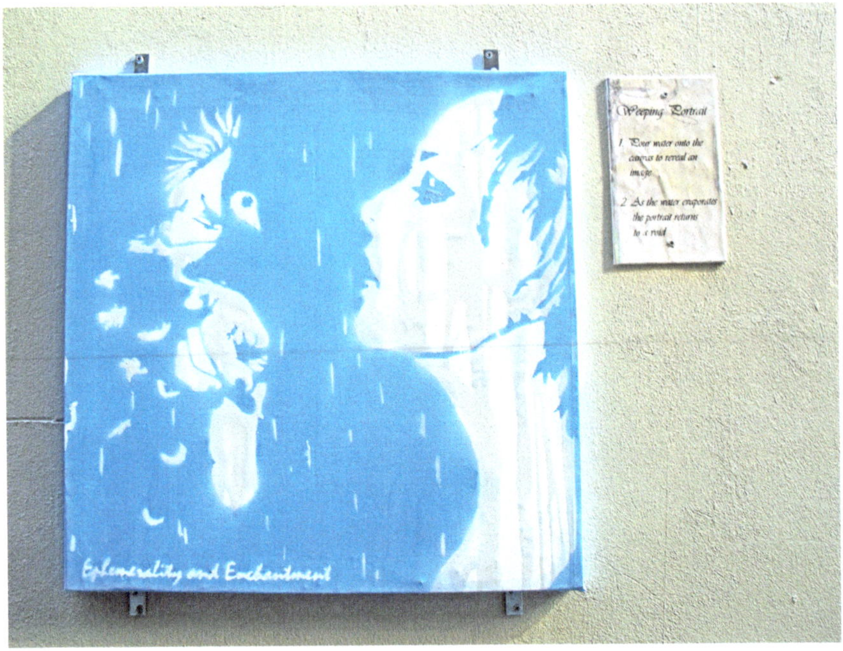



*Plate 7* CDH, 'Weeping Portrait', Melbourne 2012. Photograph © CDH.

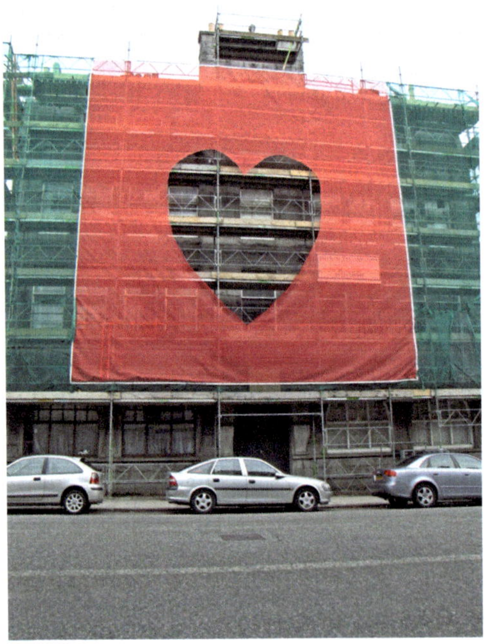

*Plate 8*
Brad Downey, 'Ladder Stick-Up', Aberdeen 2007. Photograph © the vacuum cleaner.

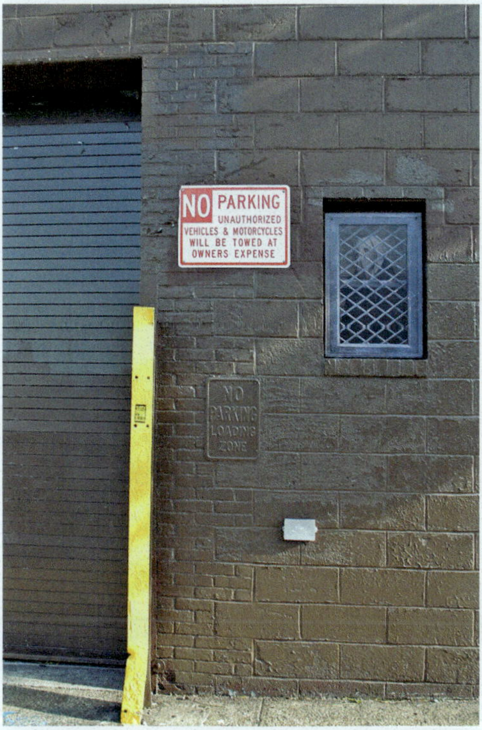


*Plate 9*
Dan Witz, New York 2011.
Photograph © Alison Young.

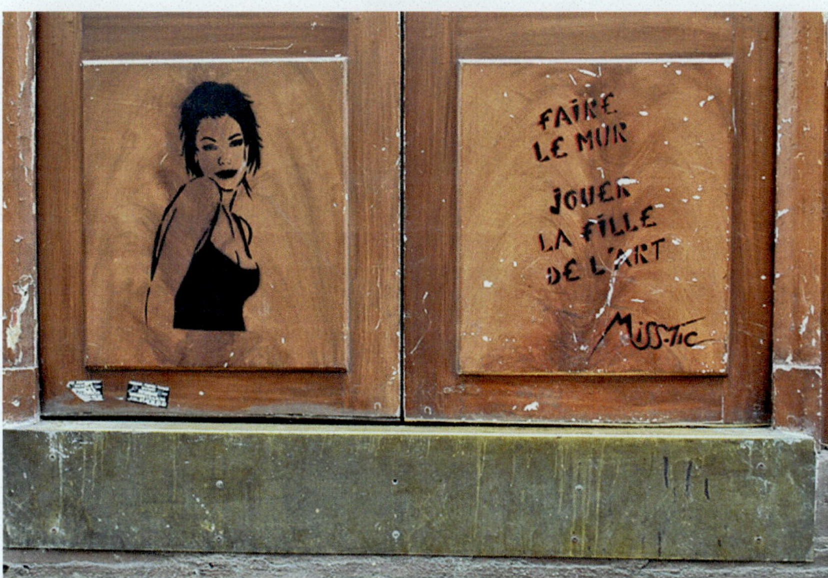


*Plate 10* Miss.Tic, Paris 2010. Photograph © Alison Young.

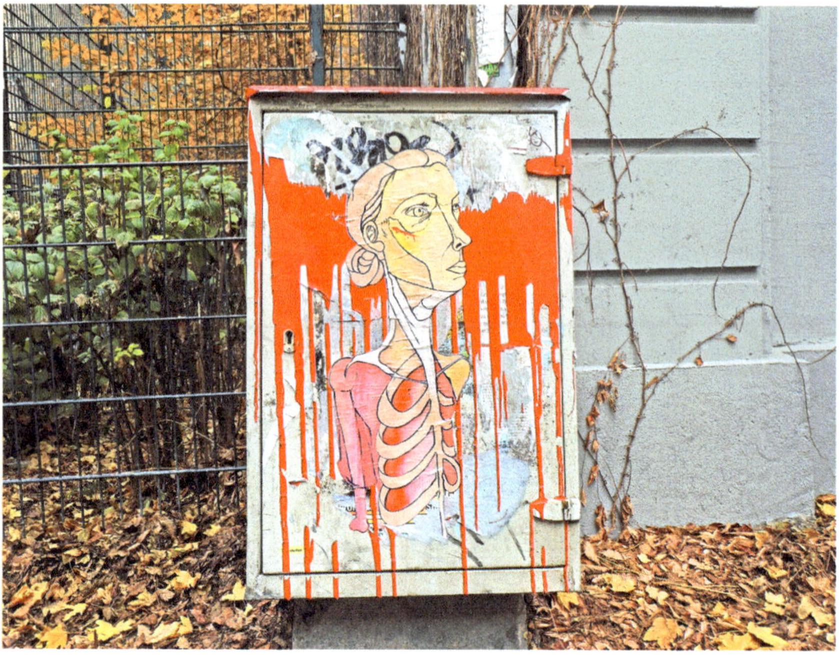

*Plate 11* Cake, Berlin 2012. Photograph © Cake.

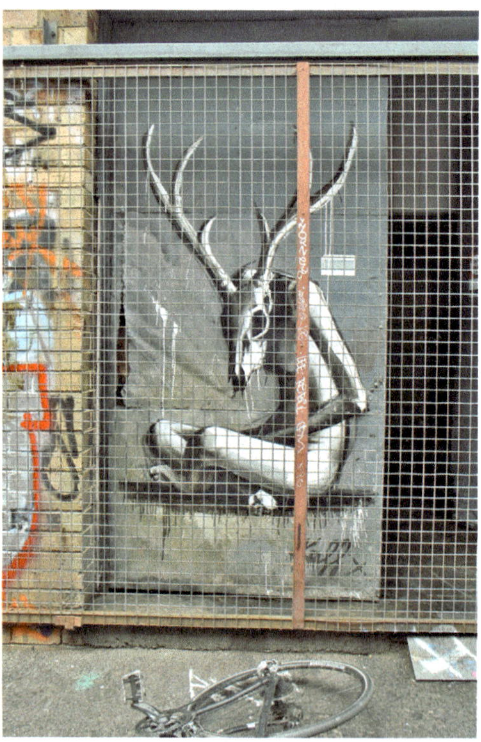

*Plate 12*
Kaff-eine, Melbourne 2012.
Photograph © Alison Young.

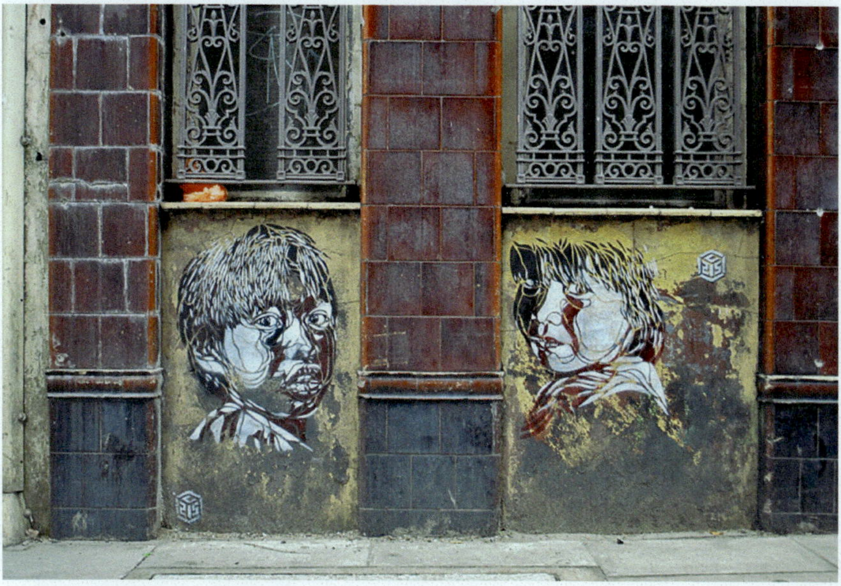

*Plate 13* C215, London 2008.
Photograph © Alison Young.

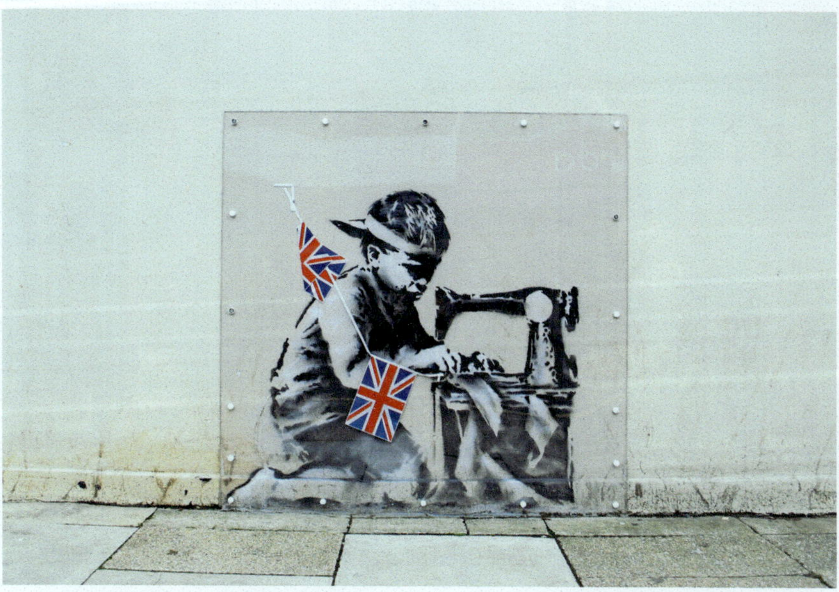

*Plate 14* Banksy, 'Slave Labour', London 2012. Photograph © Alison Young.

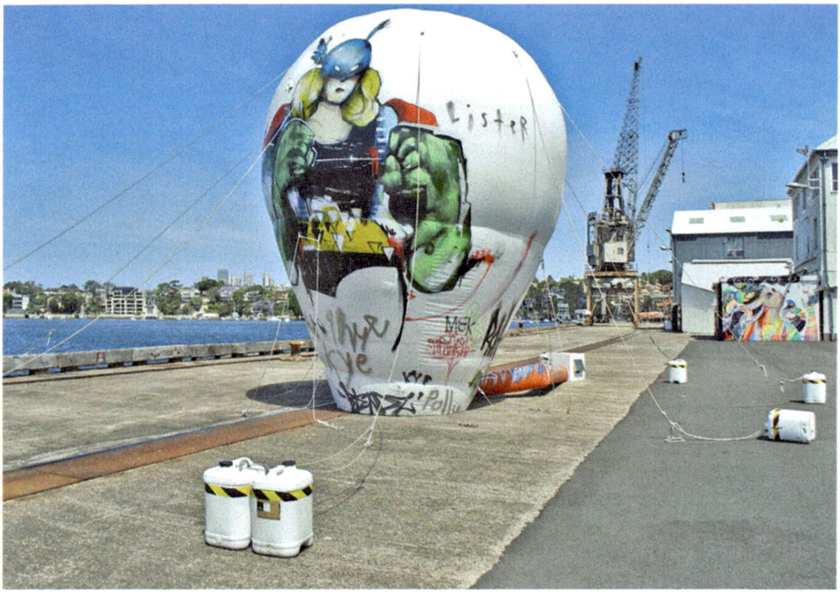


*Plate 15* Anthony Lister, Sydney 2011. Photograph © Alison Young.

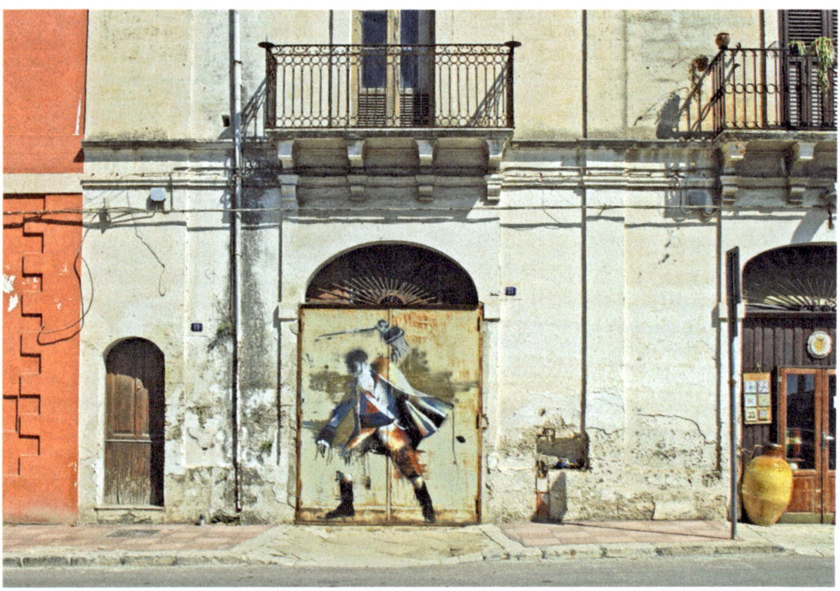

*Plate 16* Conor Harrington at FAME, Grottaglie 2012. Photograph © Alison Young.

Chapter 4

# Criminalising the image

> It's magical when it's illegal because there's nothing, and then, the next day or the next hour or whatever, there's something there, and you're like, 'I didn't see it happen, how long has it been here, how did they do it?'
>
> (Elbow-Toe, artist)

Graffiti writers and street artists around the world have been arrested, fined, subjected to community-based orders, imprisoned, blamed for encouraging social decline, and variously defined as thrill-seekers, rebellious youths or disaffected trouble-makers (Austin 2001; Dew 2007; Ferrell, Milovanovic and Lyng 2001; Ferrell 1996; Halsey and Young 2002, 2006; Iveson 2010; Millie 2008, 2011; Young 2005, 2010c). This negative socio-legal response can be understood as arising from anxiety about what graffiti and street art signify. With graffiti, much of this anxiety can be linked to the art form's enigmatic nature and insular culture. The calligraphy of graffiti writing is hard to read and most people never see a graffiti writer at work: graffiti generally appears overnight while its author remains unseen. To that extent, the censure and criminalisation of graffiti fits a pattern in which difference is abjured as a means of discursive regulation. Street art certainly provokes a broader range of social responses. However, the law does not distinguish between writing and art, and so graffiti writers and street artists are equally subject to prosecution. An image placed in public without the permission of the property owner is illegal, whether that image is someone's tag, a large hip-hop mural, a hand-drawn poster glued to a wall (a paste-up), a stencil or a political slogan. All that matters, in the eyes of the law, is whether or not an act is authorised by way of commission or the property owner's consent.

## Affect and criminalisation

Social responses to graffiti and street art vary considerably. Snyder has documented the ways in which New York graffiti writers are forced to negotiate a range of contradictions and complexities including condemnation, arrest, prosecution and incarceration at the same time as they are, thanks to their expertise, rewarded within the world of galleries, graphic design, tattooing and marketing (2009: 167–9). While the public maintain their dislike of tags – a view which may have been encouraged by official anti-graffiti campaigns (Austin 2001; Ferrell 1996; Iveson 2007) – it is clear that street art is received more positively though it often involves the same illicit activities (see Campbell (2008: 12–13) who shows tags to be the 'most objectionable' and 'pieces of art by . . . Banksy' to be the least). Stencils often meet with the greatest public approval. In 2006, when a Conservative councillor argued for the removal of a Banksy artwork from a wall in Bristol, a petition with 3,196 signatures was submitted to Council asking for the artwork to be retained. In Melbourne, the prime street-art site Hosier Lane is a popular choice for wedding photographs and has been featured in promotional materials and advertisements by Tourism Victoria.

The incursion of street art into cities and culture is everywhere evident: travel books, newspapers, magazines and online guides now regularly feature recommendations as to a city's best areas for street art; shops, bars and restaurants have commissioned street artists to paint on their premises; apparel manufacturers have hired artists and graffiti writers to design sneakers and clothing; members of the public collect photographs of street art and post images on Internet sharing sites such as Flickr, Tumblr and innumerable blogs. Where graffiti writers struggled to break into the conventional art world, street artists have met with considerable success: galleries specialising in street art can be found all over the world, and a large number of artists who began their careers placing work illicitly in the street have become commercially viable in the art market. The saleability of street art is best demonstrated by the establishment of 'urban art' listings among the world's largest auction houses such as Bonhams and Sotheby's in London (and the art world's response to situational art will be discussed in greater detail in Chapter 6).

The law, however, continues to treat street art as *criminal*. This results in part from its construction of street art as contiguous with graffiti, differing in aesthetic style but deploying similar media and with the same lack of authorisation. Graffiti is said to provoke fearfulness in citizens, in no small part due to its ability to appear independent of any obvious author, allowing the projection of anxieties as to who is responsible and why. For many years, graffiti has been represented as disgusting, unskilled and, above all, criminal. Disgust is invoked through descriptions of graffiti writers as resembling dogs marking their territory and their tags and murals as dirt, urine and rubbish (Ferrell 1996: 135–45; Young 2005: 53–5). Depicting graffiti as 'scrawl' or 'scribble' diminishes its skilfulness and categorises it instead as something done without care or respect (see Ferrell 1996: 177; Halsey and Young 2006: 283–6). Claims that graffiti writers engage in a broad range of crimes (such as theft, interpersonal violence, drug use, possession and dealing) further brand graffiti writing as a illegitimate activity with no cultural value (Ferrell 1996: 141–3; Young 2005: 56–62).

The longstanding association between graffiti, waste and criminality may relate to the challenge that it poses to the aesthetics of authority as argued by Ferrell in the context of Denver, Colorado (1996: 159–60). Indeed, many accounts of the criminalisation of graffiti writing in the 1980s and 1990s such as those offered by Ferrell (1996) and Austin (2001), confirm the importance of 'moral panic'; that is, the process whereby 'moral entrepreneurs' mobilise against the purported moral deviancy (named as criminality) of a targeted group.[1] In the context of graffiti writing, moral panic seems to have settled into an entrenched moral resentment, deeply embedded in local politics, criminal justice practice and legal discourse. Whereas it was once possible to identify discrete campaigns against graffiti in a range of jurisdictions, anti-graffiti sensibility has now colonised the terrain of authority such that it constitutes the default position for criminal justice policy and legal discourse. Such entrenched *ressentiment* constructs the illicit artist as a figure who must be excluded from the community (Girard 1977). The traces left behind by the artist – graffiti and other uncommissioned images – must therefore be eradicated such that 'a signifying practice that is, for its practitioners, profoundly about identity and existence is viewed as something to be erased' (Young 2005: 71).

It may be that such distaste arises from the affective intensity of the encounter with the uncommissioned artwork. In this chapter, I investigate the law's encounter with street art by looking at the consequences that flow from naming the situational artwork as criminal (the law's encounter with street art will be approached again in Chapter 5, focusing upon the ways in which street art contests conceptualisations of property in law). Beginning first with the experiences of street artists who have been interpellated by the authorities as criminals, I will then interrogate the ways in which the law's affective response to street art can be discerned in legislation and legal judgment. My interest here in criminalisation joins that of scholars working in the field of criminology and law who have attended to ways in which activities or behaviours come to be regarded as criminal. Such analyses have been used to reveal the interests served by the designation of certain activities as criminal (see, for example, Hillyard et al. 2004), to identify when criminalisation is occurring at an excessive level (Dubber 2001; Husak 2008) and to examine the values invested in and shored up by the identification of certain

1 Within criminology, the term 'moral panic' originates in the work of Stanley Cohen, who presented those who fuel such a panic as 'moral entrepreneurs' and those targeted by the panic as 'folk devils' (Cohen 1972). To say that it has since been widely used would be an under-statement: it appears in criminological research on behaviours and social problems ranging from drug use, through ritual abuse, child molestation, teenage 'sexting', and obscenity in art.

activities as criminal (Millie 2011). Building upon this body of literature, I suggest that the criminalisation process inherent in legislation on graffiti and street art and the judgment of graffiti writers and street artists arises out of the law's encounter with the uncommissioned word or image as something that contests the laws' investment in ownership, authority and propriety. Some of the consequences of such an investment will be revisited in Chapter 5, in examining the spatial politics of the uncommissioned image; in this chapter, the concern will be the extent to which the law's affective response to the uncommissioned image facilitates its criminalisation and judgment.[2]

## The law's encounter with street art

Encounters between graffiti writers or street artists and the law take place in a range of locations. Many involve either the decentralised authority of the police officer on the street – who might issue a caution or a fixed penalty notice – or the routinised processes of the Magistrates' Court or Children's Court. These actions are not readily available for scrutiny given that they go unreported in legal discourse. Such incidents mainly exist as data within aggregated statistics released by the police or reported in the media (see, for example, Jackson 2009). However, ethnographic research, such as that conducted by Ferrell (1996) and Snyder (2009) provides an alternative means of access to the encounter between graffiti writer or street artist and police officer. And in the present study qualitative interviews investigated artists' experiences with police, security guards, property owners and passersby. Few artists manage to avoid interactions with these various representatives of official and unofficial authorities: of the 64 street artists interviewed in my research, 42 (66 per cent) described encounters with police officers, security guards or concerned citizens. Artists recalled being moved on, being forced to take down or remove their work, being chased or subjected to physical violence. Of these, 15 (36 per cent of the artists who had had such encounters) were dealt with formally; that is, they were taken to a police station, where their details were recorded, or were charged, arrested or locked up overnight. 16 of those interviewed (40 per cent of those subject to some kind of official processing) had to appear in court on formal charges.[3]

2 In this chapter, I am thus carrying out an investigation that parallels Carr's research on social and legal responses to skateboarders in urban space. Carr writes of the need to conceptualise the criminalisation of skateboarders (part of the general tendency to associate young people in cities with crime and disorder) in a reflexive way: 'Young people should be understood as being engaged in a continual dialectical relationship with the law by which their use of the city is constantly evolving in response to a variety of legal logics – especially those of private property – which in themselves evolve to respond to these emerging practices' (Carr 2010: 990).

3 Note that in an earlier study conducted by Halsey and Young (2006), the proportion of artists and graffiti writers who had faced formal criminal justice processes was much higher

It is not surprising to find that police officers exercise considerable amounts of discretion in determining whether or not to take action, formal or otherwise, against a graffiti writer or street artist. Interviewees indicated that sometimes this decision may be based on whether or not the act is underway or merely in preparation:

> There was one time we just walked out of a friend's house. We all had bags of paint, rah, rah, rah. We weren't dressed up like Burglar Bill, don't get me wrong, but we went round the corner and then, 'Whoa' – and, oh, 'What's in the bag, son?' 'Mm, paint'. 'Where are you going?' 'We're going to paint the wall.' 'Right, go back that way, go home, we haven't seen you. If we see you, right then, that's that'.
>
> (Nick Walker)

However, a recurrent theme was that police also appear to maintain a firm distinction between graffiti and street art, with the former provoking a more punitive response than the latter. In New York, Cake declared, 'they're harder on graffiti people than the street art people, for sure', while Jordan Seiler noted that police respond differently to his politically motivated advertising take-overs compared with when he is suspected of writing graffiti:

> When I'm doing kind of personal projects like takeovers of phone booths or billboards, often the police are very – kind of calm. The space that I'm interacting with isn't like a private landowner's building. It's not – I'm not permanently destroying anything. What I'm doing can be reversed very quickly. So they will allow me a level of conversiveness with them, and eventually just say, 'Hey, I got to write you a summons'. So then you appear in front of the judge, and the judge says, 'Have you ever done this before', and you say, 'No', and he says, 'Ok, you've got six months' probation, don't let us catch you doing it again in six months'. You wait that time and your record is wiped clean. That said, I have been caught by cops that were under the assumption that I was writing graffiti, and that was a completely different experience, where they will grab you, manhandle you, throw you against a cop car, handcuff you, search everything that you have on you, without any consent, obviously, and generally scare the shit out of you.[4]

(approximately 25 per cent of the forty-four graffiti writers interviewed). Two factors explain the difference: first, the interviewees in that study were primarily recruited by social workers and youth workers, drawing on a population of individuals known to the authorities, whereas in the present study many of the street artists interviewed had managed to avoid formally entering the system. Second, that earlier study concentrated on graffiti writers: as confirmed by the respondents in the present study, agents of criminal justice are more likely to arrest graffiti writers than street artists.

4 In Melbourne, however, artist Kyle Magee discovered that even takeovers of advertising space can be thoroughly criminalised. Magee paints over adverts and was arrested doing so in a

Ellis Gallagher, also in New York, felt that the police should make more of the distinction between graffiti writing and street art. Gallagher is known for drawing shadow outlines of objects and people on sidewalks, often using chalk but also more permanent paints, and has been stopped by the police on several occasions:

> Because of my history with the police department, that means when they do stop me, they take my ID and they run my ID, and they see my graffiti arrests, I had several graffiti arrests. So they see that and they're not very happy about it, and they see a correlation between my past and what I'm doing now, they see a relation, and they try to make a connection, whereas I look at it as two separate, entirely separate, different things.

While Gallagher's previous convictions may have haunted his interactions with the police, other street artists benefited from this conceptual distinction. In Berlin, all interviewees commented that police enforce the law strictly against graffiti writers, but use a great deal of discretion with street artists. El Bocho said: 'I don't normally have problems with the police or anything because . . . if you are really friendly, then it's okay. And you say, it's only art. I'm an artist . . . it's not graffiti'. In London, after being charged with graffiti offences, Eine mobilised this distinction so as to be able to keep working on the street: 'I didn't want to stop painting and I thought yeah if I'm a little bit clever about this I can still have some fun. So . . . I moved away from graffiti and more into street art'.

Police officers also appear to exercise a degree of aesthetic judgment about the illicit artworks they confront on the street. Deadly Knitshade, a London-based member of the group Knit the City, described an encounter with two police officers after they had draped a telephone box in Parliament Square with bespoke knitting: 'One policeman . . . it was like good cop/bad cop – the bad

tram shelter outside the County Court. Magee was arrested and charged with damaging property and possessing materials for damaging property (a bucket of paint and a paintbrush). He had previous convictions for similar offences. Magee argued at trial that he was engaging in a form of political expression, protected under the Victorian Charter of Human Rights. He was convicted and fined $500, but appealed to the Victorian Supreme Court. Justice Kyrou, in September 2012, dismissed his appeal, stating that while Magee's activities were consistent with the Charter in that they expressed political views, businesses and municipalities had the right to pursue their affairs without physical interference (Magee's actions had caused $40 of damage to the tram shelter). Magee's appeal was dismissed and he was ordered to pay legal costs likely to be many thousands of dollars, in addition to the $500 fine. In New South Wales several years before Magee's case, two anti-Iraq war protesters found that the political nature of their graffiti (they wrote 'NO WAR' on top of the Sydney Opera House) did not preclude them from being sentenced to nine months' weekend imprisonment and a joint fine of $111,000: Justice Blackmore said it did not matter whether they aimed to make a political statement, their actions were still malicious damage.

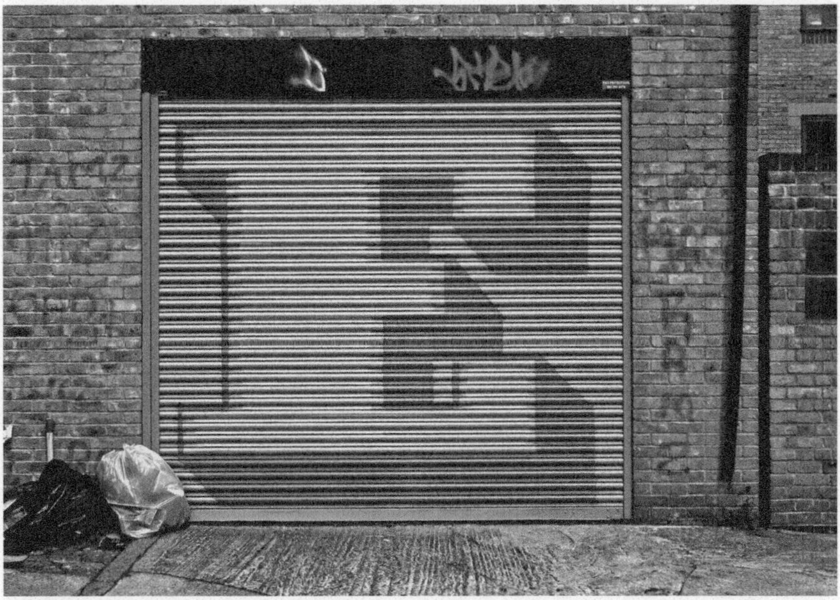

*Figure 4.1* Eine, London 2009. Photograph © Mark Rigney – Hookedblog.

cop was like "Well, you know you really shouldn't have been doing this", but the other one was taking pictures on his phone so he could show his wife when he got home.'[5] Italian artist Alice Pasquini recounted a similar experience when painting on the streets in Pigneto in Rome. Local residents had called the police. The officers pretended to write out a fine of 600 euros (in order to satisfy the angry observers) and then said to Pasquini: 'we don't understand this law, I see this as beautiful, I cannot give you a fine'.

Other artists reported encounters with security guards and property owners angered by what they regarded as property damage. A Melbourne street artist, known as the Doctor, encountered the owner of a building while she was pasting up work on the property; he said he would be calling the police but first gave her the chance to run while he did so. In New York, Cake attempted to persuade a property owner to keep her piece on his wall:

> I was putting up this piece on an abandoned building. Not abandoned, unoccupied. And a guy came out . . . and he was like, 'You have to take that down'. And I was trying to, of course, reason with him, like a stupid

5 The group members were issued with a stop-and-search notice stating 'Seen decorating a telephone box in Parliament Square'. Deadly Knitshade believes that the group members avoided arrest because they answered 'craft' instead of 'art' when asked what they were doing.

> idiot, I was like, 'No, I spent a long time on this piece, it's hand painted, let me just leave it up.' I took it down. I was trying to convince him to keep it there. But I'm sure he would have called the cops on me.

The most aggressive responses towards artists often come not from property owners but 'concerned citizens' keen to enforce the law and communicate their disapproval. Interviewees reported being verbally abused and physically assaulted by members of the public. Such encounters are often more dangerous than with police or security guards. As mentioned in Chapter 2, both Civil and his brother were assaulted by passersby; in Amsterdam, Chaz, who paints under the name The London Police, lamented:

> the weirdos that are around at three or four in the morning, like pimps or like people just on the street who are crazy, they can be pretty scary. Yeah I got punched in the face, my teeth came out, chased a bunch of times.

Street artists are extremely conscious of the risks inherent in the placing of illicit works in the street and have developed a range of risk-minimising strategies. The French artist L'Atlas, after being arrested and charged with graffiti-related offences, began wearing the white or yellow coveralls of a street-repair worker:

> I was obliged to reflect how I will continue to do my art, so I use a lot of ways to . . . put my pieces in the street in a way that I cannot be caught by the police . . . so all my performance and my art is around that subversive idea that I am doing something but I'm not allowed to do that and nobody can see me.

The idea of wearing municipal workers' uniforms to blend into urban space was made famous by the American artists Darius and Downey (Reid and Downey 2008). Some argue that it is in fact safer to put up work during the day (Sunday morning is a favourite time). Others prefer to put up work after dark (Cake said: 'I used to go in the daytime all the time. And I don't know, now that I'm older, I don't do that anymore. I do night-time. I don't feel like getting caught'.) Some use multiple tags so as to diversify their risk. Some advocate running: Shinobi, in Melbourne, said, 'I always run from security guards', while Laser 3.14, in Amsterdam, has successfully used his bicycle to escape pursuit. Others, however, see running as problematic. Melbourne artist CDH stated:

> I don't run . . . I think once you run, or if you start just becoming rude or something like that, like these are just ordinary people, you know. And a lot of the time, if you're just polite, they'll just maybe shoo you along.

> It's when you start getting confrontational that you cause a problem for yourself, I think.

Politeness is in fact a deliberate and important strategy for many street artists. A number of interviewees described situations in which they talked themselves out of difficult or dangerous encounters. Berlin-based artist Jaybo recounted: 'I [was] painting something illegal [in London], and the cops just appeared straight away, saying 'I suppose this is legal'. And I say 'yeah' and smile . . . They said 'are you sure?' and I kept smiling and they went away.' Pure Evil, also in London, managed to 'talk himself out of trouble' three times, while Nails, in Melbourne, had what he described as 'positive' encounters with the police:

> Where I've been working on something illegally and the police have kind of done their thing, they say 'What are you doing? What's going on?' and I say 'street art's a thing now, you know? It's a legitimate career and it's a profession' . . . My approach with police was always 'Okay, I've got my job to do' and that's to get my artwork out and not end up in jail. They've got their job to do, to make sure the streets are safe and to make sure that I'm not doing anything illegal, and somewhere in the middle, you kind of come to a compromise. There's no reason why I can't be a reasonable person and the response is usually is that you get a reasonable person or a reasonable person's response. So you are 'I know I'm doing something against the law. Yes, yeah, I know. It's just kind of a grey area, I know'. . . And the police are 'All right. Well, look, let's take you down and we'll just get your details. We'll take you down to the police station and we'll just check you up on the computer to make sure you haven't got outstanding or priors or anything like that'. And it's like you go through the motions and only one time I've actually had to call a lawyer to sort it out.

It is notable that this artist considered being taken to the police station and having his details checked as a 'positive' interaction. Stories like this might seem to indicate that interviewees favour decriminalisation of graffiti and street art. However, very few expressed this view. Miss.Tic, in Paris, was a rare exception:

> After having been convicted, I felt bad in my very being, because once you enter into the lion's den of the judicial process and police repression, it certainly complicates life. It's true that I would rather work with more comfort, and with more people for me than against me, and maybe legalisation would achieve that.

However, many graffiti writers and street artists seem to regard illegality as giving meaning to what they do. 16 interviewees (28 per cent) spoke of illegality in this way. Miso cited illegality as authorising councils to remove 'hate' graffiti, such as anti-Semitic or homophobic slogans. Sculptor Nick Ilton evoked illegality as giving the property owner the ability to exercise an aesthetic judgment about the uncommissioned work: 'it should definitely be illegal – if someone painted something crap on my wall, I wouldn't be happy about it.' Illegality added a semantic dimension to street art for C215 in Paris, who saw it as part of the 'poetry' of the activity. For others, illegality is tied up with pleasure: 10 out of the 64 interviewees (15.6 per cent) indicated that they derive pleasure from the illegality of street art or graffiti. Elbow-Toe, in Brooklyn, summed it up thus: 'it's magical when it's illegal'. For others, illegality raises questions about the very nature and politics of the law: Swoon, in New York, stated: 'once you start breaking the law, you start thinking, well, why can't I break the law, why is this the law, and these questions start breaking into your consciousness'.

## Legislating against uncommissioned art

What law is it that street artists are breaking? The precise definition of graffiti or street art as a crime differs from jurisdiction to jurisdiction. There exists a broad similarity, however, in structural categories such as 'criminal damage' or 'damage to property', 'vandalism' as a form of 'antisocial behaviour', various specific offences relating to property owned by transport companies, and a range of crimes dealing with proscribed activities in public space and particularly on 'the street'. Most countries have long had laws that prohibit acts damaging the property of another. In recent years specific offences have been enacted prohibiting graffiti and street art (while leaving untouched the foundational offences against property). For example, in Victoria, Australia, the main offence of criminal damage is found in the Crimes Act 1958 s197(1), while s9(1)(c) and (d) of the Summary Offences Act 1966 provide for offences of 'wilful injury' to or destruction of property and 'wilful trespass' without authority on property belonging to another, in addition to an offence of 'posting bills and defacing property' in s10.

In 2007, the State Government enacted the Graffiti Prevention Act. Andrew Millie's social constructivist analysis suggests that the values operationalised in instances of criminalisation, of which the Graffiti Prevention Act is an example, aim to safeguard a range of values including 'economic' values (usually by pointing out the financial costs of an activity) and 'prudential' values, through the implicit endorsement of a particular way of living thought to contribute to overall social welfare (2011: 283–5). The Victorian Department of Justice website explained that the Act was a response to 'community concerns about graffiti'. These concerns were said, first, to be financial ('the estimated cost of graffiti clean-up across Australia in 2003 was $300 million a year. The cost of graffiti is passed on to the community through higher service costs, insurance premiums and council rates'), thus supporting the first of

Millie's value sets. The second community concern was identified as 'environmental'. This latter point warrants explanation. 'Environmental' was defined by the Department of Justice as an activity impacting upon an individual's immediate environment in two ways: first, 'community perceptions of safety' (based on a finding in the Australian Bureau of Statistics household survey on crime that 26 per cent of Victorians regard 'graffiti and vandalism' as the third most important neighbourhood problem after dangerous driving and burglary[6]); and second, 'community perceptions of social decline'.[7]

'Environmental' concern is thus to do with the physical and material environment of the neighbourhood or city (rather than any ecological concern over the impact of paint chemicals on the inhabitants, flora or fauna of a local area). Its two cited manifestations in 'perceptions' of safety and 'perceptions of social decline' reveal that the legislation's epistemological framework derives from the 'broken windows' theory (and indeed the website makes explicit reference to this). This theory proposed that the presence of any social disorder (such as the eponymous 'broken window') represents an environment in which such crime is not regulated, encouraging the increasing incidence of such activity and gradually inviting the commission of other, more serious, crimes. This argument first appeared in 1982, in an essay in *Atlantic Monthly* by two criminologists, James Q. Wilson and George L. Kelling.

The hypothesis created a great deal of interest, within criminology and related disciplines, and in policymaking, particularly at the local governmental level, and became regarded as if it had been empirically validated, rather than the series of speculative musings that it is. In the original essay, Wilson and Kelling proposed ideas about what enables a neighbourhood to be regulated (and to self-regulate) effectively, predominantly in relation to social disorder, including public drunkenness and gang violence (there was no engagement, for example, with the problem of serious crimes experienced by many within the family home). The essay offered many wistful references to the need for the police to be able to exercise discretion as to how to enforce the law, often in ways that the authors recognised as falling outside conceptions of due process or equal treatment. The essay made only one reference to graffiti, as 'harmless display' (1982: 3) except in so far as it could symbolise disorder and incivility.

6 Thus eliding two legal categories – 'graffiti' and 'vandalism' (the latter includes activities such as window-smashing or seat-slashing on public transport) – and a crime against property with personal safety.

7 Accessed August 2008, printed out and on file with author. The web page was taken down in 2010 after a change in government: the current Department of Justice website reiterates these justifications in condensed form, stating: 'Graffiti vandalism is a highly visual problem that has associated financial costs, concerned with its prevention and removal, and social costs as it affects the visual amenity of communities and influences perceptions of public safety'. Online at www.justice.vic.gov.au/wps/wcm/connect/justlib/DOJ+Internet/Home/Community+Crime+Prevention/Action+on+Graffiti/ (accessed 28 July 2011).

There are a number of problems with the ways in which the broken windows hypothesis has been subsequently taken up in criminological research and policymaking. First, the fact that the essay is speculative is seldom acknowledged; the authors are usually cited as having proved the link between 'untended' neighbourhoods and a consequent rapid social decline into rampant criminality. Second, its claims were further investigated by Wesley Skogan (1990) in *Disorder and Decline*, which claimed to have proved that Wilson and Kelling's thesis was correct. However, subsequent testing of Skogan's dataset by Bernard Harcourt (1998) revealed serious flaws in the study. Third, the distinction between graffiti 'symbolising' and 'causing' disorder has rarely been acknowledged. If taken at its face value, the proposition that the 'otherwise harmless displays' of subway graffiti symbolise social disorder should mean either that subway riders are simply mistaken as to the presence of any disorder other than the specific infringement of rules against writing on property belonging to another, or that subway riders would benefit from learning about the purposes of subway graffiti, which are usually to do with display and communication within the community of graffiti writers.

A fourth problem relates to the reductivist interpretation of graffiti and vandalism as identical in later iterations of the hypothesis.[8] As I have argued (Young 2005), the motivations for breaking a window or slashing a seat on a train are very different from those animating the production of graffiti. Throwing a stone through a window leaves nothing but smashed glass and destroys the functionality of the window; writing a tag on a wall might be experienced as damage by the property owner, but it does not destroy the functionality of the wall. Both acts alter the look of the object they address; graffiti writing, however, adds a layer of meaning (the presence of the graffiti writer and his or her tag) to the object. Eliding graffiti with acts such as stone-throwing (which is what leads to the eponymous broken window) is based on a deliberate sophistry that overlooks important distinctions between the two activities.

Despite such problems, the eagerness of policymakers for some mechanism to curb an activity that was irritating ratepayers and voters led to the

8 I have written elsewhere (2005) about the semantic associations of the term 'vandalism' as a descriptor for property damage. As discussed in my previous research on graffiti, the word 'vandal' derives from the name of a Germanic 'Barbarian' people who lived in the area south of the Baltic between the Vistula and the Oder rivers. The Barbarian peoples are commonly remembered for inflicting a crushing defeat on the Roman legions at the battle of Adranople in 378 AD, and for following this up, in 410 AD, with an invasion of central Italy. During this invasion, they laid siege to Rome and sacked it, taking the city. For over four years the Roman army was unable to control the Vandals' activities. To name graffiti writers as 'vandals' aligns them with the barbarian horde who bring chaos and destruction to the gates of the city. The immediate response required to the vandalistic threat is defence: exclusion and eradication. Just as the Romans set an army on the Vandals, so local government and criminal justice set police officers, Neighbourhood Watch schemes and security guards on the 'vandals' who threaten the modern city.

hypothesis being used as the foundation for a range of social policies, most notably in New York City. Kelling was appointed head of the city's transit police unit and oversaw the implementation of policies designed to eradicate graffiti on the subway during the 1980s. That this project had only limited success is evidenced by the centrality still being given to graffiti in the mid-1990s, when the then Mayor, Rudy Giuliani, established the 'Anti-Graffiti Task Force', citing the broken windows theory as a cornerstone of his approach and claiming 'Where graffiti flourishes, communities suffer. Graffiti intimidates residents. It encourages street gangs. It discourages tourists, lowers property values, and it invites other kinds of crime'.[9] And the influence of the hypothesis extended beyond social policy into legislation, as can be seen from the Victorian Department of Justice's discussion of the reasoning behind the introduction of the Graffiti Prevention Act 2007: it states that the broken windows theory 'has established that' graffiti 'encourages further criminal activity which leads to economic decline and social instability'. Two and a half decades after the publication of Wilson and Kelling's suggestions, despite the hypothetical nature of the original essay and despite the contested nature of attempts to prove its validity, the assumption that the presence of graffiti leads to more graffiti and then to other types of crime is being accepted as empirically validated fact.

The overall objective of the Graffiti Prevention Act is a reduction in the incidence of graffiti. It lays out a three-pronged strategy for achieving this in s1: creating graffiti-related offences; providing search and seizure powers for the police; and providing Council with the power to enter private property so as to remove graffiti. As far as point one is concerned, six offences are listed in the statute, of which four are new: possessing a graffiti implement (defined as an aerosol paint container or any implement or substance capable of being used to mark graffiti); possessing an implement with intent to mark graffiti; advertising a prescribed graffiti implement for sale; and selling aerosol paint to a person under eighteen years old (ss7, 8, 9 and 10). The remaining offences redefine certain activities (which could have been prosecuted under the Crimes Act as criminal damage or under the Summary Offences Act as injury to property) as specific offences under this statute: 'marking graffiti in a public place' without the consent of the property owner (with the act of marking graffiti defined broadly: to 'write, draw, mark, scratch or otherwise deface property by any means so that the defacement is not readily removable by wiping with a dry cloth'); and, more seriously, 'marking offensive graffiti', which is graffiti 'visible from a public place' that would 'offend a reasonable person' (ss5 and 6).

9 From the press release issued by the Mayor's Office designating graffiti as a 'Quality of Life' crime.

The State Government may have included these latter two offences in the Act (despite the capacity of the older statutes to cover the relevant behaviours) in order to dispel any uncertainty as to whether graffiti-related activities constitute 'damage' and 'injury' to property. This, however, had already been established in a number of Victorian cases holding that 'damage' should be interpreted broadly according to the circumstances of each case. In which case, it is more likely that the State Government wanted police officers to be able to benefit from the Graffiti Prevention Act's enhanced powers not just in relation to specific offences concerning the possession or sale of aerosol cans but in the policing of graffiti or street art as an act in and of itself.

Police powers are augmented by the Act in a number of ways. First, one of the new offences (possessing a graffiti implement) reverses the onus of proof common to all possession offences (Dubber 2001). If a person is found to be in possession of a graffiti implement (aerosol cans, stencils, buckets of wheat paste or glue, paint rollers, sketchbooks of graffiti tags, and so on) on public transport, public-transport-related property (such as train stations), in an adjacent public place or in a place where the person is trespassing, they must *convince the police officer* that they have a lawful reason for the possession of that implement. If the officer is not satisfied with the reason given (such as having spray paint as part of one's employment, or for a school art project), a fixed-penalty notice can be issued (around $550); contesting the penalty risks a fine of $2500.

To facilitate the identification of individuals possessing a graffiti implement, the Act also creates powers to *search without warrant*: s13 authorises an officer to search someone if they have reasonable grounds for suspecting that a person has a graffiti implement on or near public-transport property or when they are trespassing on private property. Under Victorian law, there are two possible thresholds for authorising search without warrant: the higher of the two is 'reasonable grounds for belief'; for the Graffiti Prevention Act, the lower of the two has been selected. Further, 'suspicion' can be established if the person is present at or near a location with a high incidence of graffiti or freshly marked graffiti. Suspicion normally requires police officers to take into account factors to do with the behaviour or characteristics of an individual; under the Act, however, it is proximity to particular areas that is deemed suspicious. This provides a ready means for satisfying the Act's requirements for authorising search without warrant. Items discovered through searching then constitute the evidence needed for a charge of possessing a graffiti implement, possessing an implement with the intent to mark graffiti, or marking graffiti. In this way, enhanced police powers work to increase the likelihood of conviction by generating the necessary evidence simply through an individual's physical location in urban space. Where for the street artist, as discussed in Chapter 2, a citizen's proximity to urban surfaces authorises the adding of a situational artwork, here, for the law, proximity to certain locations authorises suspicion and possible conviction.

The Act creates a range of penalties, from on-the-spot fines to lengthy periods of incarceration (marking graffiti brings a maximum sentence of seven years' imprisonment – the most severe in Australia as noted approvingly by several Members of Parliament during the Bill's Second Reading speech). With regards to on-the-spot fines, the Act endorses a transfer of power away from the judiciary and into the hands of the police officers. An alternative approach has recently been trialled in New South Wales (NSW): the Government has opted to institutionalise the route to court for those arrested on suspicion of graffiti-related offences. Young people are compelled to attend court instead of being cautioned or fined. According to Attorney-General Greg Smith, 'Having to go to court and be dealt with, and the trauma that causes to the family and the flesh wound it makes to the family money, does have a salutary effect on the young offender.'[10] The NSW Government also wants to empower courts to cancel or restrict drivers' licences, issue fines and place individuals on Community Service Orders and Community Clean Up Orders. Charges are to be brought under a range of statutes, including the Graffiti Control Act 2008 and the Graffiti Control (Amendment) Act 2009, which allows for increased prison sentences for 'repeat offenders'. The NSW approach has been followed in Western Australia. The Criminal Code Amendment (Graffiti) Act 2009 introduced new offences alongside increased penalties for: 'acts of graffiti vandalism' (up to two years' imprisonment or a $24,000 fine); possession of a graffiti implement with intent (a $6000 fine); and possession of a 'disguise' to be worn while committing a graffiti offence (a $6000 fine). All three Australian jurisdictions (Victoria, NSW and WA) have criminalised the act of selling spray paint to individuals under the age of eighteen (in Britain, under the Antisocial Behaviour Act 2003, the threshold age is sixteen). In Western Australia, Attorney-General Christian Porter linked the sale of spray paint to the spread of 'antisocial behaviour': 'Graffiti is just one type of anti-social behaviour the people of this State are fed up with' (Perth Now, 2009).

Finally, in Britain the categorisation of graffiti as 'antisocial behaviour' has a long history.[11] Many Antisocial Behaviour Orders (ASBOs) were handed down annually under the Crime and Disorder Act 1998 and subsequent Antisocial Behaviour Act 2003 (which specifically targeted graffiti writing). In *R* v *Charan Verdi*, the defendant, who pleaded guilty to nine counts of criminal damage for spraying graffiti on London Underground trains, was

10 In an interview on ABC News, 3 June 2011, accessed 4 June 2011. www.abc.net.au/news/video/2011/06/03/3235409.htm.

11 For further discussion on antisocial behavior and graffiti, see Millie (2008). Note that the coalition government in the UK announced after its election in 2010 that the much-hated ABSO would be abolished. In May 2012 the Home Secretary, Teresa May, announced that the ASBO would be replaced with a 'criminal behavior order', whose difference from an ASBO seemed hard to discern and which was promptly nicknamed the 'CRIMBO'.

sentenced to two years' detention and placed on an ASBO for ten years. In *R* v *Michael Holmes*, a man present merely to photograph a friend writing graffiti was placed on an ASBO for three years.[12] The Antisocial Behaviour Act (as amended by the Clean Neighbourhoods and Environments Act 2005) also bestowed powers on local authorities to issue a fixed-penalty notice (usually £75) to anyone caught marking graffiti (although, unlike in Australia, no powers were enacted to issue fixed-penalty notices to those found in possession of items such as spray paint). Graffiti can also be prosecuted under the heading of 'heritage crime' (if painted on an ancient monument or a piece of public art) and under the Criminal Damage Act 1971 s6 an individual can be given a community service order or fined up to £5000 (provided the damage is less than £5000). If more than £5000 damage has been done, the case can be referred to the Crown Court, which has more extensive sentencing powers. Unlike in Australia, specific 'stop and search' powers do not exist in England or Wales.

The creation of uncommissioned words and images is certainly constructed by law as a criminal act, and both prudential and economic concerns, as Millie would put it, appear to provide the main means of authorising the law's encounter with uncommissioned images. However, whereas the law's construction of the criminality of such an act as criminal is represented as self-evident, it is important to note that property law provides an alternative perspective from which the law could engage with graffiti and street art. The appearance of an uncommissioned word or image of the wall of a property owner's house would provide evidence that their rights to enjoy property have been usurped by the graffiti writer or street artist. Instead of the raft of criminal statutes establishing the criminality of the uncommissioned image, property owners who did not appreciate the presence of such an image on their wall could utilise procedures under administrative law or property law in order to assert their rights over the property. That such a response is difficult to imagine confirms the potency of the network of associations in which illicit urban art is defined as the result of a criminal act committed by an offender. The same network of associations can also be seen at work when a graffiti writer or street artist is apprehended by a police officer and faces judgment before the criminal law.

## Judging the criminalised image

These, then, are the contours of the graffiti writer or street artist's engagement with the law with respect to placing uncommissioned words and images in public space and on private property. In addition, we must also consider the law's response when a graffiti writer or street artist appeals against a

12 See *R* v *Charan Verdi* [2005] 1 Cr. App. R. (S.) 43; *R* v *Michael Holmes* [2006] EWCA Crim 2510.

conviction to a higher court. Examination of appeals against sentencing in graffiti-related cases in Victoria, New South Wales, Western Australia, England and Wales reveals that in the majority the lower court's sentence is reduced. The lower court judge tends to prioritise general deterrence over the need to take into account the individual character of a defendant. For example, in 2009, in the case of Cheyenne Back, an eighteen year old in Sydney was convicted of 'intentionally destroying or damaging property' by tagging a café in a park. She was sentenced to three months' imprisonment by a magistrate in the Local Court. She appealed to the District Court: her sentence was reduced to a twelve-month good behaviour bond with no conviction. In his judgment, Judge Hosking commented that the previous sentence did not take into account the fact that imprisonment is only to be imposed as a matter of last resort. The judge noted that it was abnormal to impose a prison sentence on a young woman with no prior record for tagging a wall – 'as serious as that matter undoubtedly is'. The key issue, then, was the age and prior record of the defendant, as opposed to a consideration of whether or not imprisonment is an appropriate sentence for tagging a wall with a felt-tip pen.

Indeed, to ensure that his reduction of Back's sentence not be read a move in favour of graffiti, Judge Hosking commented: 'I'm not condoning what she did for a moment. People in Sydney are sick of graffiti, there's no doubt about it'. Greg Smith, then Opposition spokesperson for Justice, expressed his disappointment in this outcome. It would be unfortunate, he declared, if Judge Hosking's reduced sentence failed to deter others from 'defacing property' and, when asked if Back should be behind bars, Smith said: 'Personally, I think she should. I think graffiti is a very serious offence. I understand that the culture hasn't been to [imprison offenders] and we've got to change that culture, otherwise our city is just going to be . . . an eyesore' (quoted in Alexander 2009). As outlined in the previous section, since being appointed Attorney-General, Smith has established a system whereby all graffiti offenders are compulsorily sent to court (no cautions or on-the-spot fines) and repeat offenders to jail.

In the case of Kieran Gherardi in Perth, Western Australia, the defendant was arrested after tagging a billboard advertising new apartments. A permanent marker and some paint were found in his backpack. He pleaded guilty to the possession of these items with the intention of 'causing damage consisting of graffiti'. Magistrate Malley imposed a fine of $1000 for possession of the marker and paint and a further fine of $3000 for the criminal damage ($2800 more than the $200 it cost to remove Gherardi's tag). Although the magistrate claimed to have taken into account Gherardi's guilty plea and lack of prior convictions, he keenly emphasised 'the seriousness [of the offence] and the problem within the community and the need for deterrence'. Gherardi had asked for the conviction to be spent (for no conviction to be recorded) but the magistrate announced:

> In relation to a spent conviction, the answer is simply 'no'. In my view this is a serious matter that could well involve a custodial term. It is not a matter that happens by accident. It's not just a momentary slip. The fact is it's an intentional act by an adult who knows the consequences of what he does. In my view the deterrent element to you and to others is overwhelming. It's a discretionary matter. In my view simply because it's a first offender or there's now remorse is not sufficient to outweigh those factors.[13]

Gherardi appealed against the sentence on the grounds that the magistrate erred in passing an excessive sentence. Upon appeal, Judge Hasluck held that the magistrate had placed too much emphasis on deterrence, halved both fines (reducing Gherardi's total fine to $2000) and agreed to the request for a spent conviction. In explaining his reasons, Judge Hasluck pointed out that all Gherardi had done was write the word 'Reboot' on a surface that was 'already defaced very significantly'. The defendant had also shown remorse, was unable to pay the fine and was training to be a teacher. Nevertheless, Judge Hasluck still categorised the offence as 'serious' (56). *Gherardi* v *Pedder* would appear to indicate, once again, that a successful appeal will require a remorseful, youthful and reformed defendant, whereas the act of writing a word upon a billboard will incontrovertibly be regarded as a serious crime, no matter the extent of the damage.

Whereas Back and Gherardi had no prior convictions, in *Jones* v *Sadler (no2)*, the appellant – convicted of eight counts of unlawful damage and one count of possessing a graffiti implement (a felt-tip pen) – had two previous convictions for similar offences (in 2005, one offence of causing damage by writing on a toilet wall in a pub, and in 2006, one offence relating to graffiti on public transport).[14] This time Jones had written on a brick wall, a traffic-light signal box and a roller door. The total costs of repair were $900. He was fined $500 for possession of the felt-tip pen. However, in relation to the property damage, the magistrate sentenced him to seven months' imprisonment for each count, to be served concurrently. Although counsel for the appellant submitted that a fine would be appropriate, Magistrate Tarr responded:

> I have in mind a term of imprisonment. There is a concern in the community about this type of damage. All the councils around the metropolitan area and beyond spend thousands of dollars having to clean up after these people. While there are more cameras around now, it is still difficult to detect, and I think that a deterrent penalty needs to be

13 Magistrate S.R. Malley quoted in *Gherardi* v *Pedder* [2007] WASC 242 at 12.
14 [2010] WASC 53.

> imposed, not only to deter him but to send a message to others in the community that if they get caught then they are likely to suffer the consequences . . . I caught a train into town the other day, and every window of the train had been vandalised, and this is not the same as that but it is similar. It is people defacing property. The Criminal Code has in mind imprisonment for this sort of offence. It provides for a penalty of 12 months' imprisonment or a fine of $12,000. Imprisonment is mentioned before the fine, and the accused has two prior convictions . . . where he was fined $200 on one and $250 on another. They are paltry penalties for this sort of thing.
>
> (at 14–17)

The magistrate then addressed Jones directly:

> Just stand up, Mr Jones. I don't understand the mentality of people who go around like you and your friend have done, vandalising walls and other items around the city. It's behaviour that concerns every law-abiding citizen. They come into town and see this scribble. You only have to catch the train and see the vandalism that takes place on railway stations and on the trains themselves. As I said, I had first-hand experience of that recently and people out there are not getting the message.
>
> (at 18)

Jones appealed against his sentence. The Supreme Court of Western Australia subsequently accepted that Magistrate Tarr had erred in holding that the need for general deterrence could justify the exclusion of other penalties, such as a suspended sentence or community service, and sentenced Jones to eighty hours of community service instead.

The above statements exemplify judicial disdain for graffiti writing ('scribble'), incomprehension ('I don't understand the mentality') and a desire to effect social exclusion (when a magistrate locates himself within the 'community' along with 'every law-abiding citizen' and the graffiti writer in a group of outsiders who are 'not getting the message'). Such an affective spasm results in a sense of entitlement to bypass restrictions on the imposition of custodial sentences. It is a not infrequent judicial response to a courtroom encounter with the usually unseen graffiti writer or street artist. In New York City, Henry Matyjewicz (the main member of a group of artists who, under the name Posterboy, cut up and rearrange advertising posters) was sentenced to eleven months' imprisonment for the felony of damage to property (although this sentence was later reduced on appeal), while well-known graffiti writer Revok, whose work was being exhibited in the Museum of Contemporary Art in Los Angeles at the time of his arrest, received a sentence of 180 days' imprisonment for vandalism.

In London, six Australian graffiti writers, members of the AMF crew, were sentenced to terms of imprisonment varying from eight to fourteen months, with one of them, designated the leader of the group by the judge, also sentenced to sixteen months' imprisonment for conspiracy to commit criminal damage. Again in London, graffiti writer Tox was sentenced to twenty-seven months' imprisonment for seven counts of criminal damage, with the judge stating that the sentence was designed to deter others. Finally, Noam Jason Shoan (aka Renks of the 70k crew) was fined $30,000 in the Melbourne Magistrates' Court and ordered to carry out 250 hours of community service (see MacDowall 2006). The Office of Public Prosecution, however, appealed to the County Court, where Judge Wood agreed that the sentence was overly lenient and ordered Shoan to serve three months in prison (a sentence again overturned after Shoan appealed to the Victorian Supreme Court).[15]

Despite evidence that sentencing of graffiti writers and street artists is unnecessarily severe, the wider community still hankers after harsher punishments and greater police powers. When, a decade ago, Mark Halsey and I (2002) surveyed municipal responses to graffiti, councils were variously split between advocating zero tolerance and embracing graffiti as a means of engaging positively with youth culture. Since then, council views in Australia have hardened and very few advocate even a limited appreciation of graffiti culture by offering graffiti-related community events, workshops, mentoring, or spaces in which to do graffiti legally. In 2010, when New South Wales undertook a review of municipal and criminal responses to graffiti and street art, a number of council submissions pressed for a more punitive approach. Blacktown City Council, for example, stated:

> Council [has] gather[ed] the views of residents on graffiti since mid-2009. The overwhelming response from respondents is that the punishment for offenders is too lenient, particularly for juvenile offenders. In this regard, Council recommends the NSW government considers reducing the number of allowable cautions from three (3) to one (1), increase the penalties for graffiti related offences and require graffiti offenders to pay the full cost of repairing the damages to property resulting from the graffiti offence.
>
> (quoted in Standing Committee on Public Works, 2010: 37–8)

15 For other examples of cases in which sentences were later reduced upon appeal, see *R* v *Francisco Manuel Veira Ferreira and Sacha Belic* (1988) 10 Cr. App. R. (S.) 343; *R* v *Simon Peter Sunderland* (1996); *R* v *Robert Anthony Lee* [2005] EWCA Crim 3677; *R* v *Charan Verdi* [2005] 1 Cr. App. R. (S.) 43; *R* v *Michael Holmes* [2006] EWCA Crim 2510; *R* v *Dolan* [2008] 2 Cr. App. R. (S.) 11; *R* v *Darren Austin and others* [2009] EWCA Crim 394; *R* v *Samuel George Moore* [2011] EWCA Crim 1100; *R* v *W* [2011] EWCA Crim 1619.

The resulting report endorsed this view, recommending that the State government increase penalties for graffiti offences, which it promptly did.

Within the landscape of criminal justice, three features dominate the response to graffiti and street art. First, within the categories of 'graffiti' and 'street art', no effort is made to differentiate the various and distinctive activities that occur. Instead, the legal system has developed definitions that proceed from the point of view of the property owner: for example, any practice that results in a word or image that 'cannot be rubbed off with a dry cloth' (Victoria) or is made with 'fluid that is not water soluble' (Western Australia). Such homogenisation means there is no acknowledgement of community preferences in types of graffiti or street art or variations in the intentions of those who made the images (some writers may be seeking recognition from other graffiti writers; others may intend to show rebelliousness or destroy property; street artists may be seeking to contribute to the streetscape through creating interesting or attractive images). All uncommissioned images are treated equally as a problem to be erased just as their authors are criminals to be apprehended and punished.

Second, responses to graffiti and street art have suffered from the increasing administrativisation of criminal justice and law, which has widened the ambit of transactional justice outside of the discretionary space of the courtroom (O'Malley 2010). Lowering the threshold for suspicion and reversing the onus of proof by creating offences of possession without lawful excuse pre-emptively constructs uncommissioned images as outside the law. Enlarging police powers to include on-the-spot fines expands the network of powers and influence through which police can intervene in the everyday affairs of citizens (on on-the-spot fines, see O'Malley 2009). Renovated legislative frameworks also provide magistrates with increased sentencing powers that only receive scrutiny when an offender is able to mount an appeal against a sentence.

Third, there exists a pervasive sense that the legal response to graffiti and street art – despite significant 'net-widening' (Cohen 1985) – remains insufficient. As Greg Smith, the NSW Attorney-General stated, prison sentences will be handed down to repeat offenders. However, it is not only the persistent graffiti writer or street artist who risks receiving a prison sentence. Any individual who stands before a judge on graffiti-related charges (such as Kieran Gherardi in Australia, or the AMF crew in London) may find themselves in jail, even when it is their first offence. Perhaps this is because the defendant, in the judge's encounter with the graffiti writer or street artist, is taken as a synecdoche standing in for all the makers of unauthorised images in public space.

Consider, for example, the magistrate's comments in *Jones* v *Sadler*: 'There is a concern in the community about this type of damage. All the councils around the metropolitan area and beyond spend thousands of dollars having to clean up after these people' (14). Jones had only tagged some walls, a power control box and a roller door, yet the magistrate related his crime back to the fact that 'every window' on a train had been 'vandalised'. Although he admitted 'this is not the same as that', still he felt that 'it is similar' (17). Adverting to the *sum* total of damage in a community by *all* illicit artists (instead of focussing on the exact repair costs required in relation to the actions of a particular defendant) is repeated on government websites. In Western Australia, for example, new laws against graffiti are explained by way of the fact that graffiti costs taxpayers 'about $25 million a year'; while, as noted above, the Victorian Department of Justice cited clean-up costs across the entirety of Australia (putting the figure at $300 million).

Such gestures facilitate the evocation of a community opposed to illicit images in urban space. Magistrate Tarr in *Jones* v *Sadler* summed it up well: 'It's behaviour that concerns every law-abiding citizen. They come into town and see this scribble' (18). Even after reducing Back's sentence, Judge Hosking said: 'People in Sydney are sick of graffiti'. As a synecdoche of all graffiti writers or street artists, a defendant can be viewed as having committed a serious offence, no matter how small the specific damage. This also helps with the idea that lenient sentences are ineffective. Another slippage is made between the defendant's actual record (which may be free of prior convictions) and the continuing existence of illicit images in general. As Foucault puts it:

> the injury that a crime inflicts upon the social body is the disorder that it introduces into it: the scandal that it gives rise to, the example that it gives, the incitement to repeat it if it is not punished, the possibility of becoming widespread that it bears within it.
>
> (1977: 92)

Such slippages inevitably point judgment towards a perceived need for general deterrence. Judges are quick to cite the necessity of deterrence. In *Gherardi* v *Pedder*, Magistrate Malley said that Gherardi's sentence would 'reflect the seriousness and the problem within the community and the need for deterrence at the same time' (12). In *Jones* v *Sadler*, Magistrate Tarr fretted about the fact that 'people out there are not getting the message' (18) and declared that 'a deterrent penalty needs to be imposed, to not only deter [the appellant] but to send a message to others in the community that if they get caught then they are likely to suffer the consequences' (14). Thus, a *jurisprudence of the example* governs the judicial encounter with the illicit artist, with the 'example [acting as] a sign that serves as an obstacle' (Foucault 1977: 94). The intensity of the law's affective encounter with illicit imagery means that an artist's presence in court can lead to the imposition of a manifestly harsh sentence in the name of general deterrence, with the artist acting as a proxy for all illicit artists, sacrificed at the altar of 'the community'.

## Affect and the uncommissioned artwork

Exemplary jurisprudence bespeaks an intense anxiety in both the lawmaker and the judge, who share in what Foucault calls the 'sensibility of the reasonable man who makes the law and does not commit crime' (1977: 91). Where does this anxiety come from? The crime in question is the creation of letters or images in a word or artwork. An artwork is certainly a powerful entity (Deleuze and Guattari 1996; Grosz 2008) and its combination of colours, shapes and textures invites a response from the spectator. Artworks in galleries elicit responses that range from bliss, an appreciation of beauty, an awed awareness of the sublime, to anger and disgust at the provocations of the artwork (see Young 2005 on disgust as a response to art). Street-based images elicit an aesthetic response in much the same way; however, street art is often viewed through a prism that foregrounds the artwork's *situational illegitimacy* and its threat to property ownership and authorship (a threat that acts as an obstacle to any attempt to imagine alternative legal approaches for encountering illicit art). The artwork's illegitimacy derives from the way that property is imagined in urban space, such that any uncommissioned artwork can only be viewed as a rejection of the law of property, a rejection that is criminalised in order to shore up notions of ownership and authority. That such a task is a profound and crucial one can be seen in the intensity of the law's encounter with the illicit artist, with the affective spasm that seeks to exclude the illicit writer and erase the uncommissioned artwork focusing upon their affront to private property values and to the norms of image production in city spaces. Urban space, according to Ferrell's 'aesthetics of authority' (1996: 178), is what Deleuze and Guattari term 'striated', dominated by 'the verticals of gravity, the distribution of matter into parallel layers' (1996: 370). It is a landscape sustained by an affective investment, everything being 'ordered, numbered, monitored and controlled' (Halsey and Young 2006: 295). A graffiti writer or street artist may recast this intensely regulated city space as 'smooth' by marking them with unauthorised words and images. The nature of this performative demonstration suggests that it is impossible to contain signification within strictly delimited boundaries. In this moment of failure, which appears over and again as uncommissioned words and images appear on a city's surfaces, we find a 'levelling of terrains . . . normally taken to be replete with the signs of wealth, status and ownership' (Halsey and Young 2006: 296).

That the situational illegitimacy of the street artwork is *spatial* can be demonstrated by returning to the offence of 'marking graffiti' in the Victorian Graffiti Prevention Act 2007:

> A person must not mark graffiti on property if the graffiti is visible from a public place unless the person has first obtained the express consent of the owner, or an agent of the owner, of the property to do so.

First, a street artwork visible to the public challenges our idea of art's place. Street art resists the segregation of art within specially-designated places such as museums or galleries and therefore occupies a place and demands to be viewed in areas ordinarily used for other activities: commuting, shopping, working and so on. Second, street art depends upon property and place in order to be displayed. In galleries and museums, express or implied consent is given: the gallery owner or museum curator commissions a show or purchases a piece by an artist and in doing so consents to the presence of that work in her or his space. An illicit work in public space lacks the consent of a property owner, whether the property in question is a public asset, a train or bus, council property such as street furniture, a shop window, the wall of a warehouse or the front fence of a residence. The very notion of property ownership is tied to the idea of restraining others, so that individuals who do not own a particular property are inhibited from writing or painting on that property (or smashing its windows or burning it down): property ownership is culturally regarded both as an achievement and as a shield against others. Artists who use another's property without consent are thus taken to be flouting inviolable norms that valorise property ownership and establish legal boundaries around places drawn by the title deeds of ownership.

Delaney has argued that 'property and jurisdiction map legal meanings on to material landscapes' (2003: 71). Judges and legislators have responded to graffiti and street art in a paroxysm of anxiety occasioned by a perceived challenge to property ownership. In the affective encounter between law and the illicit image, 'the body, the imagination, pain, the heart to be respected are not, in effect, those of the criminal to be punished' (Foucault 1977: 91). It is the law's hysteria with regards to unauthorised imagery that finally counts, rather than the artist's intentions, interests or sensibilities. As far as property is concerned, graffiti writers and street artists rarely make assessments about where to write, paint, wheat paste, knit or whatever else based on the supposed ownership of a wall or fence, and not because writers and artists always want to cause annoyance or commit crimes against private property (although sometimes they do).

Artists instead make decisions about placement according to the norms of the street, which encourage placement of work in places that respect the hierarchy of graffiti writers or street artists (in the customary sense that less-experienced artists should not 'go over' or 'slash' works by artists with more experience and recognition) and away from places such as cemeteries, trees, cars and residential property (Halsey and Young 2006). An artist may also desire to place an image in a particular place consonant with her or his vision of the city; in other words, they may see urban space as a conglomeration of surfaces, to be assessed according to the aesthetics of the space, or visibility, or accessibility (Ferrell and Weide 2010; Halsey and Young 2006). In the law's encounter with the uncommissioned artwork, such nuances are repressed: the law's encounters with graffiti writers and street artists are always subject to the dominant discursive frame of their criminality. Such framing has had serious consequences for the individuals criminalised and also has prevented any chance of a dialogue as to why artists create situational art, why they place it in their selected locations, and their pleasures and desires in city spaces. There is much that we could learn from graffiti writers and street artists, in respect of their conceptualisations of city, property and authorship. Such issues are taken up in the next chapter, which investigates the ways in which property and authority in urban space are differently imagined by law and by the street artist.

encounter

# things on walls

Many cities have surveillance mechanisms, the most obvious being the closed-circuit camera. They can be seen in the streets, angling downwards from their elevated positions, like metallic carbuncles on the walls of buildings. In London, according to the website 'CCTV.co.uk', there is one camera for every fourteen people. That's around 422,000 cameras busily filming the metropolis.

A couple of decades have passed since CCTV was first introduced as a crime-fighting mechanism. The idea is that if you can see a camera, then you can be seen on camera. It was thought that (as in Foucault's reading of Bentham's Panopticon) this exposure to an authoritative and sovereign eye would result in more docile behaviour so as to avoid attracting judgment from the one who is watching. This 'Big Brother' cliché is rarely true in practice: a few years ago I visited a local council's control room and staff admitted that, with so many screens and so few staff, it was impossible to monitor behaviour on the streets with any real effectiveness. And criminological research over the last twenty years has indicated that individuals quickly become accustomed to cameras such that they lose their deterrent effect (while retaining utility in the retrospective solving of crimes).

However, cities (and private property owners) continue to invest faith (and resources – cameras are expensive) in the notion that the demands of life lived on film will make people more law abiding. In London, many buildings display notices proclaiming that you are being monitored on camera. I saw one that read: 'You are being filmed. If you graffiti our building you will be prosecuted.' Another proclaimed: 'CCTV cameras in operation. Bill stickers will be prosecuted.'

For situational artists, the camera poses a problem, since it records a criminal act. Graffiti writers and street artists often wear hoodies, hats or beanies in order to avoid being recognised on film. Selecting a suitable spot for installing a work or writing on a wall includes surveying the area for cameras. Others make artwork about the cameras. Darius and Downey turned a solitary camera into half of a lovesick duo when they welded a sculpted camera onto a wall next to a real camera in such a way that they appeared to be gazing at one another. Years later, Downey created a solo street sculptural performance in which he set a CCTV camera on fire.

And in a less dramatic, but no less effective, way an anonymous artist in London challenged the authority of CCTV. The artist took a section from one of the myriad 'CCTV CAMERAS IN OPERATION. BILL STICKERS WILL BE PROSECUTED' notices. (For decades, joking graffiti – 'Bill Stickers is innocent!', 'Free Bill Stickers!' – has been added to such notices.) The artist then reproduced the text in black lettering against a white background within a wooden picture frame. It was then hung upon a wall near Brick Lane. The will to prosecute (to 'put someone in the frame' as the police say) was transformed into an image. In a city filled with things on walls that exist to deter, record and prosecute crime, the words of the law had themselves been *framed* and put on display for passersby to see.

# Chapter 5

# Street art and spatial politics

> So people say, 'Hey, it's my property, don't paint on it'. Well, no, it's not 'your property'. You paid a lot of money for it but you're a custodian . . . Just because you paid a lot of money for it, it is actually not yours . . . Just because there's a system of breaking it up and ascribing ownership to it – it comes down to a question of legal and illegal: what is the prevailing moral code of society in which you live – but it's a shifting border.
>
> (Nails, artist)

We think of a city as an aggregation of buildings, materials, routes and images that are owned either by persons, corporations or the state. But who owns the cityscape? And what effect does such ownership have on our sense of whether spaces are *private* or *public*? In Chapter 3 I discussed the role of street art in producing the cityscape in a number of different cities, and in Chapter 4 I showed how the law views those cityscapes as composed of myriad crime scenes. This chapter will examine how the criminalisation of graffiti and street art is tied to other legal questions including the way in which an image may or may not be authorised to appear in urban space and where boundaries of permissibility are drawn. It will consider the street artwork as it exists within both city spaces *and* places; places that are owned and constructed around the artwork; and spaces which the artwork transforms and re-creates. In so doing, I will ask a number of questions about the ways in which we construct space, place and property and examine the role of the street artwork as a *spatial object* within the cityscape.

## Private space/public city

As Delaney writes: '[The] social world in which private property is a fundamental feature . . . is also territorialised with reference to public and private spaces' (2005: 5). However, public space and private space are now closely intertwined. Although we can readily point to space that appears obviously private (houses, office buildings), in fact many places that seem public are certainly privately owned, even though they are accessible to some or all of the public (shopping malls, train stations, cafés, bars, and so on). Public availability becomes contingent on permission granted by the private interests controlling a space (making ever more acute the need for extended discussions as to the existence of a commons of the urban imagination, as addressed in Chapter 2).

The increase in the private ownership of so-called public spaces in major cities around the world has been well documented (see, for example, Blomley 2004a, 2004b; Harris 1995; Iveson 2007; Keenan 2010; Loukaitou-Sideris and Ehrenfeucht 2009; Watson 2006). Most of the public spaces in cities such as New York, London, Paris, Berlin, Rome or Melbourne (parks, piazzas, squares, malls, streets and so on) are now privately owned. Very little publicly owned space exists; instead, communal spaces are usually licensed for public use (so as long as that use does not transgress the owner's expectations of what is permissible). In Australia, most jurisdictions have statutes indicating the summary offences that constitute some of these unwanted activities.[1] At other times, owners can also nominate certain behaviours as undesirable rather than illegal (think, for example, of the 'no spitting' signs that used to be common in city streets, or the 'no ball games' signs still found in various green spaces within city neighbourhoods[2]). The very idea of 'public space', then, persists in spite of the erosion of public ownership and its replacement with an extensive network of private proprietors whose ownership includes powers to exclude certain individuals from their property and a degree of authority over the permitted conduct of those who are allowed entry within their property boundaries.

Nevertheless, the idea that cities include public space remains potent. Access to public space is an important component of 'liveability' indices worldwide (Iveson 2007: 149) even though many citizens may not realise that such public spaces are privately owned. As Cooper notes, property regimes play an important role in social life because 'property is . . . a form of coding that locates relations to a thing within wider regulatory and epistemic structures' (2007: 630). Belief in the 'publicness' of public spaces persists, no doubt in part because of entrenched assumptions about freedom of movement and public space as a social asset. The 'privateness' of public space is easily

1 In Victoria, the Summary Offences Act 1966 includes provisions prohibiting certain behaviours including 'observation or visual capturing of the genital or anal region' ('upskirting'), wilfully giving false alarm of a fire, drunken and disorderly conduct, possession of housebreaking implements, flying a kite to the annoyance of any person, obstructing the footpath, and losing control of a horse-drawn vehicle, and many more.

2 Such 'no ball games' signs feature in one of Banksy's most popular artworks, depicting two children using a 'No Ball Games' sign as a ball. Some similarly particularised crimes can be seen, being gently mocked, in The Londonist's video of 'Ten Illegal Things to Do in London': http://tinyurl.com/bmstfqo.

relegated to an inconvenient aspect of modern city life that need not be confronted. Graffiti writers and street artists share in this desire to believe in extensive public space. Interviewees in my research revealed an assumption that placing an artwork in 'the street' means they have located an artwork in public space, rather than on private property; even when a wall might clearly be part of the outer boundary of a house, its exterior wall will frequently be regarded by them as *public* (for example if it abuts the thoroughfare). For graffiti writers and street artists, 'public space' tends to be defined as denoting areas in which groups of individuals congregate (open squares, piazzas, plazas, malls, train stations) or pass through (streets, laneways, underpasses, train lines, bridges, tunnels) – a publicness that derives from the *function* of a space rather than from its ownership.

It is true that the functionality of a space is an important factor in creating and maintaining a sense of 'publicness' for its users (Iveson 2007; Watson 2006). As argued in Chapter 2, graffiti writers and street artists (not to mention skateboarders, urban gardeners and many more) have shown themselves adept at finding uncommissioned cities that intertwine with the strictures of the legislated city. Yet the shrinking of publicly owned space will mean that these uncommissioned cities can be more easily characterised as *exceptional spaces*; that is, as violations of the normative regime of property rights that come about through unwanted and criminal behaviour.

Over the last two decades, scholars have engaged with the notion of 'public space' and the corresponding notion of the 'public' that has been thought to coexist with it. For Blomley (following Foucault) public space is an area of governmentality in which citizens are surveilled, regulated, policed and moved on and in which, from time to time, resistances may spring up and disrupt the legal landscape (what he calls 'unsettling' the settled spaces of the city (2004a; see also 2004b)). For Watson (2006) public space is a place of possibility in which individuals may encounter each other as intensities and potentials. Papastergiadis and Rogers (1996) focus on 'parafunctional' sites in public space; locations that seem to be unused, unwanted, sites of disrepair and decline (see also Papastergiadis 2006). Keith Hayward has also argued that parafunctional sites have developed criminological significance, since they are the locations pointed out as evidence for the broken windows thesis discussed in the previous chapter, and since they have acquired, as such, an association with criminality (real or potential).

Parafunctional sites function as symbolic markers: they prompt municipal or neighbourhood authorities in other areas to take firm stances on actual or potential criminal behaviour, in order to avoid the fate that a parafunctional location might appear to have suffered. Papastergiadis, however, points out that every such site, by virtue of its parafunctionality, is never simply one thing or another: although an area might appear forgotten or in decline, there may still be ways of using the area that provide social or cultural value for residents or passersby. As an example, graffiti writers and street artists, as noted in Chapter 3, often select abandoned buildings, derelict spaces and buildings awaiting demolition for the placement of work. Where the citizens of the legislated city might assume that an area is struggling, or unsafe, or in decline, street artists see aesthetically interesting textures and ready-made art galleries. Thinking of certain sites as parafunctional, then, leads to an enhanced understanding of 'places in terms of hidden micro-cultural practices, distinct spatial biographies, relationships (or non-relationships) with surrounding spaces/structures, intrication with different temporalities, intrinsic social role(s) – both perceived and actual – and networks of feelings and semiotic significance' (Hayward 2012: 453).

The parafunctional site is clearly a liminal one, with ambiguous worth. The liminality of other locations has led to them being characterised as 'non-places' (Augé 1995). Such places offer a reduced number of the opportunities for human interaction taken to constitute community or social life in public space. Others emphasise that the regulation or surveillance or pleasure-taking that attaches to public space is as much a product of the social worth allocated to the populations deemed to occupy sites within it: thus, the presence of the homeless might engender attempts to exclude 'strangers' from a neighbourhood, as described by Mitchell and Staeheli (2006), while Carr (2010) documents the ways in which the law has responded to the harnessing of spatial structures for use as ramps by street skateboarders. Such regulatory efforts are not new, as shown in Vorspan's (2000) account of the increasing controls exercised over public recreational activities: as industrialisation progressed throughout the nineteenth century and as individuals increasingly sought to use public space as the location for recreational pursuits, street activities were increasingly viewed as problematic, resulting in the advent of public parks and formalised sites of recreation where participants could be subject to a degree of surveillance and control.

Is public space made up of a patchwork or mosaic of privately owned property dotted with public places such as streets, parks and city squares? In a way, the answer is yes, but space is mutable, and many locations might exhibit some or all of the characteristics of 'public' places at different times according to how they are being used, interpreted and experienced. The same street may be viewed as prone to crime, as a parafunctional site, as a space of aesthetic possibility and as an interim space lacking the meaning of other, more major thoroughfares. Union Lane, in Melbourne's CBD, exemplifies this multiplicity of character. It is a long, straight lane running between Bourke Street (a major shopping area in which Melbourne's department stores are located) and Little Collins Street (also significant for shopping). In the early 2000s, Union Lane was considered a problem location: unsafe at night and unappealing during the day. There was a large civic (as opposed to 'street') mural painted on one wall. By the mid-2000s, the mural had been extensively tagged. People used the street only as a means to cut between Bourke and

Little Collins; it was a *thoroughfare* (literally a through-fare) used only to hurry through on the way from one street to another.

In 2007, the City of Melbourne decided to organise a new mural for Union Lane.[3] Dozens of graffiti writers and street artists from a range of countries worked on the wall over a period of weeks. Some were invited to particiate; others, having heard what was happening in the laneway, simply joined in. Once it was complete, the Council designated the laneway a 'permitted site' within the municipality. Others have added unauthorised tags and throw-ups to the extent that the laneway wall had to be re-painted in 2010. While this may have frustrated the Council, there can be no doubt that the experience of walking through Union Lane has been irrevocably altered. Thousands came to watch it being painted and people now linger in the laneway – they point and stare and take photos of the artworks on display – because it is no longer just a thoroughfare. It has become something else; something that is a hybrid of a gallery and a tourist destination in the cityscape. The history of this particular laneway demonstrates how difficult it can be to categorise public space as one thing or another. Such heterogeneity is not confined to sites that have been the explicit focus of redevelopment: a similar degree of heterogeneity characterises the majority of places that make up public space. The appearance of graffiti and street art confirms this: how else is it that the same location – be it a door, a wall, an alcove, an alleyway, a billboard, a street – is able to be painted by citizens of the uncommissioned city at the same time as it is being claimed as private property by the citizens of the legislated city?

Graffiti and street art problematise the very ideas of place and space. 'Place' is called into question; it cannot be taken for granted or taken as a given. The situational artwork thus helps us to see space and place as aspects of a dynamic process, produced through the intersecting activities of individuals and groups, some with more, and some with less, social capital (see Bourdieu 1984). Given this mutability and contestability, 'place-making' becomes highly significant. Place-making includes a range of behaviours and institutions from local council policies to architectural practices and planning laws (Dovey, Wood and Woodcock 2009; Dovey 2010; Dovey, Woodcock and Wollan 2012). Place-making – whether that place is a street, a municipality or a city – also depends on the production and interpretation of images. Every year, on New Year's Day, the residents in my street (in Melbourne) gather at 6pm to be photographed in the middle of the street (provided they haven't decamped to the beach). The resulting image is added to a collection on Flickr. The resulting archive could be used as a indicator of residents' ethnicities, income levels, gender and incidence of pet ownership (dog owners tend to bring their pets along to be photographed). Local councils also photograph locations

3 On the Union Lane Street Art Project, and for contributing artists bios, see: www.melbourne.vic.gov.au/Signal/WhatsHappening/AllYearRound/Pages/UnionLane.aspx (accessed on 8 April 2013).

throughout their municipality: websites and brochures include snapshots of residents happily utilising local amenities. Cities thus create images of themselves: on tourist pamphlets, architectural brochures and many everyday publications that display the place-making efforts deemed to be constitutive of 'the city'. In the present chapter, I will consider the place-making potential of street art, in the context of its inevitable challenge to regimes of property and propriety. In this chapter, I will foreground the 'uncommissioned' nature of situational art to highlight the fact that graffiti writing and street art are unauthorised under a regime of private property ownership. It is to this lack of authorisation that I now turn so as to demonstrate how graffiti writing and street art can unsettle taken-for-granted structures of ownership and control.

## Uncommissioned art

Jacques Rancière proposes that '[art] reframe[s] the way in which practices, manners of being and modes of feeling and saying are interwoven in a commonsense' (2004: 100). A 'commonsense' must locate itself; and thus uncommissioned artwork always *takes place somewhere*; it can be seen on walls, along train lines, on the rear of fences, high up on buildings, on street signs, on the pavement; in short, on almost any urban surface. It is in this unavoidable fact of *taking place* that the situational artwork's uncommissioned status presents a challenge to the commonsense regime of property and propriety that governs urban spaces.

Of course, artworks are commodities, items of property that can be bought, sold and gifted. When an artwork is bought by an individual, a corporation or a public entity such as a museum, the right to display it transfers to the purchaser. A spectator in a museum will assume that the art on display is either owned by the museum or on loan from its owner (an intuition that is no doubt correct most of the time).[4] Similarly, when visiting a friend's house, I assume that any artwork on display is legitimately owned (even though there is a thriving market in stolen art and plenty of thorny problems with provenance). Despite these potential fault lines, artworks held or displayed either at home, at work, in museums or galleries are presumed to be legally owned and to constitute property in and of themselves.

A very different set of assumptions comes into play when an artwork is placed in the street. There are plenty of commissioned images in public space: public artworks, the building-as-image that arises from architecture, official street signage and other everyday imagery. The act of commissioning is an

4 There have been a number of notable pranks involving the display of items that do not belong to a museum: Banksy famously smuggled his own work into the Metropolitan Museum in New York, the Louvre in Paris, and the Natural History Museum in London (among others) and attached it to the wall complete with accompanying didactic text for the visitor.

exercise of the rights of a propertied individual or entity. This may be a unilateral act by a sovereign actor (such as when as individual paints the outside of their house or hangs a flag from a window on national holidays). Commissioning may also involve a network of constraints and contributions: as in the fraught enterprise of re-designing the World Trade Centre in New York City, and the many reviews and public consultations that were required.[5] Even the humble street sign may be altered if it is reviewed by a government department and found to be lacking in the necessary visibility or communicative efficacy.

The artist, architect or sign maker acts as the agent of the commissioner (property owner, resident, corporation, government) and with varying degrees of autonomy. The municipal sign maker is unable to exercise aesthetic autonomy and is usually required to follow conventions and regulations as to the size, colour and shape of signs. Some artists working on a commissioned piece may have complete creative autonomy over the resulting work; others have to follow a commission with clear prescriptive dictates. Some commissioned works installed in public space have been withdrawn from display after negative public responses, as documented by Gelber (2006). Certain sites seem to invite perpetual debate and controversy such as the 'fourth plinth' in London's Trafalgar Square: public interest in the artworks periodically placed there is always intense (and sometimes critical).[6]

What, then, of the artist or writer who creates *uncommissioned* words and images in public space? They may have a great deal more autonomy than the humble sign maker; yet, at the same time, their artwork is also the result of a complicated collaborative process. Consider the factors that need to be taken into account: location; nature of the location; ease of installing the work; ability to see the work; ability to see (if installing after darkness); manifold risks (injury from falling, arrest, assault); the vagaries of the weather. Artists also pay heed to a range of conventions regarding placement including: the nature of the surface; the presence of other pre-existing artworks (in order to follow the unwritten laws of the street); the nature of the property (residential dwelling, public thoroughfare, train station) and the specific rules governing its ownership and use.

5 A process I discuss in the final chapter of *Judging the Image* (2005).

6 As Higgins commented: The Fourth Plinth would be no fun without a spot of fuss and bother; and in its eight-year history as a site of a rolling programme of temporary public sculpture it has certainly offered plenty of that' (2013: 1). At the time of writing the next sculpture intended to occupy the plinth is a giant blue cockerel by Katharina Frisch; however, planning objections have been lodged by a group called the Thorney Island Society, which calls itself a 'watchdog on local planning issues'. The group objects to the proposed sculpture on the grounds that it is 'totally inappropriate', 'unrelated to the context of Trafalgar Square' and 'adds nothing to it but a feeble distraction' (quoted in Higgins at 1-2).

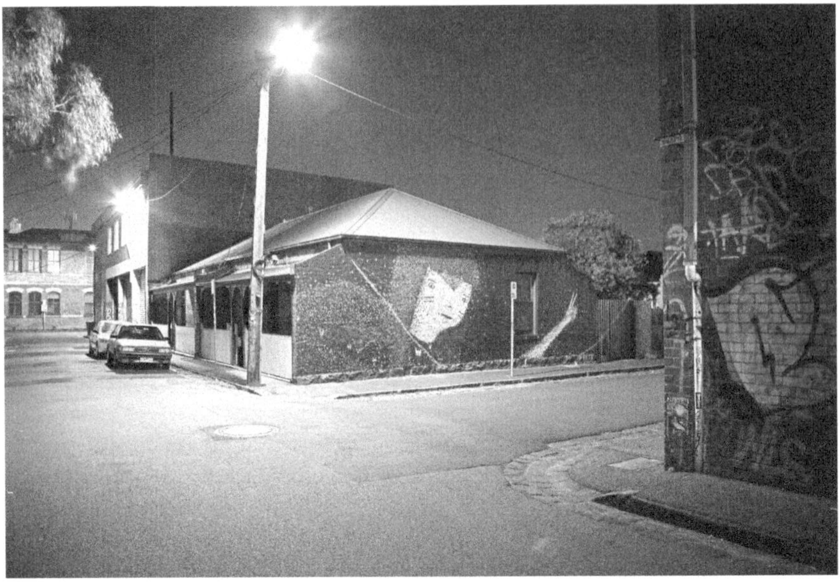

*Figure 5.1* Ghostpatrol, Melbourne 2013. Photograph © Bernard Winter.

Although situational artists sometimes create works visible on the street under commission and with a property owner's consent (see, for example, the wall by Ghostpatrol in Figure 5.1), the majority of situational artworks are done without commission.

Thinking about the street artwork as an 'uncommissioned image' helps us to see how the artwork challenges conventional conceptualisations of space and ownership through its lack of *authorisation*. Since the fifteenth century, commissioning (closely tied to the idea of patronage) has been central to the very idea of art and has connoted the authority to carry out a particular artistic enterprise (see Hollingsworth 1994). It has also, importantly, connoted a situation of *contract*; that is, an exchange of mutual consideration so as to bring each party under the authority of a shared set of terms (it also acquired particular associations such as the notion that a prime minister or president might authorise the actions of judicial, military or naval officers). When an individual, a corporation or a branch of the state commissions an artist, the commission passes authority from the property owner (controller, regulator, manager) to the artist. This authorisation is only temporary and expires (according to the terms of the implicit or explicit contract) upon completion of the work or if the terms of the contract are breached (for example if the work is installed somewhere other than the agreed location).

The street artwork, as an uncommissioned work, lacks such authorisation. It is a text without authority or, indeed, an author. It may have a maker, but that is not the same, in law, as an author. The commission (and relatedly the contract, such as exists between an artist and her gallerist or art dealer) *authorises* the creation of works; a street artwork lacks any such authorisation. A work of art created spontaneously in a studio by an artist is authorised by the artist's signature. Her signature acts not merely as an identifier – her biography and reputation – but also, as Derrida points out in *Signsponge/Signéponge* (1984), as an integral textual component of the work, unable in fact to exist outside of that artist's body of work. Neither can the signature exist outside of law, since authorisation requires an author to self-endow themselves with value. It is often said of street artworks that they simply 'appear' as if by magic in the night; as if, in other words, no one had agency in their creation and installation. This common response is not simply a result of the enchanted nature of the spectator's encounter with the street artwork; it is also symptomatic of the artwork's position outside the conventions of authority and authorisation. Since all artworks owe their existence to the law (in which case it makes sense to claim that the law itself writes or paints all texts and images) it follows that graffiti and street art (being illicit or uncommissioned) cannot properly be said, in law, to be art at all – at best, it is 'not quite art'.[7] It is a logical consequence of street art's lack of authorisation: an artwork that is not commissioned – not *author*-ised – is *not quite* an artwork.

This lack of authorisation constitutes the first of two key ways in which the situational artwork challenges conventional regimes of authority and ownership. The second relates to the fact that an artwork is illicit when it is located on property belonging to another, and without the permission of the property owner. 'Permission' attests to the dimension discussed above, since it derives from the authority of commissioning: the owner commissions or consents to an artwork and thus authorises the artist's actions. However, ownership (or the lack of it) is as important as the permission or commission in defining the legitimacy (or the lack of it) for a situational artwork.

Graffiti and street art have recently been discussed as arising in the context of an act of *trespass* (Dew 2007; McCormick et al. 2010). Trespass, as noted by McCormick, derives its semantic origins from ideas of 'offence' and 'sin' (from the Old French, *trespasser*, 'to pass beyond or across', with a contemporary gloss to be found in the modern French idiom, *trépasser*, meaning 'to die' as in to euphemistically 'pass over to the other side'). The first instance of trespass as 'to enter land unlawfully' appears around 1455 in the forest laws of Scotland: 'for whatever reason the Scots may have seen to restrict the terms under which individuals could enter their forests, we can be sure that the very fact that entry became against the law means that there was cause, if not custom, for going there in the first place' (McCormick et al. 2010: 15). Here,

7 Street art's status as 'not quite art' was addressed in the television series of that name, which aired on the ABC in 2007 and 2008.

however, (as both a Scot and a lawyer) I must point out the rather greater complexity of the situation than this implies. After the Norman Conquest, large tracts of land were reserved to the king for hunting game, both in England and in Scotland. Although the term 'trespass' was indeed first used in Scotland, the forest laws restricting access to these lands and reserving their use for hunting, were, as Barrell describes (2000: 36), rather less stringent in Scotland than their English counterparts.

Certainly, in both jurisdictions, reserved lands continued to be accessed by all sorts of individuals, who, while they may have been 'trespassing', were also contesting these new property boundaries (on the history of 'enclosures' see Linebaugh 2010). The illicit use of property belonging to another creates for the trespasser – as they cross that boundary – a sense of ownership in another's property. As José Parlá put it: 'Kids are seeing [trains] and they're like, "A perfect place to put my art because it will travel from the Bronx to Coney Island and then everyone will see it" . . . Now it becomes *your* train, you have *ownership* in something. You're thinking *politically*. You're thinking like a *pirate*' (my emphases). As long as there have been property boundaries, there have been individuals seeking to push up against them, cross them, contest them, whether in the form of burglars, poachers, pirates, or illicit artists.[8] Penalver and Sonya point out that the prohibition of the illicit use of property through trespass was always as much about status, profit, value and social hierarchy as it was ever about land: 'Laws of criminal trespass protect the boundaries around real property, established through market transactions' (2010: 11).

Trespass also derives meaning from a number of other important associations. First, it connotes 'encroaching upon land belonging to another' so that, even if an individual does not *physically enter* another's land, their actions or possessions may still be seen to have an impact upon that other person's property. Graffiti or street art that is attached to a wall belonging to another can thus be understood as trespass long after the artist has gone. Second, it connotes someone who does not respect boundaries and thus aligns the trespasser with those who, like tramps, vagabonds and nomads, have no fixed abode and hence no respect for the idea of property.[9] (Trespass is related to 'traipse', to wander without purpose or objective, of uncertain origins but possibly deriving from Middle Dutch, *trappen*, to tread, or from German, *traben*, tramp.) The notion of trespass thus invokes a semantic mesh indicating an individual with no home or social roots, no respect for the property of others, who takes or damages things belonging to others, and whose actions negatively impact on society as a whole. These associations, as I have indicated,

8 On piracy and its historical nexus arising from the enclosure of common land in Britain, Wales, Ireland and Scotland in the fifteenth and sixteenth centuries, see Linebaugh and Rediker (2000).

9 The nomad, in particular, has inspired a rich vein of postmodern thought from Nietzsche to Deleuze. See for example Deleuze (1977); Cresswell (1997).

rest upon a theological foundation in which trespass is equated with sin. Such deep-rooted associative complexity may explain some of the difficulty experienced by property owners, police and local councils in seeing graffiti and street art in a positive light.

Trespass is almost inevitable. Cities are criss-crossed with lines of ownership and exclusion; very few spaces are made available to artists. Although a 'legal' work (that is, one created with the permission of the property owner or manager, such as a commissioned mural or an image placed upon a wall authorised for graffiti by a council) is not a situational artwork in the sense that is used in this book, such legal works certainly bring street-based images into the everyday experience of citizens, and thus many street artists do sometimes produce commissioned works or seek permission from property owners.[10] CDH has sought permission to create legal artworks in Melbourne:

> I [started] a non-profit organisation to organise legal spaces for street artists to paint. I went door knocking, asking for permission to paint people's walls . . . I would knock on a door and I'd say, your wall's pretty badly tagged and the paint's peeling, and I'm a street artist and we do legal murals . . . So many times I'd get this answer; 'Yes, great idea, we're really on board with it, we'd love to have a mural, but we're not the owners of the building, we're just tenants in the store'. So then I'd email or ring up the real estate agent, and I could predict what the reaction was going to be: 'We need to speak to the owner'. And then what I discovered was these buildings are in our community, but the people who own the buildings, the people who are responsible for the aesthetic of the buildings, are completely removed from the community. A lot of the time they're like a small corporate investment group, or it's an owner that doesn't live

10 See Kramer (2010) on legal painting in New York City, and, as examples of legal sites, see the wall known as the May's Lane Art Project in Sydney, which displays works by a rotating series of artists. The wall is at the rear of a building containing a graphic design business whose owner organised (and thus authorised) the site. In London the famed Southbank skate park provides an example of a legal spot in the centre of a city where graffiti is authorised, although contributors to the user forum on 'Legal Walls', a site aiming to help writers 'find legal walls around the world', sometimes exhibit skepticism as to whether a site with considerable CCTV surveillance is a safe place to paint: see comments at www.legal-walls.net/#lat=47.5378&lng=8.773270000000025&zoom=2 (accessed 30 January 2013). In his analysis of the role of legal walls within cityscapes, McAuliffe notes, in the context of one particular municipality, 'The legal walls manifested an attempt by [Paramatta City Council] to create a geography of managed 'hot spots', away from commercial and residential premises, and away from the transport corridors so popular with graffiti writers' (2013: 525) and that legal walls 'territorialise the deterritorialised practice of graffiti; by fixing the space of legal activity, they make visible a group living beyond visibility as transgressive actors on the fringe of socially acceptable behaviour' (2013: 528). That such territorialisation is often tied to efforts to reduce graffiti or street art elsewhere in a city can be seen in the account by Craw et al. (2006) regarding the effectiveness of legal murals as graffiti deterrence.

> in Melbourne . . . Their motivation is to get a good return from their investment property, and the idea of having somebody come along and paint a mural that could be some huge headache, and it's like, why bother? This is what convinced me of the value of illegal street art, because a lot of the time, the people that are responsible for the aesthetic of our community have no connection to our community. They don't even live in our community. And the people who do live there and have to look at this wall every day are completely disempowered. And fundamentally that just doesn't seem right.

This is not to say that permission cannot be obtained. Many legitimate murals exist in London, Melbourne, New York, Paris and so on. But the very requirement that an artist seek permission arises from the fact that graffiti and street art are considered a crime against property. Legal walls are still objects owned by another; the artist is only temporarily permitted to carry out the activity of creating an artwork. It is an exceptional moment within a matrix constituted by the criminal law and the law of property, outside both of which lies situational art. And authorised artworks constitute a very small minority of the words and images placed in cityscapes by graffiti writers and street artists. Situational art, then, is not simply criminalised (indeed, over-criminalised as demonstrated in Chapter 4); it is also *unauthorised*. Graffiti writers and street artists thus exist without a voice, without standing, without sensibility. Meanwhile, the cityscape is configured as a conglomeration of crime scenes, which result from acts of trespass across boundaries that are supposedly impregnable.

## Commissioning through social policy

Can social policy mitigate the effects of the law? According to Philippopoulous-Mihalopoulos: 'the city finds itself within the law and lends itself to juridical architectonics, just as the law finds itself inhabiting buildings and getting lost behind street corners' (2007: 4). So too, I would argue, does municipal policymaking, through a web of social policies issued, reviewed and revised by its municipalities. After several years of analysing municipal responses to graffiti (see, for example, Halsey and Young 2002), I was invited in June 2004 to develop a management policy for graffiti and street art in the City of Melbourne (encompassing the CBD and neighbouring suburbs Carlton, Parkville and South Melbourne). Enthused by the opportunity to engage directly with the object of my research, I hoped to deploy my knowledge in a manner that would be helpful to graffiti writers and street artists, individuals who are conventionally not even conceptualised as 'stakeholders' in terms of municipal policymaking. I hoped, in other words, to be able to shift local policy away from the default regulatory position in which uncommissioned words and images are held to be social problems.

In any policymaking exercise constraints are endemic, and I was aware of the ways in which social policy can negatively impact on certain groups. My aim was to formulate a policy that took the most reflexive approach possible within the framework created by the City of Melbourne's existing policy obligations, notably the Victorian State Government strategy, *Grappling with Graffiti* (2003). Its core components centre on what is called the three E's of good policy: *eradication*, *education* and *enforcement*. In the proposed strategy, I added a fourth E: *engagement* (with the communities of graffiti writers and street artists) by emphasising a 'partnerships' model and broadly defining the agencies sought after for participation: graffiti writers, street artists, residents, traders, community groups, galleries, transport companies, utility providers, police, construction companies and hoarding manufacturers. I avoided the standard definition of partnerships in which a council seeks partners with an agency in order to generate data about censured behaviour so as to 'correct' problematic behaviour (see Iveson 2006; 2007). Instead, partnerships would generate opportunities for graffiti writers and street artists including access to spaces in which they could put up work without fear of arrest (and without the council being able to use these partnerships to stamp out graffiti in the city).

It was under 'Eradication' that the Strategy diverged most noticeably from conventional municipal regulatory approaches. I proposed that the municipality should contain three types of zones. First, a 'zero tolerance' zone (this included council assets). Second, areas of limited tolerance, in which the fate of graffiti and street art would be left to property owners. In the event of a disagreement, between neighbours for example, the council would facilitate a resolution (rather than simply removing the offending artwork). Third, areas of 'high tolerance', in which graffiti and street art would not be removed by council; that is, areas in which stakeholders would let graffiti or street art self-regulate. A number of laneways in the CBD (Hosier Lane, Caledonian Lane and Centre Place) were already exhibiting self-regulation; graffiti writers and street artists hoped that this might continue without council intervention. The proposed strategy thus recognised aspects of Melbourne's urban geography (the myriad laneways so vital for graffiti and street art) and its developed cultures of graffiti and street art.[11]

The council's response to the proposal was initially positive. Further, public consultation was undertaken and public submissions invited.[12] Seventy-nine

11 Some elements of the Strategy were mandatory, such as a time limit for removal of 'hate' graffiti, and a process through which Council could assist individuals with graffiti removal. I tried to make positive use of some constraints: for example, I redefined the notion of 'stakeholder' to include those routinely left out – graffiti writers, street artists, young people generally and even people who like to look at street art. I similarly reworked the notion of 'rights' so that citizens would be able to assert their right to retain graffiti and street art in their neighbourhood (especially if it had been zoned as zero or limited tolerance).

submissions were received, of which nineteen were unfavourable and sixty were favourable. Almost 75 per cent of submissions were thus supportive of the Strategy either wholly or in part. As expected, opposition focused on the proposed tolerance zones. It was argued that residents would be forced to put up with graffiti and street art that they found offensive. Others argued that cleaning costs would be increased. Some claimed that the City of Melbourne would be in contravention of the law by establishing zones of self-regulation. This, however, was based on a misunderstanding of the legal position: graffiti or street art done with the property owner's consent does not constitute a criminal offence and any such zone would of course only come into existence after property owners had given their consent. Despite the misgivings of some of the submissions, the overall reception of the proposal was strongly in favour and preparations were made for the proposal to be presented to the council for adoption.

But one morning my telephone rang and I was informed that the policy was being abandoned. The Engineering staff would write a new one. When I pressed for information, I was told that the decision had made 'at the highest level' within the council.[13] Four months later, a 'zero tolerance' Management Plan was adopted by the council. It acknowledged that 'murals' could have aesthetic value but promised the swift removal of 'tags and stand-alone stencils'. Since there are relatively few large murals and a preponderance of tags and stencils, the municipality was in effect declaring war on graffiti and street art.[14] The Plan stated: 'graffiti is not acceptable in the municipality and the City of Melbourne will do everything in its power to eradicate this vandalism'.[15] It located graffiti management within the council's 'service arrangements for street cleaning and waste removal' and promised to 'tackle graffiti head-on' and 'get tough on graffiti' with its 'rigorous enforcement regime'.

12 Accessed August 2008, printed out and on file with author. The web page was taken down in 2010 after a change in government: the current Department of Justice website reiterates these justifications in condensed form, stating: 'Graffiti vandalism is a highly visual problem that has associated financial costs, concerned with its prevention and removal, and social costs as it affects the visual amenity of communities and influences perceptions of public safety'. Online at www.justice.vic.gov.au/wps/wcm/connect/justlib/DOJ+Internet/Home/Community+Crime+Prevention/Action+on+Graffiti/, accessed 28 July 2011.

13 I was also instructed to refrain from making any comments to the media.

14 Policy fluctuations are common in the political process. However, this outcome was unexpected for two reasons: first, because it represented a wholesale reversal of an approach that had been agreed upon at every level (except the highest, that of the CEO who was reportedly responsible for the reversal) rather than a negotiated variation; and second, because it ignored the public consultation findings which supported the adoption of the Draft Strategy.

15 All quotations taken from the City of Melbourne Graffiti Management Plan 2006, downloaded from www.melbourne.vic.gov.au/info.cfm?top=145&pg=1108 on 15 March 2006.

The Graffiti Management Plan undertook to inform residents and traders how to remove graffiti from their property and how to deter 'vandals' and to 'ensure vandals are aware that their activities are unwelcome and they run a real risk of detection and apprehension'. The Plan announced a commitment to assisting Victoria Police in the prosecution of graffiti writers and street artists by photographing tags and stencils and making these available to the police, and that the City of Melbourne would advocate for legislative changes to make it easier to prosecute, arm judges with harsher penalties, and widen the City of Melbourne's ability to remove graffiti and street art from private and public property throughout the municipality. It distinguished tagging from 'murals or street art' and added a permit system for the commissioning and retention of street art. The council thus arrogated to itself the authority as to whether or not any existing piece of street art should be allowed to survive or even to come into existence.

It was envisaged by Council that the permit system would operate in a manner similar to the system for building alterations. Forms would need to be filled in by the graffiti writer, street artist or property owner and a notice displayed at the site for four weeks, after which a sub-committee of the Engineering Department (including a police officer) would adjudicate on the application. An online register was established so as to 'help people find those legal sites that have a Street Art permit'.[16] By June 2009, twenty-four applications had been made, with permits granted to all except one ('withdrawn') and another that was refused. These statistics give the impression that the system promoted street art. There were, however, a number of ambivalences not revealed by the permit system. First, the register did not actively 'help people' find sites with permits other than by providing a bureaucratic list of address and outcomes. Little detail was provided as to the nature of the artwork. No images were uploaded. In short, there was no real attempt to encourage people to view street art. Second, neither the register nor the Council website acknowledged that the City of Melbourne compelled many property owners and traders to submit retrospective applications for permits to cover pre-existing artworks in the laneways (Hosier Lane, Caledonian Lane, Rutledge Lane).[17] Third, these retrospective applications created confusion in that pre-existing artworks suddenly appeared to have been 'commissioned' by the City of Melbourne and in that many writers and street artists did not understand this new permit system and went over a number of existing

16 Stated on the City of Melbourne website, at www.melbourne.vic.gov.au/info.cfm?top=145&pg=3274 . The Register is at www.melbourne.vic.gov.au/info.cfm?top=145&pa=3274&pg=3842 (accessed on 14 June 2009).

17 I'm grateful to Andrew McDonald, then director of Citylights Project (Hosier Lane and Centre Place) and the Until Never gallery (Hosier Lane), for providing me with information as to the Council's insistence on retrospective permits.

works now bearing a Council permit number, either believing that walls with 'City of Melbourne Permit' on them were legal walls open to everyone, or as a gesture of disdain for the Council's attempt to control the space.[18]

After the advent of the Graffiti Prevention Act 2007 (see Chapter 4) it became apparent that a regulatory synergy existed between municipalities and the State Government. The Act not only added to the criminalisation of graffiti, it created new powers for Councils to remove graffiti from private property. The Council's divided position with respect to graffiti and street art is evident in the following statement on its website:

> The City of Melbourne recognises there is widespread concern about graffiti tagging within the municipality. At the same time, tourists and visitors regularly view street art murals.
>
> [The Graffiti Management Plan] plan distinguishes between the need to remove unwanted graffiti applied without permission and street art murals placed on walls and infrastructure with the blessing of property owners and in accordance with the Council's approval criteria and planning laws.[19]

There is a deliberate use of the language of authorisation. Property owners were invited to telephone in and discuss potential commissions for new work. With regards to existing work, property owners were advised as follows:

> If you are a property owner or manager and you have existing graffiti on your property which is a potential street art site, you will need to decide whether you would like it to stay or whether you want it removed.

18 The saga of one of Banksy's Melbourne stencils, known as the 'Little Diver' (also discussed in the encounter 'Banksy under glass'), reveals a number of tensions in the City of Melbourne's system. The Council's Graffiti Management Plan had outlawed 'stand-alone stencils' and thus the 'Little Diver' stencil should have been regarded as illegal. However, by 2006, Banksy had become the most famous street artist in the world and his Melbourne stencils (from a visit in 2003) had become valuable assets rather than vandalism (see Banksy 2002, 2003, 2005b; Manco 2002). An application to retain the 'Little Diver' stencil was submitted to the City of Melbourne. The application was not only approved but a sheet of protective plexiglass was bolted on top of the stencil. This provoked a predictably cynical response from the local artistic community: the council were seen to be keen to 'protect' and 'preserve' Banksy's works but not those done by other artists. Then, in December 2008, someone poured silver paint behind the plexiglass. On top of the plexiglass, the words 'Banksy woz ere' were written in black marker pen. No doubt, this Banksy stencil would have been erased anyway (most of his other Melbourne works had already been buffed or painted over). Yet the 'Little Diver' episode reveals that both the permit system and Council's desire to preserve some works and not others were regarded as hypocritical and misplaced by the local artistic community.

19 At www.melbourne.vic.gov.au/AboutCouncil/PlansandPublications/strategies/Pages/Graffiti managementplan.aspx (accessed on 14 June 2009).

> If you would like the work to remain and it meets City of Melbourne's approval guidelines, you will need to sign a Street Art approval form which will ensure that the site is not cleaned by the City of Melbourne.[20]

The Council was no doubt being cautious after public condemnation of its accidental removal of another Banksy stencil, a parachuting rat, in one of the city's most popular street art laneways. Yet this comment also demonstrates the precarious position of the street artwork, in that removal is the default position, whereas an extra bureaucratic mechanism must come into play if a work is to be spared.

Even commissioned works struggle to exist in such a hostile climate. In September 2010, the well-known artist Anthony Lister painted a large artwork on a wall in a vacant piece of ground in Brisbane. He was given permission by the owner of the land. However, within forty-eight hours it was painted over by a council cleaning crew. In the ensuing debate over whether the artwork had any 'right' to be there, the very fact of the commission was disputed, with some claiming that the artist should have sought permission from the owner of the wall rather than the owner of land overlooked by the wall (in which he stood while painting).[21]

Council policy regarding graffiti and street art can sometimes shift when management changes. The City of Melbourne is, at the time of writing, attempting to work more directly with graffiti writers and street artists in order to encourage artwork in locations such as Hosier Lane and Rutledge Lane. This is a welcome alternative to the more repressive strategy of installing CCTV cameras suggested by Victoria Police. In Western Australia, Fremantle City Council is seeking community feedback on a strategy that focuses its removal efforts on 'offensive graffiti and tags'. When it comes to other types of situational art:

> Graffiti that falls into the category of *pieces*, *slogans* or *stencils* may have artistic or cultural merit and considered to be 'unauthorised street art' and will be photographed and referred to the Director Community Development for a decision about its removal or retention . . . Unauthorised street art on private property deemed to have artistic or cultural merit will be left in place unless there is a request to have it

20 Both statements on the City of Melbourne website at www.melbourne.vic.gov.au/ForResidents/StreetCleaningandGraffiti/GraffitiStreetArt/Pages/Whatisstreetart.aspx (accessed on 14 June 2009).

21 See the discussion in Dickinson (2010). In 2012, residents of a neighbourhood in Atlanta painted over a mural by Roti, created with permission from the property owners, during the Living Walls street art event in 2012. The protesting residents complained that they had not been consulted as to whether they liked the mural: see Jarvie (2012).

> removed made by the property owner. A register of retained street art will be kept. (italics in original)[22]

Anything deemed 'unauthorised street art' is thus being given the chance of an authorised existence. This revised strategy has been hailed as a radical step for the municipality. However, there are clear conditions that need to be met (permission sought, no request for removal, council approval). The situational artwork is thus, once again, in a precarious position. These municipal regulations are also designed to mesh with the criminal law, as is evident from the FAQs provided on the council website:

> Q. Are there locations in Fremantle where I can do graffiti without getting arrested?
> A. No. There are no sites in the City where you do not run the risk of getting arrested for graffiti. Unauthorised art or marking a wall without permission was, and continues to be a criminal offence.
>
> Q. What if I get arrested by the police for doing graffiti and you like my graffiti so you keep it?
> A. The act of marking a wall is an offence no matter how good your work is. If you are caught doing unauthorised artwork you can be arrested and charged. This is a police matter.[23]

As progress goes, this is glacially slow. Even these councils seeking a 'less repressive' approach cannot help but frame graffiti and street art as something to be managed, limited, controlled and, as Brighenti (2010b) would put it, territorialised.

Will the experience of creating and viewing graffiti and street art in these municipalities be altered in any way? It is highly unlikely. Perhaps the problem is that to be 'less repressive' is such a grudging objective. McAuliffe (2013) has noted how much artists stand to lose when legal walls are removed or abolished (as recently happened in Paramatta and in Nottingham in the United Kingdom). Inexperienced artists, in particular, often use legal walls to improve their skills. And legal walls have educational benefits for ordinary citizens who are able to see graffiti writers and street artists at work during daylight hours and to speak with them about the artwork. But initiatives such

22 In the Draft Revised Graffiti Strategy, Fremantle City Council, September 2012, available online at www.fremantle.wa.gov.au/cityoffremantle/Community_engagement/Community_consultation_projects/Revised_Graffiti_Policy (accessed on 26 January 2013).

23 The FAQs and responses can be found at: www.fremantle.wa.gov.au/home/List_of_News_and_Media/2013/February/Revised_graffiti_policy_FAQ (accessed on 26 January 2013).

as legal walls or street art permits come at a high price: that of the legal system's refusal to acknowledge the artist's autonomy to create public works without the authorisation of property owners. More than this, these initiatives continue to demand that the street artist subordinates any possibility of self-commissioning authority in favour of that of the pre-existing authority of a council, a resident or a police officer. The commission is still paramount. The public city is still held at bay by the pervasive investment in the private authority of the proprietor.

## Spatial politics

A number of graffiti writers and street artists interviewed for this book argued that their work is at its best when it is illegal. On that basis, they rejected the idea that it should be decriminalised. Similarly, I would argue, street art needs no commission. It has its greatest affective impact when uncommissioned. Legal walls and murals play a beneficial role in accustoming citizens to the presence of certain aesthetic genres. Yet the authorities (property owners, police, councils, governments) retain control of these sites and refuse to recognise the situational artist as a maker of legal artwork. Despite such restrictions, innumerable graffiti writers and street artists create illicit work every day and thus demonstrate their agency and their ability to self-commission, to authorise their own actions. Street art thus *makes its own space*, not as a partitioned, permitted, semi-tolerated activity, but as an emergent, *autopoietic* practice, a de-territorialising tactic that exposes the multiple boundaries and borders of the propertied cityscape.

The challenge, then, is for us to imagine how graffiti writers and street artists can continue to exist outside of the dominant property paradigm, since knowledge that the street artwork is unauthorised and hence illicit is crucial (as I argued in Chapter 1) to its affective charge.[24] In this chapter, then, I have questioned the authority of 'the authorities' given that public space is used by a heterogeneous mix of citizens. In particular, I have asked why situational art presents such a challenge to the modernist territorialisation of urban space. As Carter has argued, we have passed from 'a discourse of grounding to one of territorialisation in which the rules of sociality are replaced by a preoccupation with limits' (2007: 431). Such territorialisation mitigates against the possibility of experiencing the enchantment that Bennett and others propose is essential to an ethical aesthetics and that I have argued in Chapter 2 is a necessary precondition for new genres of urban experience (Bennett 2001, 2010; Watson 2006). Instead of a territorialised city, situational artists point instead to the possibility of a public city founded on 'communication'; that is, a space founded through the urban imagination and

24 See Brook (2007) on the link between aesthetics and authorisation.

the circulation of signs (see also Nancy 1991). The 'urban inscription' created by graffiti writers and street artists allows the such a space to become known and experienced, 'through the bodily, rhythmic writing and re-writing of it', as Dickens puts it (2002: 27), for it is in each and every singular encounter with the street artwork that the possibility of a public city is reiterated.

encounter

# Banksy under glass

Banksy doesn't sign his street works. The provenance of a Banksy is considered to be established when a photograph of the work *in situ* appears on Banksy's website. Many of his early works have faded and many have been buffed. Some have been painted over by other artists as part of the usual turnover of works on the street (and especially during a long-running struggle over certain spaces with Robbo, a London graffiti writer, and the members of his crew). Some have been accidentally painted over, as when a Melbourne cleaning crew removed a Banksy rat in 2010. A few have been destroyed, deliberately, or by chance, as when a Melbourne plumber drilled through another Banksy rat while carrying out construction work on a building in 2012.

At the same time as Banksy's street pieces have been experiencing the usual deleterious effects of weather, time and cleaning crews, his canvases and prints have been selling for higher and higher prices at auction, on eBay and through galleries. Suddenly, property owners began to look twice at Banksy-painted walls. Banksy pieces had become valuable. They could lead to an increase in property prices (a direct reversal of the broken windows thesis discussed in Chapter 4). They were also thought to add character to a neighbourhood: some councils started fixing sheets of plexiglass over Banksy works in order to conserve them and thus prolong the urban coolness that an area might acquire from them. No street artist has had their work covered with plexiglass more often than Banksy.

I've seen several pieces by Banksy under glass. Near the former location of Black Rat Projects gallery in Shoreditch, in the forecourt of a bar called Cargo, two covered artworks by Banksy can be seen. One is his 'Designated Graffiti Area'; the other, 'His Master's Voice', in which he reworks the EMI logo (associated with that phrase) to show a dog firing a rocket launcher into an old-fashioned record player. Both are classic examples of Banksy's style. They have to be viewed now under a thick layer of plexiglass that makes it hard to see the texture of the wall and hard to photograph, thanks to the unavoidable reflections from the plasticky overlay. One London friend told me about encountering a man who had just discovered that his wall had been painted by Banksy. He realised that the work had value and was immediately focusing on the related problems of how to preserve the work and how to monetise it for himself.

But the preservation of a street artwork – and especially a Banksy – is trickier than it might seem. In 2003, Banksy visited Melbourne and put up a lot of work. Most were eventually buffed, painted over or faded from sight. However, one, the 'Little Diver' (also discussed in Chapter 5), remained for a number of years, probably escaping the buff because it was situated low on a wall in a very small street. It depicted a small figure wearing a diver's helmet, opened to show an empty space where the head should be. A question mark next to the figure completed the image. As Banksy's fame grew, the building owner, with the city council's agreement, affixed plexiglass on top of the artwork.

While the image itself had not changed, at some point the 'Little Diver' had become significant to certain members of its audience. It was no longer an illicit stencil in the street; it was a valuable artwork. The plexiglass, however, triggered a further transformation. This protective covering signified to other artists that a hierarchy of value was at work; that the 'Little Diver' was different. It may, then, have been in protest against such assumptions that, in December 2008, someone poured silver paint behind the plexiglass, obliterating the stencil, and wrote 'Banksy woz ere' on the glass.

Melbourne media mourned the loss of the 'Little Diver' and lamented the 'vandalism' of the silver paint. But the event is more complex. First, what was done to the image (pouring paint behind the plexiglass) draws our attention to its covering as much as the image itself. It therefore invites us to think about the hypocrisy of protecting some works and not other, equally deserving ones. Second, the words 'Banksy woz ere' require analysis. The words literally point out what happened: a Banksy stencil *was* here but is no longer. The words also suggest that Banksy was once here in person. Finally, they evoke the famous 'Kilroy was here' of the 1970s, written by anonymous graffiti writers all over the world.

The 'Little Diver' stencil was later restored to Melbourne, albeit in thoroughly postmodern fashion. In 2010, local street artist Phoenix placed a paste-up version of the image exactly where Banksy's had been. Phoenix also created a second version in another laneway and a further replacement for the original replica when it faded.

Screwing plexiglass into a wall in order to preserve an artwork (and the value it adds to a property or an area) might meet with derision from street artists. But such acts seem mild in comparison with those who remove artworks from their original location in order to sell them on the private market. In 2007, a Banksy rat was cut out of a wall in London, and in 2008 a section of wall with a Banksy image on it was removed using a power saw in Kingston, Jamaica; it appeared for sale on eBay (without finding a buyer).

The removal was videoed and an account of its removal can be found on the website 'The Afflicted Yard'. In recent years there has been much discussion (and condemnation) of the removal of these works. However, it is clear that a definite trend had begun.

In 2010, a wall in Los Angeles painted in the run-up to the Academy Awards (when Banksy's film *Exit Through the Gift Shop* was nominated for 'Best Documentary Film') was removed, again by power saw. In 2012, a man removed a Banksy known as 'Sperm Alarm' from a wall in central London and offered it for sale on eBay for £17,000.

And, since then, there has been the saga of the Banksy work on the side wall of a cut-price shop, Poundland, in Whymark Avenue, Wood Green. The work appeared in May 2012. It was placed low down on Poundland's wall and depicted a small boy bent over a sewing machine, making bunting for the upcoming Diamond Jubilee celebrations (and which would no doubt do double duty a few months later when the Olympic Games would be hosted in London). A string of plastic bunting stretched up from the stenciled image and was attached to the wall.

The appearance of the work caused great excitement. People rushed to photograph it. Someone removed the plastic bunting; a friend told me he heard a man say he was taking it as a souvenir. Within a few days, plexiglass had been placed over it (see Plate 14). The location became so popular as a destination that Transport For London staff placed a sign in the foyer of Turnpike Lane station, the nearest Underground stop to Whymark Avenue, giving directions to Poundland 'if you are looking for Banksy'.

In February 2013, locals noticed that scaffolding swathed in plastic sheeting covered the site of Poundland's Banksy. News soon leaked out that the image had been cut from the wall. It turned up under the name of 'Slave Labor (Bunting Boy)', listed for auction at Fine Art Auctions Miami in the Modern, Contemporary and Street Art sale, with a starting bid of $400,000 USD and a suggested price range of $500–700,000. Poundland issued a statement saying that they were not responsible for the work's removal. The auction house issued a statement saying that they were selling the work with all necessary authority to do so. The FBI asked the British police to investigate the circumstances in which the work came to be offered for sale. Shortly before auction, the Banksy was removed from sale. Most commentators speculated that the building owner (as distinct from Poundland, the tenants) had authorised the work's removal. The result was a public shambles and a much-loved street artwork being lost to the public sphere. At the time of writing, 'Slave Labour' has reappeared: it is being offered for auction by the Sincura Auction Group, at a private auction in London on 2 June 2013. The auction group stated that the work has been 'sensitively restored'; Alan Strickland, a councillor for Wood Green, said he would continue the fight to have the artwork returned to Whymark Avenue.

When a situational artwork is taken from a wall using power tools and then sold for profit, how should we describe such an act? Is it 'removal' – like a version of the buff? Is it greed? Is it *theft*? We might initially say that an uncommissioned artwork has no owner and thus cannot be capable of being stolen. Yet the individual who in 2012 cut Banksy's 'Sperm Alarm' from a wall in London was charged with handling stolen goods and attempting to convert criminal property.

Such moments indicate that there are shifts taking place in how we view street art. Putting glass on top of an artwork attempts to freeze something that was intended to be ephemeral. Prosecuting individuals who remove street artworks from walls indicates that the situational artwork is in the process of accruing value in law *as property* even as the law continues to categorise it as an offence *against property*.

There is much that we have to thank Banksy for in the short but intense history of street art. But, most of all, his artworks provoke reactions, which demonstrate that the encounter with situational art is always in flux. Yesterday's vandalism may yet be tomorrow's heritage.

Chapter 6

# Transformations

## Urban imagination in the public city

Having travelled through the cityscape, considering various dimensions of the ways in which we encounter situational art, there is also a story to be told about *transformation*. I have visited London many times over the last decade as part of my research. Each time, I arrive at Heathrow after a long flight from Melbourne and hail a taxi to wherever I am staying. The driver almost always asks: 'What are you doing while you are in London? Holiday? Work?' I always answer, 'I am here doing research on street art.' In 2003, the driver said, 'Never heard of it.' In 2005, the response was: 'Street art – that's like graffiti, isn't it?' Three years later, in 2008, the driver said: 'Street art – have you met Banksy then?' In 2010, the driver nodded judiciously and said, 'Some of that stuff's not bad, especially that Banksy'. Finally, in 2012, the driver commented: 'Oh yeah, I saw some of that street art on *The Apprentice*.'[1]

This trajectory indicates a shift in the popular conception of situational art: by the spectator, the artist and the city itself. Graffiti and street art have moved from relative obscurity into a more mainstream cultural position thanks to a decade in which they were subjected to the market forces of the art world, the judgments of criminal law and intellectual property, the machinations of local government policy, and the forces of commodification in fashion, music, publishing and architecture.

How do private and public tastes change? How has street art moved from a minoritarian practice in the early 2000s to mainstream popularity in 2012? This bespeaks the evolution of *taste* as a dynamic aspect of the cultural field (Bourdieu 1984; Bourdieu and Johnson 1993). This evolution may have far-reaching social effects including changes in school curriculum, the generation of profit in the art market, changes in curatorial practice as galleries adapt to

1 Shortly before this fieldwork trip, the British version of the television series, *The Apprentice* (in which individuals who aspire to success in the world of business compete for an apprenticeship with a well-known executive) screened an episode in which the competitors were informed that street art was one of the 'next big things' in the art world and were set the task of selecting artists and artworks for a pop-up show, in order to sell artworks to collectors. The show featured the artists Pure Evil, Nathan Bowen, Copyright and James Jessop.

the difficulties of exhibiting work originally meant for the street, and architectural developments incorporating graffiti and street art into urban design.[2] The street aesthetic has helped to give birth to new ways of thinking about art, architecture, education and many others domains of contemporary life.

Thinking about how public imagination has evolved through architecture, education and fashion is important for a number of reasons. First, the contemporary meaning of graffiti and street art will have changed – both for me as a researcher and for anyone reading this book – as opposed to five or ten years ago (as it has for London's taxi drivers). We cannot go back to a time when these cultural practices were still obscure and marginal. Second, for graffiti writers and street artists, this 'mainstreaming' now means that it is possible for them to make a living from their artwork. Although critics decry the commercialisation of graffiti and street art, for many artists it has made them financially sustainable. It is also symbolically important that an illegal activity is highly valued in other spheres. Taste, in this regard, is making the criminalisation of situational art look ever more anachronistic. It no longer seems implausible to imagine artists citing cultural attitudes as part of their legal defence or as an element mitigating sentence. Nor is it impossible to imagine that there might be a debate, at some point in the future, as to whether uncommissioned words and images should be illegal in the first place.

Taste, then, has effects that extend far beyond the aesthetic. This chapter considers ways in which such transformations in public taste come about.

2 In respect of art education in schools, the curriculum from 2010–14 for secondary schools in Victoria suggests that students might choose to research the differences between early street artists (such as Keith Haring, Jean-Michel Basquiat and Barry McGee) and those of contemporary times (such as Blu, Banksy, Faile and Sixarte). That street art now occupies a place in the mainstream educational landscape is also evidenced by the fact that students can purchase a standardised essay on 'street art in museums and cities' from an online essay mill: www.essaysprofessors.com/samples/Art/museums-and-street-art-in-cities.html. Key moments in the art market's relationship with street art would include the sale at Sotheby's in February 2007 of Banksy's 'Bombing Middle England' for £102,000 and the exorbitant prices subsequently achieved at the October 2007 Bonhams auction in London. These sales helped to create the 'art bubble', which deflated somewhat over the next few years as the global financial crisis took effect in the art world (Editorial, 2009). Street art, however, had achieved – and managed to retain – a validated position within auction houses, many of which (such as Artcurial in Paris, and Bonhams and Dreweatts in London) began 'urban art' lists. Museums and galleries have sought to do justice to the ephemeral and street-based nature of situational art, by staging live painting events as part of exhibitions of street art, projecting images onto walls, and offering spaces for artists to sticker within the gallery (all of these were incorporated into the National Gallery of Australia's street art exhibition, 'Space Invaders', in 2010; the Tate Modern in London created a walking tour of the surrounding area and offered temporary wall space for visitors to tag). In terms of architectural innovation, some house deigns have utilised a street art or graffiti aesthetic: in Melbourne, on Victoria Street in Fitzroy a development of apartments features wild-style writing along the lower levels of its outer walls, while in Sutton Place in Carlton, the 'Hive Graffiti Apartments' created outer walls sculpted into the shape of tags.

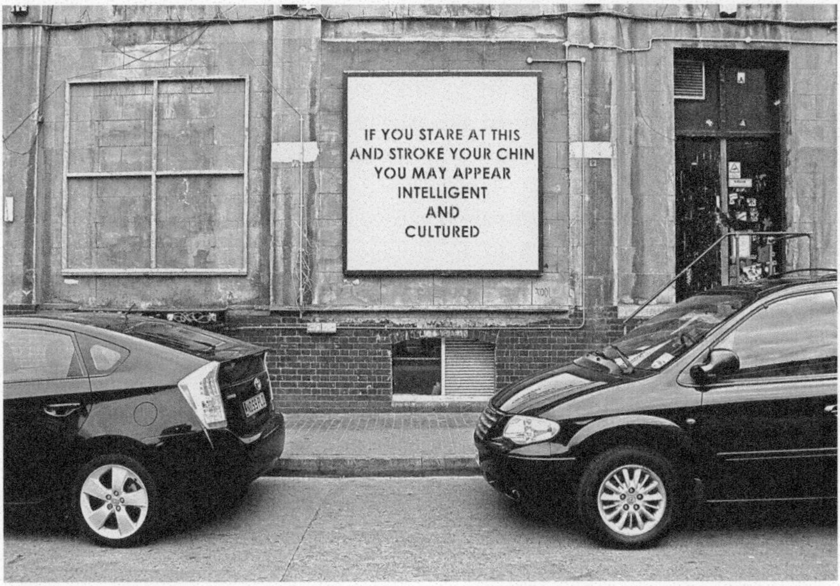


*Figure 6.1* Mobstr, London 2012. Photograph © Alison Young.

It shows how taste may be created and structured (even if it is a taste for something that is illegal or which derives its meaning and affective charge from illegality). And the aura of edginess that still attaches to street art means that, for some, the acquisition of a liking for its aesthetic allows the spectator to construct herself as 'cool' (a dynamic satirised in one of Mobstr's street pieces in London).

As Bourdieu notes, definitions of 'culture' are associated with the holdings of major museums, which are assumed to purchase and display art of the greatest cultural and artistic value. In relation to situational art, however, national and state museums have shown a somewhat conflicted attitude. On the one hand, artworks by José Parlá and Swoon have been bought by the Museum of Modern Art (MoMA) in New York City, while Paul Insect and Miss.Tic are part of the collection of the Victoria and Albert Museum in London. Several museums have held significant exhibitions of graffiti and street art.[3] On the other hand, there has been a certain hesitation to fully embrace the art of the street. Thus, although the Tate Modern put on a high-profile show, it actually involved only six artworks confined to the exterior façade of

3 The key exhibitions to note are: 'Art in the Streets' (2011) at the Museum of Contemporary Art (MoCA) in Los Angeles; 'Street Art' (2008) at Tate Modern in London; 'Space Invaders' (2010) at the National Gallery of Australia in Canberra; and 'Né Dans La Rue' ('Born in the Street') (2009) at Fondation Cartier and 'Au Delà du Street Art' ('Beyond Street Art)' (2013)

the museum's own building (enormous and impressive though they were) and while the National Gallery of Australia's exhibition of street artworks was a significant moment in indicating a shift in the status of the art form within Australia, the exhibition featured a relatively small proportion of its collection of street artworks and the show was confined to a small space within the museum.

National and state museums are regarded as the gatekeepers and guardians of cultural heritage. For them to engage with graffiti and street art is significantly validating, and they will likely have played a major role in communicating the street aesthetic to the public.[4] However, of perhaps further reaching impact have been the activities of private or commercial galleries. While museums such as the Tate bestow aesthetic authority on graffiti and street art, private galleries augment cultural value in two significant ways. First, there is the commercial value attached to displayed artworks. As a commercial enterprise, a private gallery generates a metonymic association through which artworks acquire a sense of value (cultural and financial) which, in turn, is transferred to the purchaser of the artwork. Dickens (2009) documented the two commercial enterprises run by D*Face: the first, the Outside Institute, never became financially viable because it was located in an area in which there was little street art and because the street art aesthetic had not yet made an impact on the public imagination. D*Face explained:

> I ran it for a year. I lived and breathed it. I lost my hair because of it, and that's no joke. It was a nightmare from beginning to end. It was far too big a beast for me to run on my own and I literally didn't leave the place for a year. I was trying to do my own work and I was trying to run a gallery, I was trying to organise the artists, I was trying to make the sales. It was an absolute nightmare . . . But we had a brilliant time doing it and we were the first gallery – probably the first gallery in Europe to be doing anything like that, on the scale that we were doing it. We were the first gallery to get [the artist] SEEN: the 'Godfather of Graffiti' had never been to London . . . We put his first show on and had absolute chaos because of it. We did a lot of cool things.

at the Musée de la Poste in Paris. See also a panel discussion held at MoMA in New York in January 2013, hailed by local writer Emily Colucci as the moment when MoMA 'made a serious step forward in recognising the cultural importance of graffiti, writing and hip hop': see Colucci (2013).

4 The 'Art in the Streets' exhibition and the NGA's 'Space Invaders' exhibition both met with hostile media coverage. The Los Angeles press denounced the exhibition as responsible for an increase in property crime perpetrated by featured artists and visitors to the show: see Blankstein, Winton and Ng (2011). When 'Space Invaders' toured to Melbourne, the *Herald Sun* criticised the NGA's involvement in an exhibition that featured criminal activity: see Craven (2011).

D*Face's second enterprise, StolenSpace, has enjoyed cultural and financial success from the outset. It is located in the heart of London's street art scene (near the Truman Brewery site) and has benefited from the city's newfound respect for street art as a cultural practice (on the Outside Institute and StolenSpace, see Dickens 2009).

Second, private galleries have extended public awareness of the cultural value of street art through their sheer proliferation. Once street art started to snowball commercially in the art world, a great many private galleries sprang up solely for the purpose of selling street art. These galleries often presented themselves as user-friendly and egalitarian in ways that old-fashioned galleries associated with the fine arts were not. One gallerist said that people feel welcome viewing street art because they have seen it on the street (as opposed to a traditional art space): 'They feel that this is their street, this is their artwork, so when they see something similar through the window of a gallery, they go "Oh, it's there too. Let's go have a look"'.[5]

Through museums and private galleries, then, street art has acquired three core cultural values: a sense of heritage, an egalitarian ethos and profitability. A similarly paradoxical combination can be seen in the way that street art has been bought and sold over the decade. In the early 2000s, artworks were initially traded among artists (such as at the Seesaw get-togethers in Melbourne parks). Then there were small-scale events such as Finders Keepers in Shoreditch, London, where D*Face, Dave the Chimp and Mysterious Al painted on scavenged detritus and displayed the results for one night, after which they would be offered to the public (see Dickens 2009). Many artists used 'drops'; that is, they left artworks in public for people to find and take home.[6] The possibility that an individual might remove an artwork has always existed with street artists expressing varying opinions about the acquisitive practices of their fans. Some feel that the desire to keep a piece of art is entirely understandable, whereas others argue that removal of a work deprives others of the chance of enjoying it. Pure Evil said:

> If you do stuff on the street it's going to get gone: someone's going to take it, or it's going to get destroyed pretty fast. But that's always been the kind of consideration, it's always been quite a zen thing to leave stuff on the street.

5 Swoon also commented that she enjoyed doing street art because it provided her with an opportunity to interact with people who might feel excluded from the perceived elitism of a contemporary art gallery.

6 Adam Neate in London is the artist most associated with this practice. Over the course of several years, Neate left thousands of works around the streets of London. In 2008, during the course of one night, he and a team of assistants left 1,000 works for members of the public to find (or not). The event is documented in Neate and MacKinnon (2009).

Removing an artwork for the purposes of selling it has attracted much greater criticism. The practice of tearing down pasted-up artworks, chipping off glued-on mosaics, or even (as discussed in the case of some Banksy images) using power tools to remove whole sections of wall, began in earnest once street art acquired financial value. Artworks were no longer something simply to be looked at on the street, or removed for personal possession, they were objects to be bought and sold in myriad ways and at hugely varying price points. Santa's Ghetto (an annual pre-Christmas exhibition and sales event begun by Banksy and Steve Lazarides in 2002) provided one of the spurs for this, as did the periodic releases of prints by Banksy and others through Pictures on Walls (POW), a screen-printing company set up by Lazarides and a small number of friends. Both Santa's Ghetto and POW were ostensibly about encouraging the availability of affordable art.[7] Ellsworth-Jones (2012) recounted how punters keen to buy Banksy prints through POW would queue overnight or spend hours on the Internet hitting the 'refresh' button in the hope of securing a limited-edition print. Dickens (2009) described the frenzy that accompanied Banksy's 'Barely Legal' exhibition in Los Angeles in 2007: 'Within minutes of the first print . . . being put on the POW website for sale, server activity . . . went from 2mbps to 172mbps instantly' (363). Despite the obvious size of the market, POW maintained its commitment to affordable art. London-based artist Eine, who worked as a printmaker at POW, commented that Banksy 'always wanted to keep [prices] as low as possible and [prints] started off at £150 and they slowly went up to £500. But they always tripled at least in price on the secondary market the day after'.

This secondary market was swift to develop. At first, it was confined to the exchange of artworks among enthusiasts who frequented websites such as eBay Banksy and Wallkandy. One collector noted that these sites started out with a strong sense of community, with members sharing information about upcoming print releases and freely exchanging opinions about artworks, before this communitarian spirit was replaced by a profit motive:

> The forums started to have these rich boys who were very annoying, because we'd all been talking about 'will I buy this for 30 quid or that for 30 quid', and all of sudden it was like people were saying, 'oh, yeah, well, you know, I think I'll buy this, it's only £30,000, in fact I'll have two, as they're such an investment'. There had been some really interesting characters, like one student who . . . bought canvasses, all sorts, created a major collection in this country, one of the first big ones, and he made a massive fortune, and there was a really nice guy who lives in the countryside, who basically cashed in at the end of the bubble and he was able to buy a house. His portfolio, as it were, was absolutely unbelievable.

7 On Pictures on Walls, see Dickens (2009) and (2010).

> He'd managed to get several small originals [by major artists] because he was just there at the beginning. So there were people who made money, because it was incidental to their love of the art. What changed were these people coming in who were ripping us off for our knowledge, really, to make investments for their future.

Then art galleries began to participate in the secondary market. The Banksy show at Andipa Gallery in London in 2008 was a key event. Partly this was because it sold out all the works on display, but also, because it demonstrated – spectacularly – that Banksy's work could be separated from those individuals directly connected to Banksy. Until this point, Banksy's work could only be purchased through strictly controlled outlets (via the forums, Pictures On Walls, and Steve Lazarides, who was acting as Banksy's agent). The Andipa show sent a message to art collectors that Banksy's work was desirable, valuable and could be had without queuing overnight or maintaining a presence in online forums. On the contrary, they could be bought the old-fashioned way: by being the highest bidder.

Subsequent events produced even higher prices. In October 2006, Sotheby's achieved record prices for Banksy images. In 2007, at both Sotheby's and Bonhams, prices for Banksy works hit record levels (including £102,000 for 'Bombing Middle England'). While the market fixated on Banksy, other artists also began to sell for substantial sums (in 2006, Nick Walker's 'Moona Lisa' sold at Bonhams for £54,000, and Adam Neate's 'Suicide Bomber' at Sotheby's for £78,500). By the end of 2006, people were talking about a 'Banksy effect'.[8] Sales figures in 2007 indicated that an 'art bubble' was inflating street art just as it was fine art (artists who had previously painted on walls suddenly realised they could actually sell the same image on canvas). At the height of the bubble, buyers began 'flipping' artworks; that is, buying them at shows and on-selling them immediately (often on eBay or online forums). At the height of the bubble, according to one gallerist, it was possible to see:

> people flipping things in opening nights. One of my colleagues overheard someone . . . saying 'I own those two things over there, if you give me this for them you can have them now' . . . That kind of frenzy buying.

8 The phrase was used in a news report on CNN on 4 December 2006; transcript accessible online at http://transcripts.cnn.com/TRANSCRIPTS/0612/04/ywt.01.html (accessed on 6 March 2013). In early 2007, the influential street art website Wooster Collective published a short piece analyzing the nature and impact of 'the Banksy effect', and endorsing it as overwhelmingly positive in introducing the general public to street art and allowing artists other than Banksy himself to benefit from the new-found market for street artworks. The piece can be found at http://www.woostercollective.com/post/the-banksy-effect (accessed on 6 March 2013).

> It's orgiastic and quite disgusting to see. It doesn't indicate long term collecting.[9]

In 2008, with prices still high, Eine noted the impact upon well-meaning enthusiasts who lacked financial resources:

> A print that was for £150 four years ago is now £6,000. So it's a guaranteed easy way of making money; spend £500 one day, the next week collect £2,000. Even if you hate it. Even if you've never heard of him, you've got no idea what he does, where else can you be guaranteed to make £2,000. So in that respect it's turned into a bit of a monster. You know, we weren't able to sell to the people that really wanted to buy it and stick it on their walls.

When the bubble burst, thanks to the global financial crisis, sales figures plummeted for many artists. However, some gallerists and auction houses indicated that the downturn was merely a return to what was realistic for young artists in an emerging field. One staff member in a London auction house described the transition from 2007 to 2012 as follows:

> Everyone was jumping on the bandwagon in 2007 and 2008, and everyone was a stencil artist and all sorts of people, galleries and dealers, auction houses included, were selling work by artists that were not particularly well established and very much just part of the trend. So what's happened really is quite interesting: the good ones have stayed and the prices are now steadily increasing; well, they leveled off, and now are steadily increasing, and that's gone all the way through the field from the artists and the galleries and the dealers and the agents . . . So I think for the markets it's a very positive move, because what we've got left are the best.

One gallerist told me that the bubble had not inflated street art to the same extent that it had elsewhere (regarding the work of Damien Hirst, for example) and so the collapse was felt less acutely: 'everything quietened down for a while but [street art] didn't go away and the market re-corrected with steady sales.' Not all gallerists would be so phlegmatic: some of the smaller galleries set up in the heady days of 2007 did not survive the downturn (one individual commented: '[the scene] lost a lot of galleries and dealers and agents, but most

9 A number of gallerists interviewed for my research stated that they had instituted strategies to identify those profiteering through artworks, such as monitoring websites to determine who of their clients was flipping artworks; and refusing to sell multiple copies of prints to clients (a popular means of increasing prices was to buy multiple prints, keep one, and sell on the rest using the demand available on online forums from those who had missed out on the initial sale of the edition).

of those that have gone were very much new galleries that just literally set up with a number of new street artists').

Unlike many art forms, the myriad means of exchanging, selling and displaying street art meant that it could potentially appeal *to everyone*. In Chapter 1, the notion of making 'art for everyone' was discussed as a key motivation for graffiti writers and street artists; here, however, this idea resurfaces as a selling point and a symptom of street art's inevitable commodification. For those with no money, street art can be found in the street (or ripped from the walls). For those on a tight budget, print releases offer something 'like' an original artwork (even if that means getting one of an edition of 500). For those with deep pockets, 'urban art' could be absorbed into existing collections on a more or less equal footing with works by established artists (and so works by Banksy suddenly appeared on lists of holdings alongside those of Picasso and Van Gogh).

Not all taste-making is so obviously connected with money. The Internet played a crucial role in familiarising the public imagination with street art. It helped to create a networked community of street art practitioners, fans, critics and collectors through a range of specialised websites and its capacity more generally for connectedness and information-sharing. In the late 1990s and early 2000s, very few websites featured situational art; those that did were mostly graffiti-related (such as Art Crimes). By 2005, there were images of street art on Flickr, videos of people making street art on YouTube, and specialised sites such as Stencil Revolution and Wooster Collective had attracted thousands of readers. Those numbers will have multiplied again: there are now hundreds of websites featuring street art, including influential blogs like Vandalog, Unurth, Juxtapoz and Arrested Motion. Some sites exist in information-sharing mode; some feature only images; others provide short essays in addition to photographs. Locality drives content for some (such as Hooked, which concentrates on street art in East London, or Invurt and Land of Sunshine, which tend to feature artwork in Melbourne, or Fitzroy Flasher, focusing on artwork found in the suburb of Fitzroy, and Melbourne Street Art 86, which showcases artworks found along the 86 tram route). For others, the aim is more global. Juxtapoz, although American, features articles about street art events in Italy and Norway; Wooster Collective quickly expanded its purview from a single neighbourhood in New York (in which its authors lived) to the entire world. Vandalog is probably the most successful global street art website: it features images and short essays on international street art events, works and issues, and has a team of contributors based in New York, London, Melbourne and other locations. Street artists also maintain their own websites, providing information about artworks for sale and upcoming shows.

This online proliferation has meant that the experience of viewing street art is no longer confined to the encounter with uncommissioned art in urban space. Urban space has become virtual space. As the Italian artist Alice

Pasquini commented: 'It's funny how this is internet art most of the time.' A perhaps unintended consequence is that the spectator often views street art in an environment utterly alienated from the artwork's location. Website authors would no doubt encourage individuals to seek out artworks in their physical location, but it is undeniable that many readers will regard viewing online images as sufficient. Certainly, the Internet makes it possible to see artwork on the other side of the world (when very few people can afford to buy a plane ticket for the purposes of viewing art in other cities); but then again, given the ways in which street art is linked to its physical location in public space, there is something of an irony in the fact that it can be viewed so readily in a space that is purely virtual.

Walking tours are another prominent component in the taste-making process. Such tours have both built upon and helped to build public interest in street. Cities around the world offer a range of options from small-scale tours (among friends) to large public tours. Some are free of charge (see, for example, the Wooster Collective's walking tours of the Lower East Side and SoHo in New York in 2005). Others require payment and are run by a local council or business. Whatever the format, walking tours trade upon the notion that walking-and-looking is an unmediated phenomenon. Participants are encouraged to feel that they inhabit the street in a manner identical to the citizen who happens upon an artwork in urban space (much as a visitor to a zoo is encouraged to look at the exhibits without noticing the bars that separate non-human animal from animal). Walking tours also rely upon the experience of *walking*, that is, they emphasise the physical experience of being in public space as creating a subject-position radically different from that of looking at online websites.[10]

This orchestration of experience is replicated on a larger scale in the street art festival, such as Outpost!, held in Sydney in November 2011 (see Plate 15). Some have been so successful they have taken place over a period of years including the Stencil Art Festival in Melbourne, Living Walls in Atlanta, Pow Wow in Hawai'i, FAME in Grottaglie in Italy, and Nuart in Stavanger in Norway. For a weekend, a week, a month, street art is displayed, workshops are held, discussion forums formed and the city is also reflected back to its citizens (see Plate 16). At FAME, visitors are presented with a map showing the locations of newly created artworks (as well as those from previous years). Visitors are encouraged to walk, cycle or drive around the town. Since Grottaglie has over seventy artworks now on display the map presents something of a challenge. How many works can one see in forty-eight hours? Some seek to manage the task by viewing only the newly installed works;

10 A viewpoint that many, post-de Certeau, would endorse, and which has animated much of my own research. Note that some tours seek to combine the virtual and the actual, producing a subject position that experiences public space but is driven by a website or a phone app that dictates the itinerary and makes sense of the experience, also allowing it to be relived as a virtual memory after the tour is over.

others search out works by their favourite artists and ignore walls painted by others. Festival attendees are usually comprised of collectors, gallerists, enthusiasts, die-hard fans, curious locals and others who come for the social side of things (the young Italians lured by FAME's all-night party did not seem to care much for street art). Festivals are also attended by artists seeking gallery representation or looking to enhance their reputation by painting walls on location.

While cities such as Melbourne and London have sufficiently large populations to guarantee participation in events and viewing of artworks, in smaller towns such as Stavanger or Grottaglie festivals attract more outsiders than locals. The prospect of a boost to the local economy provides an incentive to host such an event and turn a blind eye to any possible contraventions of the law (if contributing artists or visitors put up illicit artworks). The street art festival, then, demonstrates in microcosm the ways in which street art traverses the cultural field and the range of ways in which it is presently consumed, acquired, travelled to, learned about, bought, sold and enjoyed as an aesthetic object.

Given the extensive popularity enjoyed by street art as a result of these transformations in taste and in cultural status, it may seem strange to then raise the question of its demise. However, people have been pondering the 'death of street art' for years. At the FAME festival in Grottaglie, in September 2011, an arts journalist said to me: 'Well, street art is dead, anyway. All that's happening now is mural projects.' On another occasion, I was told the story of a well-known street artist who, in some circles, prefers not to discuss his street art background, emphasising instead that he is a 'contemporary artist'. Others have been wondering whether capitalism killed off street art: certainly one night, as I watched a television advertisement showing a car prowling through city streets past artworks in the style of Rone and M-City, I found myself wondering whether street art *might* be dead.

In some ways, it would seem to be an empirically unfounded suggestion. Hundreds of artists continue to venture out each night painting, postering, stickering and writing on the walls of cities around the world. The aesthetic of graffiti and street art clearly has an appeal that many feel transcends consumption. So, of course, street art is not (yet) dead. However, as tensions and complications have attached themselves onto the very idea of situational art, the repeated claim that 'street art is dead' indicates an unease, or anxiety, about what it is today, and what it might yet become in the future.

What, then, is this unease, or anxiety? Despite the increase in public interest in street art, there is a clear perception among many of its practitioners and supporters that *something has been lost*.[11] That street art may soon be

11 See, for example, the article by CDH, a practicing street artist, in which he laments street art as having lost its political edge, its authenticity and its passionate commitment to an economy of the gift: in CDH (2013) forthcoming.

considered one aspect of 'contemporary art' would support the notion that it has lost something of its critical or contestatory stance (its do-it-yourself emphasis and willingness to exhibit art outside mainstream art institutions) and may be in the process of being subsumed like other art movements in history. Alternatively, we might say that going mainstream has led to a reduced appreciation of street art's history, nuances and intentions. In other words, a triumph of surface over depth that goes against the professed aim of street artists in making 'art for everyone' (or gallerists attempting to avoid the staid elitism of the art establishment).

Another aspect of this relates to the claim that street art has lost its critical edge; that street art no longer seeks to contest law, authority and status. If this claim is correct, then street art has been co-opted by the system it sought to challenge. But such co-optation cannot be clearly identified. Councils still buff walls; homeowners still paint over tags; newspapers still fulminate against 'vandals' as if our cities were already burning to the ground. Writers and artists continue to be arrested and subjected to the exemplary jurisprudence of the criminal law. So where, then, does this claim of co-optation come from?

As with the other variants of the perception that something has been lost, this account displaces the anxiety occasioned by transformation. Transformation forces an acknowledgement that *art changes*. It changes social arrangements and it itself changes. In the midst of such processes of transformation and the resulting anxieties as to loss, how should we understand street art – not street art as it was in 2002 or 2003 but street art as a process, a movement in flux and undergoing change even as it itself evolves? Perhaps we should approach it as art existing continually in paradox: it is an art of contradiction, of encounter. It is an art existing always *in its situation*, and the situation of street art in public space (actual or virtual) is one that necessitates an encounter irrevocably with authority. When we encounter an uncommissioned artwork or word in public space it is not possible to view it as other than precariously present in public space. When we encounter an 'urban artwork' in an auction house or a 'street artwork' in a museum, it brings with it a history of artists working without commission or permission, at risk of arrest, offering images to the city in a way that is always subject to rejection as much as pleasure (and a rejection that often results in the utter destruction of the artwork, not simply a critical review or a raised eyebrow). Even in the gallery, the auction house and on the Internet, the situational artwork speaks of the question of authority in public spaces and in the urban imagination. As such, it draws our attention to the ways in which the citizen's right to public spaces (online, in the gallery, in the street) is always contingent, subject to reduction or revocation. It draws our attention to the ways in which uses of public space are both authorised and unauthorised.

While this chapter has focused on the transformation of street art's cultural value, in many ways 'transformation', broadly conceived, is a theme that has permeated this entire book. Preceding chapters have recounted instances of transformation in which the topography of the street has been converted into the architecture of a gallery; and the individuals who have installed street artworks in these settings have been redefined by the law as criminals rather than as artists. With particular artworks and artists, activity that would otherwise be called vandalism has been discursively categorised as art, accessible only to those wealthy enough to pay high sums of money. And in the graffiti management strategies of local councils and the statutes enacted against graffiti, we have seen the ideology of private property and ownership rights transformed into social policy that perpetuates the territorialisation of cities and reduces the possible forms of citizenship available to their inhabitants. This book has travelled through the space of the cityscape attending to different aspects of the encounter with situational art; but it has also told a story about the *time* of street art, and how our encounter with it has changed, just as street art itself changes the ways in which we experience urban space.

Transformation, like movement through urban space, is not in itself problematic. The task at hand is to identify the interests served by the social, legal, economic and political forces acting upon the cityscape and the ways we talk about situational art. The fact that an exemplary jurisprudence converts minor property crime into an offence demanding a prison sentence or large fine indicates that the transformative processes at work when we think about situational art can have serious negative consequences for a group of individuals. The relentless repetition of tired catachreses such as 'vandalism' and 'broken windows' demonstrates the way in which something that could be thought of as art is being repeatedly excluded from the realm of aesthetics and restricted to the arena of petty crime, again with considerable negative consequences for those attempting to add to the amenity of urban spaces by practicing what they see as an art form.

Situational art has been subjected to a regime of discursive practices that threaten to diminish its contributions to the life of the city. My aim, in this book, has been to point out the effects of those representational practices and to argue that it is time for us to leave them behind. I do not mean to suggest that we should simply flip categories of discourse such that all illicit words and images in urban space automatically are to be categorised as 'art', or that no-one should be prosecuted for engaging in street art or graffiti. Such an inversion would smack of an oppositional ideology and risk achieving no real social change. Instead, I suggest that we seek a conversation between those who wish to 'protect' their property and those who experience a sense of entitlement to add to it; between those who want to adapt city spaces to their own ends and those who believe that the authority to do so is vested only in government agencies or through property ownership. It is not that we should ignore one position in favour of the other. It is not that the uncommissioned should win out over the authority of law. But my purpose is to ask: what is at stake, in both perspectives, in the refusal to entertain the views of the other side? Is it possible to move between both? Can we accept ownership and adaptive uses? Can we love both the experience of commissioned art *and* the enchanting, uncanny intervention that occupies a space belonging to another? If we can, it is along such lines that we might find that we are able to inhabit a public city that we have made our very own.

# Bibliography

Alexander, H. (2009) 'Graffiti Girl Wins Appeal against Jail', *The Age*, 4 March.

Amin, A. and Thrift, N. (2002) *Cities: Reimagining the Urban*, London: Polity Press.

Attoh, K.A. (2011) 'What Kind of a Right Is the Right to the City?', *Progress in Human Geography*, 35: 669–85.

Augé, M. (1995) *Non-Places: Introduction to an Anthropology of Supermodernity*, London: Verso Books.

Austin, J. (2001) *Taking the Train: How Graffiti Art Became an Urban Crisis in New York City*, New York: Columbia University Press.

—— (2004) 'Two Tagged Stories from the USA' in No Author (ed.) *King Size: A Project About Tags, Diy-Craft & Subcultural Globalization*, Norhaven: Adams.

—— (2010) 'More to See Than a Canvas in a White Cube: For an Art in the Streets', *City*, 14(1/2): 33–47.

Banet-Weiser, S. (2011) 'Convergence on the Street', *Cultural Studies*, 25(4/5): 641–58

Banksy (2002) *Existstencillism*, London: Weapons of Mass Distraction.

—— (2003) *Banging Your Head Against a Brick Wall*, London: Weapons of Mass Distraction.

—— (2005a) *Banksy: Wall and Piece*, London: Random House.

—— (2005b) *Cut It Out*, London: Weapons of Mass Distraction.

Barrell, A. (2000) *Medieval Scotland*, Cambridge: Cambridge University Press.

Bartholome, L. and Snyder, P. (2004) 'Is It Philosophy or Pornography? Graffiti at the Dinosaur Bar-B-Que', *The Journal of American Culture*, 27(1): 86–98.

Bell, D.A. and de-Shalit, A. (2011) *The Spirit of Cities: Why the Identity of a City Matters in a Global Age*, Princeton, NJ: Princeton University Press.

Benjamin, W. (trans. R. Tiedemann) (1999) *The Arcades Project*, Cambridge, MA: Harvard University Press.

Bennett, J. (2001) *The Enchantment of Modern Life: Attachments, Crossings and Ethics*, Princeton, NJ: Princeton University Press.

—— (2005) *Empathic Vision*, Palo Alto, CA: Stanford University Press.

—— (2010) *Vibrant Matter: A Political Ecology of Things*, Durham, NC: Duke University Press.

Berg, A. (2004) 'Graffiti Is Vandalism', in No Author (ed.) *King Size: A Project About Tags, Diy-Craft & Subcultural Globalization*, Norhaven: Adams.

Blankstein, A., Winton, R. and Ng, D. (2011) 'Tagging Outside an L.A. Street Art Exhibit Fuels Debate', *Los Angeles Times*, 20 April 2013.

Blomley, N. (2004a) 'Un-Real Estate: Proprietary Space and Public Gardening', *Antipode*, 36(4): 614–41.

—— (2004b) *Unsettling the City: Urban Land and the Politics of Property*, New York: Routledge.

—— (2008) 'Enclosure, Common Right and the Property of the Poor', *Social & Legal Studies*, 17(3): 311–31.

—— (2011) *Rights of Passage: Sidewalks and the Regulation of Public Flow*, New York: Routledge.

Borden, L. (2000) 'Speaking the City: Skateboarding Subculture and Recompositions of the Urban Realm', *Research in Urban Sociology*, 5(1): 135–54.

Bou, L. (2005) *Street Art: The Spray Files*, New York: Collins Design.

Bourdieu, P. (trans. R. Nice) (1984) *Distinction: A Social Critique of the Judgement of Taste*, Cambridge, MA: Harvard University Press.

Bourdieu, P. and Johnson, R. (1993) *The Field of Cultural Production: Essays on Art and Literature*, Cambridge: Polity Press.

Brighenti, A.M. (2009) *The Wall and the City*, Trento: Professional Dreamers.

—— (2010a) 'Lines, Barred Lines. Movement, Territory and the Law', *International Journal of Law in Context*, 6(3): 217–27.

—— (2010b) 'On Territorology', *Theory, Culture & Society*, 27(1): 52–72.

Brook, I. (2007) 'Aesthetic Aspects of Unauthorised Environmental Interventions', *Ethics, Place and Environment*, 10(3): 307–18.

Buchanan, R. and Johnson, R. (2009) 'Strange Encounters: Exploring Law and Film in the Affective Register', *Studies in Law, Politics and Society*, 46: 33–60.

Buck-Morss, S. (1991) *The Dialectics of Seeing: Walter Benjamin and the Arcades Project*, Boston: MIT Press.

Butler, C. (2012) *Henri Lefebvre: Spatial Politics, Everyday Life and the Right to the City*, London: Routledge.

Campbell, F. (2008) *Good Graffiti, Bad Graffiti? A New Approach to an Old Problem*, Wigan, UK: Environmental Campaigns Limited.

Careri, F. (2002) *Walkscapes: Walking as an Aesthetic Practice*, Barcelona: Editorial Gustavo Gili.

Carr, J. (2010) 'Legal Geographies – Skating around the Edges of the Law: Urban Skateboarding and the Role of Law in Determining Young People's Place in the City', *Urban Geography*, 31(7): 988–1003.

Carter, P. (2007) 'Public Space: Its Mythopoetic Foundations and the Limits of the Law', *Griffith Law Review*, 16: 430.

Castleman, C. (1984) *Getting Up: Subway Graffiti in New York*, Boston: MIT Press.

CDH (2013, forthcoming) 'Notes on the Commodification of Street Art', *Art Monthly Australia*, (June).

Certeau, M. de (trans. S. Rendall) (1984a) *The Practice of Everyday Life*, Berkeley: University of California Press.

—— (ed.) (1984b) 'Walking in the City', in *The Practice of Everyday Life*, Berkeley: University of California Press.

—— (1985) 'Practices of Space', in M. Blonsky (ed.) *On Signs*, Baltimore: Johns Hopkins University Press.

Chalfant, H. and Prigoff, J. (1987) *Spraycan Art*, New York: Thames and Hudson.

Chatterton, P. (2010) 'Seeking the Urban Common: Furthering the Debate on Spatial Justice', *City*, 14(6): 625–28.

Chiu, C. (2009) 'Contestation and Conformity', *Space and Culture*, 12(1): 25–42.

Cohen, S. (1972) *Folk Devils and Moral Panics*, St Albans: Paladin.

—— (1985) *Visions of Social Control: Crime, Punishment and Classification*, Cambridge: Polity Press.

Colucci, E. (2011) 'Who Is the Artist? Thoughts on Anonymous Street Art', *Hyperallergic*, 29 August, online at http://hyperallergic.com/33957/anonymous-street-art/

—— (2013) 'The Vandals are No Longer Too Hot to Handle at MoMA', *Hyperallergic*, 14 January, online at http://hyperallergic.com/63498/the-vandals-are-no-longer-too-hot-to-handle-at-moma/

Cook, P. (2011) 'When Edgy Turns Stodgy: Gentrification and the Angst of the Urban Under-Class', *Architectural Review*, 230(1375): 35.

Cooper, D. (2006) '"Sometimes a Community and Sometimes a Battlefield": From the Comedic Public Sphere to the Commons of Speakers' Corner', *Environment and Planning D*, 24(5): 753.

—— (2007) 'Opening up Ownership: Community Belonging, Belongings, and the Productive Life of Property', *Law & Social Inquiry*, 32(3): 625–64.

Cooper, M. and Chalfant, H. (1988) *Subway Art*, New York: Holt Paperbacks.

Craven, J. (2011) 'Government-Sponsored Graffiti Art Show Angers Campaigners', *Herald Sun*, 1 September.

Craw, P.J., Leland Jr, L.S., Bussell, M.G., Munday, S.J. and Walsh, K. (2006) 'The Mural as Graffiti Deterrence', *Environment and Behavior*, 38(3): 422–34.

Cresswell, T. (1997) 'Imagining the Nomad: Mobility and the Postmodern Primitive', *Space and Social Theory: Interpreting Modernity and Postmodernity*, 360–79.

—— (2006) 'The Right to Mobility: The Production of Mobility in the Courtroom', *Antipode*, 38(4): 735–54.

Cresswell, T. and Merriman, P. (2011) *Geographies of Mobilities: Practices, Spaces, Subjects*, Burlington, VT: Ashgate.

Croy, L. (2013) 'Police Target Graffiti Vandals,' *The West Australian*, 3 May.

Cunningham, S. (2012) *Melbourne*, Sydney: University of New South Wales Press.

Dallen, T. and Boyd, S. (2006) 'Heritage Tourism in the 21st Century: Valued Traditions and New Perspectives', *Journal of Heritage Tourism*, 1(1): 1–16.

Danysz, M. and Dana, M-N. (2010) *From Style Writing to Street Art: A Street Art Anthology*, Paris: Drago.

Davison, G. (2012) '"Keeping Dalston Different": Defending Place-Identity in East London', *Planning Theory & Practice*, 13(1): 47.

Del Nevo, M. (2011) *The Work of Enchantment*, New Brunswick, NJ: Transaction Publishers.

Delaney, D. (2003) *Law and Nature*, Cambridge: Cambridge University Press.

—— (2005) *Territory: A Short Introduction*, London: Wiley-Blackwell.

—— (2010) *The Spatial, the Legal and the Pragmatics of World-Making: Nomospheric Investigations*, London: Routledge.

Deleuze, G. (1977) 'Nomad Thought', *The New Nietzsche*: 142–9.

Deleuze, G. and Guattari, F. (1996) *What Is Philosophy?*, New York: Columbia University Press.

DeLillo, D. (1997) *Underworld*, New York: Scribner.

Derrida, J. (trans. Rand, R.) (1984) *Signéponge/ Signsponge*, New York: Columbia University Press.

Dew, C. (2007) *Uncommissioned Art: An A–Z of Australian Graffiti*, Melbourne: Melbourne University Press.

Dickens, L. (2002) '"Finders Keepers": Performing the Street, the Gallery and the Spaces In-Between', *Liminalities*, 4(1): 1–30.

—— (2009) *The Geographies of Post-Graffiti: Art Worlds, Cultural Economy and the City*, PhD thesis, Royal Holloway College, London.

—— (2010) 'Pictures on Walls? Producing, Pricing and Collecting the Street Art Screen Print', *City*, 14(1/2): 63–81.

Dickinson, A. (2010) 'Graffiti Artwork by Anthony Lister Commissioned by Property Owner Rubbed out by Brisbane City Council', *Courier Mail*, 14 September.

Dovey, K. (2010) *Becoming Places: Urbanism/ Architecture/ Identity/ Power*, London: Routledge.

—— (2011) 'Uprooting Critical Urbanism', *City*, 15(3–4): 347–54.

Dovey, K., Wood, S. and Woodcock, I. (2009) 'A Test of Character: Regulating Place-Identity in Inner-City Melbourne', *Urban Studies*, 46/1(2): 1–21.

Dovey, K., Woodcock, I. and Wollan, S. (2012) 'Placing Graffiti: Creating and Contesting Character in Inner-City Melbourne', *Journal of Urban Design*, 17(1): 21–41.

Drissel, D. (2011) 'Anarchist Punks Resisting Gentrification: Countercultural Contestations of Space in the New Berlin', *International Journal of the Humanities*, 8(10): 19–44.

Droney, D. (2010) 'The Business of "Getting Up": Street Art and Marketing in Los Angeles', *Visual Anthropology*, 23(2): 98–114.

Dubber, M.D. (2001) 'Policing Possession: The War on Crime and the End of Criminal Law', *The Journal of Criminal Law and Criminology*, 91(4): 829–996.

Editorial (2009) 'The Art-Market Bubble', *New Criterion*, 27(5): 2–3.

Ellsworth-Jones, W. (2012) *Banksy: The Man Behind the Wall*, London: St. Martin's Press.

Ferrell, J. (1994) *Confronting the Agenda of Authority: Critical Criminology, Anarchism, and Urban Graffiti*, Westport, CT: Praeger Publishers.

—— (1995) 'Urban Graffiti Crime, Control, and Resistance', *Youth & Society*, 27(1): 73–92.

—— (1996) *Crimes of Style: Urban Graffiti and the Politics of Criminality*, Boston: Northeastern University Press.

—— (1997) 'Youth, Crime, and Cultural Space', *Social Justice*, 24/4(70): 21–38.

—— (1998) 'Freight Train Graffiti: Subculture, Crime, Dislocation', *Justice Quarterly*, 15(4): 587–608.

Ferrell, J., Milovanovic, D. and Lyng, S. (2001) 'Edgework, Media Practices, and the Elongation of Meaning: A Theoretical Ethnography of the Bridge Day Event', *Theoretical Criminology*, 5(2): 177–202.

Ferrell, J. and Weide, R.D. (2010) 'Spot Theory', *City*, 14(1–2): 48–62.

Fleming, J. (2001) *Graffiti and the Writing Arts of Early Modern England*, Philadephia: University of Pennsylvania Press.

Foster, S.R. (2011) 'Collective Action and the Urban Commons', *Notre Dame Law Review*, 87(1).

Foucault, M. (trans. A. Sheridan) (1977) *Discipline and Punish*, New York: Pantheon.

Frederick, U.K. (2009) 'Revolution Is the New Black: Graffiti/Art and Mark-Making Practices', *Archaeologies*, 5(2): 210–37.

Ganz, N. and Manco, T. (2009) *Graffiti World: Street Art from Five Continents*, New York: Abrams.

Gastman, R. and Neelon, C. (2010) *The History of American Graffiti*, New York: Harper Design.

Gelber, K. (2006) 'Distracting the Masses: Art, Local Government and Freedom of Political Speech in Australia', *Law Text Culture*, 10: 195.

Giles, K. and Giles, M. (2010) 'Signs of the Times: Nineteenth–Twentieth Century Graffiti in the Farms of the Yorkshire Wolds', in J. Oliver and T. Neal (eds) *Wild Signs: Graffiti in Archaeology and History*, Oxford: Archaeopress.

Girard, R. (trans P. Gregory) (1977) *Violence and the Sacred*, Baltimore: Johns Hopkins University Press.

Gomez, M.A. (1992) 'The Writing on Our Walls: Finding Solutions through Distinguishing Graffiti Art from Graffiti Vandalism', *University of Michican Journal of Law Reform*, 26: 633.

Graham, N. (2011) *Lawscape: Property, Environment, Law*, London: Routledge.

Grant, C.(2012) 'Knitting a Nicer World', *The Hoopla*, 16 August, online at http://thehoopla.com.au/knitting-nicer-world/.

Grosz, E.A. (2008) *Chaos, Territory, Art: Deleuze and the Framing of the Earth*, New York: Columbia University Press.

Hall, S., Critcher C., Jefferson T., Clarke J. and Roberts B. (1978) *Policing the Crisis: Mugging, the State, and Law and Order*, London: MacMillan.

Halsey, M. and Young, A. (2002) 'The Meanings of Graffiti and Municipal Administration', *Australian and New Zealand Journal of Criminology*, 35(2): 165–86.

—— (2006) '"Our Desires Are Ungovernable": Writing Graffiti in Urban Space', *Theoretical Criminology*, 10(3): 275–306.

Hansen, N. (2005) *Rash*, Melbourne: Madman Entertainment.

Harcourt, B.E. (1998) 'Reflecting on the Subject: A Critique of the Social Influence Conception of Deterrence, the Broken Windows Theory, and Order-Maintenance Policing New York Style', *Michigan Law Review*, 97: 291.

Hardt, M. and Negri, A. (2009) *Commonwealth*, Cambridge, MA: Belknap Press.

Harris, J. (1995) 'Private and Non-Private Property: What Is the Difference?', *Law Quarterly Review*, 111: 421–44.

Harvey, D. (2006) *Spaces of Global Capitalism*, London: Verso Books.

—— (2011) 'The Future of the Commons', *Radical History Review*, 109: 101–7.

Haworth, B., Bruce, E. and Iveson, K. (2013) 'Spatio-Temporal Analysis of Graffiti Occurrence in an Inner-City Urban Environment', *Applied Geography*, 38: 53–63.

Hayward, K.J. (2012) 'Five Spaces of Cultural Criminology', *British Journal of Criminology*, 52(3): 441–62.

Hickey-Moody, A. and Malins, P. (2007) *Deleuzian Encounters: Studies in Contemporary Social Issues*, London: Palgrave Macmillan.

Higgins, C. (2013) 'Planning Cock Up on Trafalgar Square's Fourth Plinth', *The Guardian*, 4 May.

Hillyard, P., Sim, J., Tombs, S. and Whyte, D. (2004) '"Leaving a 'Stain Upon the Silence": Contemporary Criminology and the Politics of Dissent', *British Journal of Criminology*, 44(3): 369–90.

Holder, J.B. and Flessas, T. (2008) 'Emerging Commons', *Social & Legal Studies*, 17(3): 299–310.

Hollingsworth, M. (1994) *Patronage in Renaissance Italy: From 1400 to the Early Sixteenth Century*, London: John Murray.

Hughes, R. (1997) *American Visions: The Epic History of Art in America*, New York: Alfred A. Knopf.

Husak, D. (2008) *Overcriminalization: The Limits of the Criminal Law*, New York: Oxford University Press.

Iveson, K. (2006) 'Cities for Angry Young People? From Inclusion and Exclusion to Engagament in Urban Policy', in B. Gleeson and N. Snipe (eds) *Creating Child Friendly Cities*, London, Routledge.

—— (2007) *Publics and the City*, Oxford: Blackwell.

—— (2010) 'The Wars on Graffiti and the New Military Urbanism', *City*, 14(1/2): 115–34.

—— (2013) 'Cities within the City: Do-It-Yourself Urbanism and the Right to the City', *International Journal of Urban and Regional Research*, 37(3): 941–56.

Jackson, A. (2009) 'Graffiti Tags Help Police Put Names to Offenders', *The Age*, 22 December.

Jacob, K. (2008) *Street Art in Berlin*, Berlin: Jaron.

Jarvie, J. (2012) 'The Limits of Commissioned Street Art', *The Atlantic Cities*, 11 December.

Jenkins, S. (2007) 'In a War Zone Wide Awake: Jon Naar in New York C. 1973', in J. Naar (ed.) *The Birth of Graffiti*, Munich: Prestel Verlag.

Kane, S.C. (2009) 'Stencil Graffiti in Urban Waterscapes of Buenos Aires and Rosario, Argentina', *Crime, Media, Culture*, 5(1): 9–28.

Keenan, S. (2010) 'Subversive Property: Reshaping Malleable Spaces of Belonging', *Social & Legal Studies*, 19(4): 423–39.

Kramer, R. (2010) 'Moral Panics and Urban Growth Machines: Official Reactions to Graffiti in New York City, 1990–2005', *Qualitative Sociology*, 33(3): 297–311.

Lacayo, R. and Miranda, C.A. (2005) 'Takin' It to the Streets', *Time*, 166(17): 104–9.

Lanchester, J. (2012) *Capital*, London: Faber and Faber.

Lefebvre, H. (1996) *The Right to the City*, Oxford: Blackwell.

Lethem, J. (2003) *The Fortress of Solitude*, New York: Doubleday.

Leung, I.S. (2009) 'What Does "Recovery" Look Like in the Art World? Or, Surviving the Next Art Market Bubble', *Ctrl + P Journal of Contemporary Art*, September: 6–10.

Lewisohn, C. (2008) *Street Art: The Graffiti Revolution*, London: Tate.

Linebaugh, P. (2010) *Enclosures from the Bottom Up*, Durham: Duke University Press.

Linebaugh, P. and Rediker, M. (2000) *The Many-Headed Hydra: The Hidden History of the Revolutionary Atlantic*, Boston: Beacon Press.

Linn, K. (2007) *Building Commons and Community*, Oakland, CA: New Village Press.

Lorimer, H. (2011) 'Walking: New Forms and Spaces for Studies of Pedestrianism', in T. Cresswell and P. Merriman (eds), *Geographies of Mobilities : Practices, Spaces, Subjects*, Burlington, VT: Ashgate.

Loukaitou-Sideris, A. and Ehrenfeucht, I. (2009) *Sidewalks: Conflict and Negotiation over Public Space*, Cambridge, MA: MIT Press.

McAuliffe, C. (2012) 'Graffiti or Street Art? Negotiating the Moral Geographies of the Creative City', *Journal of Urban Affairs*, 34(2): 189–206.

—— (2013) 'Legal Walls and Professional Paths: The Mobilities of Graffiti Writers in Sydney', *Urban Studies*, 50(3): 518–37.

McCormick, C., Schiller, M., Schiller, S. and Seno, E. (2010) *Trespass: A History of Uncommissioned Urban Art*, Koln: Taschen.

MacDowall, L. (2006) 'In Praise of 70k: Cultural Heritage and Graffiti Style', *Continuum: Journal of Media & Cultural Studies*, 20(4): 471–84.

McGaw, J. (2008) 'Complex Relationships between *Détournement* and *Récupération* in Melbourne's Street (Graffiti and Stencil) Art Scene', *Architectural Theory Review*, 13(2): 222–39.

Mailer, N. (2009) *The Faith of Graffiti*, New York: Harper Collins.

Manco, T. (2002) *Stencil Graffiti*, New York: Thames & Hudson.

Massumi, B. (1992) *A User's Guide to Capitalism and Schizophrenia: Deviations from Deleuze and Guattari*, Boston: MIT Press.

—— (2002) *Parables for the Virtual: Movement, Affect, Sensation*, Durham: Duke University Press Books.

Meagher, S.M. (2007) 'Philosophy in the Streets', *City*, 11(1): 7–20.

Miéville, C. (2009) *The City & the City*, New York: Del Rey Ballantine Books.

—— (2012) *London's Overthrow*, London: Westbourne Press.

Millie, A. (2008) 'Anti-Social Behavior, Behavioural Expectations and an Urban Aesthetic', *British Journal of Criminology*, 48(3): 379–94.

—— (2011) 'Value Judgments and Criminalization', *British Journal of Criminology*, 51(2): 278–95.

Milun, K. (2011) *The Political Uncommons: The Cross-Cultural Logic of the Global Commons*, Farnham, England: Ashgate.

Mitchell, D. (2003) *The Right to the City: Social Justice and the Fight for Public Space*, New York: Guilford Press.

Mitchell, D. and Staeheli, L. (2006) 'Clean and Safe? Property Redevelopment, Public Space, and Homelessness in Downtown San Diego', in S. Low and N. Smith (eds) *The Politics of Public Space*, New York: Routledge.

Mitchell, J. (2008) 'What Public Presence? Access, Commons and Property Rights', *Social & Legal Studies*, 17(3): 351–67.

Morris, B. (2004) 'What We Talk About When We Talk About "Walking in the City"', *Cultural Studies*, 18(5): 675–97.

Naar, J. (2007) *The Birth of Graffiti*, New York: Prestel.

Nancy, J.-L. (1991) *Inoperative Community*, Minneapolis: University of Minnesota Press.

Neate, A. and MacKinnon, F. (2009) *The London Show*, London: Elms Lesters.

Netz, R. (2004) *Barbed Wire: An Ecology of Modernity*, Middletown, CT: Wesleyan University Press.

O'Malley, P. (2009) 'Theorizing Fines', *Punishment & Society*, 11(1): 67–83.

—— (2010) 'Simulated Justice: Risk, Money and Telemetric Policing', *British Journal of Criminology*, 50(5): 795–807.

Oliver, J. and Neal, T. (2010) *Wild Signs: Graffiti in Archaeology and History*, Oxford: Archaeopress.

Ostrom, E. (1990) *Governing the Commons: The Evolution of Institutions for Collective Action*, Cambridge: Cambridge University Press.

—— (2000) 'Collective Action and the Evolution of Social Norms', *The Journal of Economic Perspectives*, 14(3): 137–58.

—— (2008) 'The Challenge of Common Pool Resources', *Environment*, 50(4).

Papastergiadis, N. (2006) *Spatial Aesthetics*, London: Rivers Oram Press.

Papastergiadis, N. and Rogers, H. (1996) 'Parafunctional Spaces', *Art and the City*, London: Academy Group.

Papen, U. (2012) 'Commercial Discourses, Gentrification and Citizens' Protest: The Linguistic Landscape of Prenzlauer Berg, Berlin', *Journal of Sociolinguistics*, 16(1): 56–80.

Penalver, E.M. and Sonya, K. (2010) *Property Outlaws*, New Haven, CT: Yale University Press.

Perth Now (2009) 'Graffiti Penalties Set to Double', *Perth Now*, 31 December.

Philippopoulos-Mihalopoulos, A. (2007) *Law and the City*, New York: Routledge-Cavendish.

—— (2010a) 'Law's Spatial Turn: Geography, Justice and a Certain Fear of Space', *Law, Culture and the Humanities*, 7(2): 187–202.

—— (2010b) 'Spatial Justice: Law and the Geography of Withdrawal', *International Journal of Law in Context*, 6(3): 201–16.

—— (2013) 'Atmospheres of Law: Senses, Affects, Lawscapes', *Emotion, Space and Society*, 7: 35–44.

Philippopoulos-Mihalopoulos, A. and FitzGerald, S. (2008) 'From Space Immaterial: The Invisibility of the Lawscape', *Griffith Law Review*, 17(2): 438–53.

Pinder, D. (2011) 'Errant Paths: The Poetics and Politics of Walking', *Environment and Planning D: Society and Space*, 29: 672–92.

Pye, M. (1993) *Maximum City: The Biography of New York*, London: Sinclair-Stevenson.

Rancière, J. (trans. G. Rockhill) (2004) *The Politics of Aesthetics: The Distribution of the Sensible*, London: Continuum Publishing.

Reid, L. and Downey, B. (2008) *The Adventures of Darius and Downey and Other True Tales of Street Art as Told to Ed Zipco*, London: Thames & Hudson.

Riggle, N.A. (2010) 'Street Art: The Transfiguration of the Commonplaces', *Journal of Aesthetics & Art Criticism*, 68(3): 243–57.

Rose, C.M. (1994) *Property and Persuasion: Essays on the History, Theory, and Rhetoric of Ownership*, Boulder: Westview Press.

Saler, M. (2006) 'Modernity and Enchantment: A Historiographic Review', *American Historical Review*, 111(3): 692.

Sassen, S. (1991) *The Global City: New York, London, Tokyo*, Princeton, NJ: Princeton University Press.

Shaw, K. (2005) 'The Place of Alternative Culture and the Politics of Its Protection in Berlin, Amsterdam and Melbourne', *Planning Theory & Practice*, 6(2): 149–69.

Sinclair, I. (1997) *Lights out for the Territory*, London: Granta.

Skogan, W.G. (1990) *Disorder & Decline: Crime and the Spiral of Decay American Neighborhoods*, Berkeley: University of California Press.

Smallman, J. and Nyman, C. (2005) *Stencil Graffiti Capital: Melbourne*, New York: Mark Batty Publisher.

Snyder, G.J. (2006) 'Graffiti Media and the Perpetuation of an Illegal Subculture', *Crime Media Culture*, 2(1): 93.

—— (2009) *Graffiti Lives: Beyond the Tag in New York's Urban Underground*, New York: New York University Press.

Spiers, A. (2011) '"It's Not Easy to Sell Friendship": On Participation and Audience Engagement', *LALA*, 23 August, online at http://lalaishere.net/2011/08/it%E2%80%99s-not-easy-to-sell-friendship-on-participation-and-audience-engagement/.

Stewart, S. (1993) *On Longing: Narratives of the Miniature, the Gigantic, the Souvenir, the Collection*, Durham: Duke University Press Books.

Taussig, M. (1999) *Defacement: Public Secrecy and the Labor of the Negative*, Palo Alta, CA: Stanford University Press.

Thompson, D. (2008) *The $12 Million Stuffed Shark : The Curious Economics of Contemporary Art and Auction Houses*, London: Aurum.

Valverde, M. (2011) 'Seeing Like a City: The Dialectic of Modern and Premodern Ways of Seeing in Urban Governance', *Law & Society Review*, 45(2): 277–312.

Vorspan, R. (2000) 'Rational Recreation and the Law: The Transformation of Popular Urban Leisure in Victorian England', *McGill Law Journal*, 45: 891.

Wacławek, A. (2011) *Graffiti and Street Art*, New York: Thames & Hudson.

Watson, S. (2006) *City Publics: The (Dis)Enchantments of Urban Encounters*, New York: Routledge.

White, E. (2008) *The Flâneur*, London: Bloomsbury.

Whybrow, N. (2005) *Street Scenes: Brecht, Benjamin, and Berlin*, Portland, OR: Intellect Books.

Wilson, J.Q. and Kelling, G.L. (1982) 'Broken Windows: The Police and Neighborhood Safety', *Atlantic Monthly*, 249(3): 29–38.

Witz, D. (2010) *Dan Witz: In Plain View: 30 Years of Artworks Illegal and Otherwise*, Berkeley, CA: Gingko Press.

Workhorse and PAC (2012) *We Own the Night: The Art of the Underbelly Project*, New York: Rizzoli

Young, A. (2005) *Judging the Image: Art, Value, Law*, New York: Routledge.

—— (2010a) 'Legal/ Illegal: Street Art in Australia', in J. Babington (ed.) *Space Invaders*, Canberra: National Gallery of Australia.

—— (2010b) 'Negotiated Consent or Zero Tolerance? Responding to Graffiti and Street Art in Melbourne', *City*, 14(1/2): 99–114.

—— (2010c) *Street/Studio: The Place of Street Art in Melbourne*, Melbourne: Thames & Hudson.

—— (2011) 'The Art of Public Secrecy', *Australian Feminist Law Journal*, 57(35): 57–74.

Ziegler, G. (2004) 'The Politics of the Third Rail', *Space and Culture*, 7(3): 283–301.

# Index